To

From

Date

THE

LUCADO
INSPIRATIONAL
READER

THE
LUCADO
INSPIRATIONAL
READER

HOPE *and* ENCOURAGEMENT
for YOUR EVERYDAY LIFE

MAX LUCADO

THOMAS NELSON
Since 1798

NASHVILLE   DALLAS   MEXICO CITY   RIO DE JANEIRO

Published in Nashville, Tennessee, by Thomas Nelson. Thomas Nelson is a registered trademark of Thomas Nelson, Inc.

Page design by Mandi Cofer.

Thomas Nelson, Inc. titles may be purchased in bulk for educational, business, fund-raising, or sales promotional use. For information, please e-mail SpecialMarkets@ThomasNelson.com.

Scripture quotations marked NKJV are from the New King James Version®. © 1982 by Thomas Nelson, Inc. Used by permission. All rights reserved. Scripture quotations marked KJV are from the King James Version. Scripture quotations marked MSG are from *The Message* by Eugene H. Peterson. © 1993, 1994, 1995, 1996, 2000. Used by permission of NavPress Publishing Group. All rights reserved. Scripture quotations marked NCV are from the New Century Version®. © 2005 by Thomas Nelson, Inc. Used by permission. All rights reserved. Scripture quotations marked NLT are from the Holy Bible, New Living Translation. © 1996, 2004, 2007. Used by permission of Tyndale House Publishers, Inc., Wheaton, Illinois 60189. All rights reserved. Scripture quotations marked NIV are from the Holy Bible, New International Version®, NIV®.© 1973, 1978, 1984 by Biblica, Inc.™ Used by permission of Zondervan. All rights reserved worldwide. Scripture quotations marked PHILLIPS are from *The New Testament in Modern English, Revised Edition.* © J. B. Phillips 1958, 1960, 1972. Used by permission of Macmillan Publishing Co., Inc. Scripture quotations marked RSV are from the Revised Standard Version. © 1946, 1952 by Division of Christian Education of the National Council of the Churches of Christ in the United States of America. Scripture quotations marked TLB are from *The Living Bible.* © 1971 by Tyndale House Publishers, Wheaton, Illinois 60187. All rights reserved. Scripture quotations marked NRSV are from the New Revised Standard Version of the Bible. © 1989 by the Division of Christian Education of the National Council of the Churches of Christ in the U.S.A. All rights reserved. Scripture quotations marked NASB are from the New American Standard Bible®, © 1960, 1962, 1963, 1968, 1971, 1973, 1975, 1977, 1995 by The Lockman Foundation. Scripture quotations marked NEB are from the New English Bible © 1961, 1970 by the Delegates of the Oxford University Press and the Syndics of the Cambridge University Press. Scripture quotations marked ESV are from the English Standard Version. © 2001 by Crossway Bibles, a division of Good News Publishers.

Any italic in scripture quotations reflects the author's own emphasis.

Library of Congress Cataloging-in-Publication Data

Lucado, Max.
The Lucado inspirational reader : hope and encouragement for your everyday life / Max Lucado.
   p. cm.
Includes bibliographical references.
ISBN 978-0-8499-4830-5 (hardcover)
1. Christian life--Miscellanea. I. Title. II. Title: Inspirational reader.
BV4501.3.L84605 2011
248.4--dc23

2011033369

Printed in the United States of America
11 12 13 14 15 QG 6 5 4 3 2 1

*To Marcelle Le Gallo–celebrating thirty years
of glad service at the Oak Hills Church*

Contents

CONTENTS

Acknowledgments

$\mathcal{H}$eartfelt thanks to the hundreds of folks who have contributed time and talent to the creation of these books for the last twenty-five-plus years. Editors, publishers, designers, printers, sales teams, bookstore workers, illustrators, publicists–I'm grateful.

A few key team members have provided oversight to every single page of each book: Karen Hill, Liz Heaney, Carol Bartley, Steve and Cheryl Green, Susan Ligon, and David Moberg. I cannot say enough about your contributions. Thank you.

And deepest love to the dearest family this side of heaven.

The Bible

A Mine to Be Quarried

*O*n a trip to the United Kingdom, our family visited a castle. In the center of the garden sat a maze. Row after row of shoulder-high hedges, leading to one dead end after another. Successfully navigate the labyrinth, and discover the door to a tall tower in the center of the garden. Were you to look at our family pictures of the trip, you'd see four of our five family members standing on the top of the tower. Hmmm, someone is still on the ground. Guess who? I was stuck in the foliage. I just couldn't figure out which way to go.

Ah, but then I heard a voice from above. "Hey, Dad." I looked up to see Sara, peering through the turret at the top. "You're going the wrong way," she explained. "Back up and turn right."

Do you think I trusted her? I didn't have to. I could have trusted my own instincts, consulted other confused tourists, sat and pouted and wondered why God would let this happen to me.

But do you know what I did? I listened. Her vantage point was better than mine. She was above the maze. She could see what I couldn't.

Don't you think we should do the same with God? "God is . . . higher than the heavens" (Job 22:12 TLB). "The LORD is high above all nations" (Ps. 113:4 NASB). Can he not see what eludes us? Doesn't he want to get us out and bring us home? Then we should do what Jesus did.

Rely on Scripture. Doubt your doubts before you doubt your beliefs. Jesus told Satan, "Man shall not live on bread alone, but on every word that proceeds out of the mouth of God" (Matt. 4:4 NASB). The verb *proceeds* is literally "pouring out." Its tense suggests that God is constantly and aggressively communicating with the world through his Word. God is speaking still!

—*NEXT DOOR SAVIOR*

If we are to be just like Jesus, we must have a regular time of talking to God and listening to his Word.

—*JUST LIKE JESUS*

*T*rust {God's} Word. Don't trust your emotions. Don't trust your opinions. Don't even trust your friends. In the wilderness heed only the voice of God.

Again, Jesus is our model. Remember how Satan teased him? "If you are the Son of God . . ." (Luke 4:3, 9 NCV). Why would Satan say this? Because he knew what Christ had heard at the baptism. "This is My beloved Son, in whom I am well-pleased" (Matt. 3:17 NASB).

"Are you really God's Son?" Satan is asking. Then comes the dare—"Prove it!" Prove it by doing something:

"Tell this stone to become bread" (Luke 4:3 NASB).

"If You worship before me, it shall all be Yours" (v. 7 NASB).

"Throw Yourself down from here" (v. 9 NASB).

What subtle seduction! Satan doesn't denounce God; he simply raises doubts about God. Is his work enough? Earthly works—like bread changing or temple jumping—are given equal billing with heavenly works. He attempts to shift, ever so gradually, our source of confidence away from God's promise and toward our performance.

Jesus doesn't bite the bait. No heavenly sign is requested. He doesn't solicit a lightning bolt; he simply quotes the Bible. Three temptations. Three declarations.

"It is written . . ." (v. 4 NASB).

"It is written . . ." (v. 8 NASB).

"It is said . . ." (v. 12 NASB).

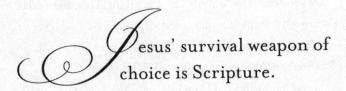

Jesus' survival weapon of choice is Scripture.

Jesus' survival weapon of choice is Scripture. If the Bible was enough for his wilderness, shouldn't it be enough for ours? Don't miss the point here. Everything you and I need for desert survival is in the Book. We simply need to heed it.

—*NEXT DOOR SAVIOR*

*T*hrough the words of the prophets, {God} used Scripture to reveal his will. Doesn't he do the same today? Open the Word of God and you'll find his will.

—*THE GREAT HOUSE OF GOD*

*G*od speaks to us through his Word. The first step in reading the Bible is to ask God to help you understand it. "But the Helper will teach you everything and will cause you to remember all that I told you. This Helper is the Holy Spirit whom the Father will send in my name" (John 14:26 NCV).

Before reading the Bible, pray. Don't go to Scripture looking for your own idea; go searching for God's. Read the Bible prayerfully. Also, read the Bible carefully. Jesus told us, "Search, and you will find" (Matt. 7:7 NCV). God commends those who "chew on Scripture day and night" (Ps. 1:2 MSG). The Bible is not a newspaper to be skimmed but rather a mine to be quarried. "Search for it like silver, and hunt for it like hidden treasure. Then you will understand respect for the LORD, and you will find that you know God" (Prov. 2:4-5 NCV).

Here is a practical point. Study the Bible a little at a time. God seems to send messages as he did his manna: one day's portion at a time. He provides "a command here, a command there. A rule here, a rule there. A little lesson here, a little lesson there" (Isa. 28:10 NCV). Choose depth over quantity. Read until a verse *bits* you, then stop and meditate on it. Copy the verse onto a sheet of paper, or write it in your journal, and reflect on it several times.

On the morning I wrote this, for example, my quiet time found me in Matthew 18. I was only four verses into the chapter when I read, *"The greatest person in the kingdom of heaven is the one who makes himself humble like this child"* (NCV). I needed to go no further. I copied the words in my journal and have pondered them on and off during the day. Several times I asked God, "How can I be more childlike?" By the end of the day, I was reminded of my tendency to hurry and my proclivity to worry.

Will I learn what God intends? If I listen, I will.

Don't be discouraged if your reading reaps a small harvest. Some days a lesser portion is all we need. A little girl returned from her first day at school. Her mom asked, "Did you learn anything?" "I guess not," the girl responded. "I have to go back tomorrow and the next day and the next day . . ."

Don't go to Scripture looking for your own idea; go searching for God's.

Such is the case with learning. And such is the case with Bible study. Understanding comes a little at a time over a lifetime.

—*Just Like Jesus*

You have a Bible? Read it.

Has any other book ever been described in this fashion: "For the word of God is living and active. Sharper than any double-edged sword, it penetrates even to dividing soul and spirit, joints and marrow; it judges the thoughts and attitudes of the heart" (Heb. 4:12 NIV)?

"Living and active." The words of the Bible have life! Nouns with pulse rates. Muscular adjectives. Verbs darting back and forth across the page. God works through these words. The Bible is to God what a surgical glove is to the surgeon. He reaches through them to touch deep within you.

Haven't you felt his touch?

In a late, lonely hour, you read the words "I will never desert you, nor will I ever forsake you" (Heb. 13:5 NASB). The sentences comfort like a hand on your shoulder.

—*Facing Your Giants*

The words of the Bible have life! . . . God works through these words.

People have been known to justify stupidity based on a "feeling." "I felt God leading me to cheat on my wife . . . disregard my bills . . . lie to my boss . . . flirt with my married neighbor." Mark it down: God will not lead you to violate his Word. He will not contradict his teaching. Be careful with the phrase "God led me . . ." Don't banter it about. Don't disguise your sin as a leading of God. He will not lead you to lie, cheat, or hurt. He will faithfully lead you through the words of his Scripture and the advice of his faithful.

—*FACING YOUR GIANTS*

The following paragraphs document the degeneration of this author into criminal activity. The facts are true, and no names have been changed. I confess. I have violated the law. What's worse, I don't want to stop!

My felonious actions began innocently. My route to the office takes me south to an intersection where I and every other person in Texas turn east. Each morning I wait *long* minutes in a *long* line at a *long* light, always mumbling, "There must be a better way." A few days back I found it. While still a half mile from the light, I spotted a shortcut, an alley behind a shopping center. It was worth a try. I turned on my blinker, made a quick left, bid farewell to the crawling commuters, and took my chances. I weaved in between the Dumpsters and over the speed bumps and voilà. It worked! The alley led me to my eastbound avenue several minutes faster than the rest of society.

Lewis and Clark would have been proud. I certainly was. From then on, I was ahead of the pack. Every morning while the rest of the cars waited in line, I veered onto my private autobahn and smugly applauded myself for seeing what others missed. I was surprised that no one had discovered it earlier, but then again, few have my innate navigational skills.

One morning Denalyn was with me in the car. "I'm about to remind you why you married me," I told her as we drew near to the intersection. "See that long line of cars? Hear that dirge from the suburbs? See that humdrum of humanity? It's not for me. Hang on!"

Like a hunter on a safari, I swerved from the six-lane onto the one-lane and shared with my sweetheart my secret expressway to freedom. "What do you think?" I asked her, awaiting her worship.

"I think you broke the law."

"What?"

"You just went the wrong way on a one-way street."

"I did not."

"Go back and see for yourself."

I did. She was right. Somehow I'd missed the sign. My road-less-taken was a route-not-permitted. Next to the big orange Dumpster was a "Do Not Enter" sign. No wonder people gave me those looks when I turned into the alley. I thought they were envious; they thought I was deviant.

But my problem is not what I did before I knew the law. My problem is what I want to do now, after I know the law. You'd think that I would have no desire to use the alley, but I do! Part of me still wants the shortcut. Part of me wants to break the law. (Forgive me, all you patrolmen who are reading this book.) Each morning the voices within me have this argument:

My "ought to" says, "It's illegal."

My "want to" answers, "But I've never been caught."

My "ought to" reminds, "The law is the law."

My "want to" counters, "But the law isn't for careful drivers like me. Besides, the five minutes I save I'll dedicate to prayer."

My "ought to" doesn't buy it. "Pray in the car."

Before I knew the law, I was at peace. Now that I know the law, an insurrection has occurred. I'm a torn man. On one hand I know what to do, but I don't want to do it. My eyes read the sign "Do Not Enter," but my body doesn't want to obey. What I should do and end up doing are two different matters. I was better off not knowing the law.

Sound familiar? It could. For many it is the itinerary of the soul. Before coming to Christ we all had our share of shortcuts. Immorality was a shortcut to pleasure. Cheating was a shortcut to success. Boasting was a shortcut to popularity. Lying was a short-cut to power.

Then we found Christ, we found grace, and we saw the signs. . . .
All these years you've been taking shortcuts, never seeing
the "Do Not Enter" sign. But now you see it. Now you know it. I
know, I know . . . it would have been easier had you never seen the
sign, but now the law has been revealed. So what do you do?

Your battle is identical to the one within the heart of Paul.

But I need something *more!* For if I know the law but still can't
keep it, and if the power of sin within me keeps sabotaging my
best intentions, I obviously need help! I realize that I don't
have what it takes. I can will it, but I can't *do* it. I decide to do
good, but I don't *really* do it; I decide not to do bad, but then
I do it anyway. My decisions, such as they are, don't result in
actions. Something has gone wrong deep within me and gets
the better of me every time.

It happens so regularly that it's predictable. The moment
I decide to do good, sin is there to trip me up. I truly delight
in God's commands, but it's pretty obvious that not all of me
joins in that delight. Parts of me covertly rebel, and just when
I least expect it, they take charge. (Rom. 7:17-23 MSG)

The civil war of the soul.

Let me give you a second truth to take to the battlefield. The
first was your position: you are a child of God. The second is your
principle: the Word of God.

When under attack, our tendency is to question the validity of God's commands; we rationalize like I do with the one-way street. *The law is for others, not for me. I'm a good driver.* By questioning the validity of the law, I decrease in my mind the authority of the law.

For that reason Paul is quick to remind us, "the law is holy, and the command is holy and right and good" (7:12 NCV). The root word for *holy* is *hagios*, which means "different." God's commands are holy because they come from a different world, a different sphere, a different perspective.

In a sense the "Do Not Enter" sign on my forbidden alley was from a different sphere. Our city lawmakers' thoughts are not like my thoughts. They are concerned for the public good. I am concerned with personal convenience. They want what is best for the city. I want what is best for me. They know what is safe. I know what is quick. But they don't create laws for my pleasure; they make laws for my safety.

The same is true with God. What we consider shortcuts God sees as disasters. He doesn't give laws for our pleasure. He gives them for our protection. In seasons of struggle we must trust his wisdom, not ours. He designed the system; he knows what we need.

—*IN THE GRIP OF GRACE*

The Church

God's Family

*W*e are, incredibly, the body of Christ. And though we may not act like our Father, there is no greater truth than this: We are his. Unalterably. He loves us. Undyingly. Nothing can separate us from the love of Christ (Rom. 8:38–39).

—*A GENTLE THUNDER*

*S*cripture calls the church a poem. "We are His workmanship" (Eph. 2:10 NKJV). "Workmanship" descends from the Greek word *poeo* or "poetry." We are God's poetry! What Longfellow did with pen and paper, our Maker does with us. We express his creative best.

You aren't God's poetry. I'm not God's poetry. *We* are God's poetry. Poetry demands variety. "God works through different men in different ways, but it is the same God who achieves his purposes through them all" (1 Cor. 12:6 PHILLIPS). God uses all types to type his message. Logical thinkers. Emotional worshipers. Dynamic leaders. Docile followers. The visionaries who lead, the studious who ponder, the generous who pay the bills. Action-packed verbs. Rock-solid nouns. Enigmatic question marks. Alone, we are meaningless symbols on a page. But collectively, we inspire. "All of you *together* are Christ's body, and each one of you is a separate and necessary part of it" (1 Cor. 12:27 NLT).

—*CURE FOR THE COMMON LIFE*

In 1976, tremors devastated the highlands of Guatemala. Thousands of people were killed and tens of thousands were left homeless. A philanthropist offered to sponsor a relief team from our college. This flyer was posted in our dormitory: "Needed: students willing to use their spring break to build cinder-block homes in Quetzaltenango." I applied, was accepted, and began attending the orientation sessions.

There were twelve of us in all. Mostly ministry students. All of us, it seemed, loved to discuss theology. We were young enough in our faith to believe we knew all the answers. This made for lively discussions. We bantered about a covey of controversies. I can't remember the list. It likely included the usual suspects of charismatic gifts, end times, worship styles, church strategy, and so forth. By the time we reached Guatemala, we'd covered the controversies and revealed our true colors. I'd discerned the faithful from the infidels, the healthy from the heretics. I knew who was in and who was out.

But all of that was soon forgotten. The destruction from the earthquake dwarfed our differences. Entire villages had been leveled. Children were wandering through rubble, calling the names of their parents. Long lines of wounded people awaited medical attention. Our opinions seemed suddenly petty. The disaster demanded teamwork. The challenge created a team.

The task turned rivals into partners. I remember one fellow in particular. He and I had distinctly different opinions regarding the style of worship music. I, the open-minded, relevant thinker, favored contemporary, upbeat music. He, the stodgy, close-minded caveman, preferred hymns and hymnals. Yet when stacking bricks for houses, guess who worked shoulder to shoulder? As we did, we began to sing together. We sang old songs and new, slow and fast. Only later did the irony of it dawn on me. Our common concern gave us a common song.

This was Jesus' plan all along. None of us can do what all of us can do. Remember his commission to the disciples? "You {all of you collectively} shall be My witnesses" (Acts 1:8 NASB). Jesus didn't issue individual assignments. He didn't move one-by-one down the line and knight each individual.

"You, Peter, shall be my witness . . ."

*N*one of us can do what all of us can do. . . . Jesus works in community.

"You, John, shall be my witness . . ."

"You, Mary Magdalene, shall be my witness . . ."

But rather, "You (the sum of you) shall be My witnesses . . ." Jesus works in community. For that reason, you find no personal pronouns in the earliest description of the church.

—*Outlive Your Life*

*P*eople on a plane and people on a pew have a lot in common. All are on a journey. Most are well-behaved and presentable. Some doze, and others gaze out the window. Most, if not all, are satisfied with a predictable experience. For many, the mark of a good flight and the mark of a good worship assembly are the same. "Nice," we like to say. "It was a nice flight/It was a nice worship service." We exit the same way we enter, and we're happy to return next time.

A few, however, are not content with nice. They long for something more. The boy who just passed me did. I heard him before I saw him. I was already in my seat when he asked, "Will they really let me meet the pilot?" He was either lucky or shrewd because he made the request just as he entered the plane. The question floated into the cockpit, causing the pilot to lean out.

"Someone looking for me?" he asked.

The boy's hand shot up like he was answering his second-grade teacher's question. "I am!"

"Well, come on in."

With a nod from his mom, the youngster entered the cock-pit's world of controls and gauges and emerged minutes later with eyes wide. "Wow!" he exclaimed. "I'm so glad to be on this plane!"

No one else's face showed such wonder. I should know. I paid attention. The boy's interest piqued mine, so I studied the faces of the other passengers but found no such enthusiasm. I mostly saw contentment: travelers content to be on the plane, content to be closer to their destination, content to be out of the airport, content to sit and stare and say little.

There were a few exceptions. The five or so mid-age women wearing straw hats and carrying beach bags weren't content; they were exuberant. They giggled all the way down the aisle. My bet is they were moms-set-free-from-kitchens-and-kids. The fellow in the blue suit across the aisle wasn't content; he was cranky. He opened his laptop and scowled at its screen the entire trip. Most of us, however, were happier than he and more contained than the ladies. Most of us were content. Content with a predictable, uneventful flight. Content with a "nice" flight.

And since that is what we sought, that is what we got. The boy, on the other hand, wanted more. He wanted to see the pilot. If asked to describe the flight, he wouldn't say nice. He'd likely produce the plastic wings the pilot gave him and say, "I saw the man up front."

Do you see why I say that people on a plane and people on a

pew have a lot in common? Enter a church sanctuary and look at the faces. A few are giggly, a couple are cranky, but by and large we are content. Content to be there. Content to sit and look straight ahead and leave when the service is over. Content to enjoy an assembly with no surprises or turbulence. Content with a *nice* service. "Seek and you will find," Jesus promised (Matt. 7:7 NIV).

And since a nice service is what we seek, a nice service is usually what we find.

A few, however, seek more. A few come with the childlike enthusiasm of the boy. And those few leave as he did, wide-eyed with the wonder of having stood in the presence of the pilot himself. . . .

Do you come to church with a worship-hungry heart? Our Savior did.

May I urge you to be just like Jesus? Prepare your heart for worship. Let God change your face through worship. Demonstrate the power of worship. Above all, seek the face of the pilot. The boy did. Because he sought the pilot, he left with a changed face and a set of wings. The same can happen to you.

—*JUST LIKE JESUS*

*O*ddly, some people enjoy the shade of the church while refusing to set down any roots. God, yes. Church, no. They like the benefits, but resist commitment. The music, the message, the clean conscience–they accept church perks. So they date her, visit her. Enjoy an occasional rendezvous. They use the church. But commit to the church? Can't do that. Got to keep options open. Don't want to miss out on any opportunities.

I propose they already are. Miss the church and miss God's sanctioned tool for God promotion. For church is a key place to do what you do best to the glory of God.

—*Cure for the Common Life*

I'm writing this . . . on a Saturday morning in Boston. I came here to speak at a conference. After I did my part last night, I did something very spiritual: I went to a Boston Celtics basketball game. I couldn't resist. Boston Garden is a stadium I'd wanted to see since I was a kid. Besides, Boston was playing my favorite team, the San Antonio Spurs.

As I took my seat, it occurred to me that I might be the only Spurs fan in the crowd. I'd be wise to be quiet. But that was hard to do. I contained myself for a few moments, but that's all. By the end of the first quarter I was letting out solo war whoops every time the Spurs would score.

People were beginning to turn and look. Risky stuff, this voice-in-the-wilderness routine.

That's when I noticed I had a friend across the aisle. He, too, applauded the Spurs. When I clapped, he clapped. I had a partner. We buoyed each other. I felt better.

At the end of the quarter I gave him the thumbs-up. He gave it back. He was only a teenager. No matter. We were united by the higher bond of fellowship.

That's one reason for the church. All week you cheer for the visiting team. You applaud the success of the One the world opposes. You stand when everyone sits and sit when everyone stands.

At some point you need support. You need to be with folks who cheer when you do. You need what the Bible calls *fellowship*. And you need it every week. After all, you can only go so long before you think about joining the crowd.

—*WHEN GOD WHISPERS YOUR NAME*

*G*od has only one flock. Somehow we missed that. Religious division is not his idea. Franchises and sectarianism are not in God's plan. God has one flock. The flock has one shepherd. And though we may think there are many, we are wrong. There is only one.

Never in the Bible are we told to create unity. We are simply told to maintain the unity that exists. Paul exhorts us to preserve "the unity which the Spirit gives" (Eph. 4:3 NEB). Our task is not to invent unity, but to acknowledge it.

I have two sisters and a brother. We are siblings because we came from the same family. We have the same father and mother. I'm sure there have been times when they didn't want to call me their brother, but they don't have that choice.

Nor do we. When I see someone calling God *Father* and Jesus *Savior*, I meet a brother or a sister–regardless of the name of their church or denomination.

By the way, the church names we banter about? They do not exist in heaven. The Book of Life does not list your denomination next to your name. Why? Because it is not the denomination that saves you. And I wonder, if there are no denominations in heaven, why do we have denominations on earth?

What would happen (I know this is a crazy thought.), but what would happen if all the churches agreed, on a given day, to change their names to simply "church"? What if any reference to any denomination were removed and we were all just Christians? And then when people chose which church to attend, they wouldn't do so by the sign outside . . . they'd do so by the hearts of the people inside. And then when people were asked what church they attended, their answer wouldn't be a label but just a location.

And then we Christians wouldn't be known for what divides us; instead we'd be known for what unites us–our common Father.

Crazy idea? Perhaps.

But I think God would like it. It was his to begin with.

—*A Gentle Thunder*

When I see someone calling God *Father* and Jesus *Savior*, I meet a brother or a sister—regardless of the name of their church or denomination.

*G*od is building a family. A permanent family. Earthly families enjoy short shelf lives. Even those that sidestep divorce are eventually divided by death. God's family, however, will outlive the universe. "When I think of the wisdom and scope of his plan I fall down on my knees and pray to the Father of all the great family of God—some of them already in heaven and some down here on earth" (Eph. 3:14–15 TLB).

Jesus even defined his family according to faith not flesh. "A multitude was sitting around Him; and they said to Him, 'Look, Your mother and Your brothers are outside seeking You.' But He answered them, saying, 'Who is My mother, or My brothers? . . . Whoever does the will of God is My brother and My sister and mother'" (Mark 3:32–33, 35 NKJV).

Common belief identifies members of God's family. And common affection unites them. Paul gives this relationship rule for the church: "Be devoted to one another in brotherly love" (Rom. 12:10 NIV). The apostle plays the wordsmith here, bookending the verse with fraternal-twin terms. He begins with *philostorgos* (*philos* means "friendly"; *storgos* means "family love") and concludes with *philadelphia* (*phileo* means "tender affection"; *adelphia* means "brethren"). An awkward but accurate translation of the verse might be "Have a friend/family devotion to each other in a friend/family sort of way." If Paul doesn't get us with the first adjective, he catches us with the second. In both he reminds us: the church is God's family.

Common belief identifies members of God's family. And common affection unites them.

You didn't pick me. I didn't pick you. You may not like me. I may not like you. But since God picked and likes us both, we are family.

—*Cure for the Common Life*

*W*e are in this together. We are more than followers of Christ, disciples of Christ. "We are parts of his body" (Eph. 5:30 NCV). "He is the head of the body, which is the church" (Col. 1:18 NCV). I am not his body; you are not his body. We–together–are his body.

—*Outlive Your Life*

Comfort

God in the Hurts of Life

*M*artha sat in a damp world, cloudy, tearful. And Jesus sat in it with her. "I am the resurrection and the life. Those who believe in me, even though they die like everyone else, will live again" (John 11:25 NLT). Hear those words in a Superman tone, if you like. Clark Kent descending from nowhere, ripping shirt and popping buttons to reveal the *S* beneath. *"I AM the Resurrection and the Life!!!"* Do you see a Savior with Terminator tenderness bypassing the tears of Martha and Mary and, in doing so, telling them and all grievers to buck up and trust?

I don't. I don't because of what Jesus does next. He weeps. He sits on the pew between Mary and Martha, puts an arm around each, and sobs. Among the three, a tsunami of sorrow is stirred; a monsoon of tears is released. Tears that reduce to streaks the watercolor conceptions of a cavalier Christ. Jesus weeps.

He weeps with them.

He weeps for them.

He weeps with you.

He weeps for you.

He weeps so we will know: Mourning is not disbelieving. Flooded eyes don't represent a faithless heart. A person can enter a cemetery Jesus-certain of life after death and still have a Twin Tower crater in the heart. Christ did. He wept, and he knew he was ten minutes from seeing a living Lazarus!

And his tears give you permission to shed your own. Grief does not mean you don't trust; it simply means you can't stand the thought of another day without the Jacob or Lazarus of your life. If Jesus gave the love, he understands the tears. So grieve, but don't grieve like those who don't know the rest of this story.

—*NEXT DOOR SAVIOR*

*C*arlos Andres Baisdon-Niño lay down with his favorite Bible storybook. He began with the first chapter and turned every page until the end. When he finished, he blew his good-night kisses to Mami and Papi, to his three *niñas*, and then, as always, he blew one to Papa Dios. He closed his eyes, drifted off to sleep, and awoke in heaven.

Carlos was three years old.

When Tim and Betsa, his parents, and I met to plan the

funeral, they wanted me to watch a video of Carlos." You've got to see him dancing," Tim told me. One look and I could see why. What little Carlos did to the rhythm of a Latin song can't be described with words. He shook from top to bottom. His feet moved, his hands bounced, his head swayed. You got the impression that his heart rate had switched over to his native Colombian beat.

We laughed, the three of us did. And in the laughter, for just a moment, Carlos was with us. For just a moment there was no leukemia, syringes, blankets, or chemotherapy. There was no stone to carve or grave to dig. There was just Carlos. And Carlos was just dancing.

But then the video stopped, and so did the laughter. And this mom and dad resumed their slow walk through the valley of the shadow of death.

Are you passing through the same shadow? Is this book being held by the same hands that touched the cold face of a friend? And the eyes that fall upon this page, have they also fallen upon the breathless figure of a husband, wife, or child? Are you passing through the valley? If not, {these thoughts} may seem unnecessary. Feel free to move on—{they} will be here when you need {them}.

If so, however, you know that the black bag of sorrow is hard to bear.

It's hard to bear because not everyone understands your grief.

They did at first. They did at the funeral. They did at the graveside. But they don't now; they don't understand. Grief lingers.

As silently as a cloud slides between you and the afternoon sun, memories drift between you and joy, leaving you in a chilly shadow. No warning. No notice. Just a whiff of the cologne he wore or a verse of the song she loved, and you are saying good-bye all over again.

Why won't the sorrow leave you alone?

Because you buried more than a person. You buried some of yourself. Wasn't it John Donne who said, "Any man's death diminishes me"? It's as if the human race resides on a huge trampoline. The movements of one can be felt by all. And the closer the relationship, the more profound the exit. When someone you love dies, it affects you. . . .

Why does grief linger? Because you are dealing with more than memories—you are dealing with unlived tomorrows. You're not just battling sorrow—you're battling disappointment. You're also battling anger.

It may be on the surface. It may be subterranean. It may be a flame. It may be a blowtorch. But anger lives in sorrow's house. Anger at self. Anger at life. Anger at the military or the hospital or the highway system. But most of all, anger at God. Anger that takes the form of the three-letter question—why? Why him? Why her? Why now? Why us?

God is a good God . . . Though we don't understand his actions, we can trust his heart.

You and I both know I can't answer that question. Only God knows the reasons behind his actions. But here is a key truth on which we can stand.

Our God is a good God.

"You are good, LORD. The LORD is good and right" (Ps. 25:7–8 NCV).

"Taste and see that the LORD is good" (Ps. 34:8 NIV).

God is a good God. We must begin here. Though we don't understand his actions, we can trust his heart.

—*TRAVELING LIGHT*

"*S*urprise!"

Add to the list of sorrow, peril, excitement, and bedlam the word *interruption*. Jesus' plans are interrupted. What he has in mind for his day and what the people have in mind for his day are two different agendas. What Jesus seeks and what Jesus gets are not the same.

Sound familiar?

Remember when you sought a night's rest and got a colicky baby? Remember when you sought to catch up at the office and got even further behind? Remember when you sought to use your Saturday for leisure, but ended up fixing your neighbor's sink?

Take comfort, friend. It happened to Jesus too.

His pulse has raced. His eyes have grown weary. His heart has grown heavy . . . He knows how you feel.

In fact, this would be a good time to pause and digest the central message . . .

Jesus knows how you feel.

Ponder this and use it the next time your world goes from calm to chaos.

His pulse has raced. His eyes have grown weary. His heart has grown heavy. He has had to climb out of bed with a sore throat. He has been kept awake late and has gotten up early. He knows how you feel.

You may have trouble believing that. You probably believe that Jesus knows what it means to endure heavy-duty tragedies. You are no doubt convinced that Jesus is acquainted with sorrow and has wrestled with fear. Most people accept that. But can God relate to the hassles and headaches of my life? Of your life?

For some reason this is harder to believe.

Perhaps that's why portions of this day are recorded in all the Gospel accounts (Matt. 14:1-33; Mark 6:1-54; Luke 9:1-27; John 6:1-24). No other event, other than the Crucifixion, is told by all four Gospel writers. Not Jesus' baptism. Not his temptation. Not even his birth. But all four writers chronicle this day. It's as if Matthew, Mark, Luke, and John knew that you would wonder if God understands. And they proclaim their response in four-part harmony:

Jesus knows how you feel.

—*In the Eye of the Storm*

$\mathcal{T}$wo days ago I read a word in the Bible that has since taken up residence in my heart.

To be honest, I didn't quite know what to do with it. It's only one word and not a very big one at that. When I ran across the word (which, by the way, is exactly what happened; I was running through the passage, and this word came out of nowhere and bounced me like a speed bump), I didn't know what to do with it. I didn't have any hook to hang it on or category to file it under.

It was an enigmatic word in an enigmatic passage. But now, forty-eight hours later, I have found a place for it, a place all its own. My, what a word it is. Don't read it unless you don't mind changing your mind because this little word might move your spiritual furniture around a bit.

Look at the passage with me.

Then Jesus left the vicinity of Tyre and went through Sidon, down to the Sea of Galilee and into the region of the Decapolis. There some people brought to him a man who was deaf and could hardly talk, and they begged him to place his hand on the man.

After he took him aside, away from the crowd, Jesus put his fingers into the man's ears. Then he spit and touched the man's tongue. He looked up to heaven and with a deep sigh said to him, *"Ephphatha!"* (which means, "Be opened!"). At this, the man's ears were opened, his tongue was loosened and he began to speak plainly. (Mark 7:34–35 NIV)

Quite a passage, isn't it?

Jesus is presented with a man who is deaf and has a speech impediment. Perhaps he stammered. Maybe he spoke with a lisp. Perhaps, because of his deafness, he never learned to articulate words properly.

Jesus, refusing to exploit the situation, took the man aside. He looked him in the face. Knowing it would be useless to talk, he explained what he was about to do through gestures. He spat and touched the man's tongue, telling him that whatever restricted his speech was about to be removed. He touched his ears. They, for the first time, were about to hear.

But before the man said a word or heard a sound, Jesus did something I never would have anticipated.

He sighed.

I might have expected a clap or a song or a prayer. Even a "Hallelujah!" or a brief lesson might have been appropriate. But the Son of God did none of these. Instead, he paused, looked into heaven, and sighed. From the depths of his being came a rush of emotion that said more than words.

Sigh. The word seemed out of place.

From the depths of his being came a rush of emotion that said more than words.

I'd never thought of God as one who sighs. I'd thought of God as one who commands. I'd thought of God as one who weeps. I'd thought of God as one who called forth the dead with a command or created the universe with a word . . . but a God who sighs?

Perhaps this phrase caught my eye because I do my share of sighing.

I sighed yesterday when I visited a lady whose invalid husband had deteriorated so much he didn't recognize me. He thought I was trying to sell him something.

I sighed when the dirty-faced, scantily dressed six-year-old girl in the grocery store asked me for some change.

And I sighed today listening to a husband tell how his wife won't forgive him.

No doubt you've done your share of sighing.

If you have teenagers, you've probably sighed. If you've tried to resist temptation, you've probably sighed. If you've had your motives questioned or your best acts of love rejected, you have been forced to take a deep breath and let escape a painful sigh.

I realize there exists a sigh of relief, a sigh of expectancy, and even a sigh of joy. But that isn't the sigh described in Mark 7. The sigh described is a hybrid of frustration and sadness. It lies somewhere between a fit of anger and a burst of tears.

The apostle Paul spoke of this sighing. Twice he said that Christians will sigh as long as we are on earth and long for heaven.

The creation sighs as if she were giving birth. Even the Spirit sighs as he interprets our prayers (Rom. 8:22–27).

All these sighs come from the same anxiety: recognition of pain that was never intended or of hope deferred.

Man was not created to be separated from his creator; hence he sighs, longing for home. The creation was never intended to be inhabited by evil; hence she sighs, yearning for the Garden. And conversations with God were never intended to depend on a translator; hence the Spirit groans on our behalf, looking to a day when humans will see God face to face.

And when Jesus looked into the eyes of Satan's victim, the only appropriate thing to do was sigh. "It was never intended to be this way," the sigh said. "Your ears weren't made to be deaf; your tongue wasn't made to stumble." The imbalance of it all caused the Master to languish.

So I found a place for the word. You might think it strange, but I placed it bedside the word *comfort*, for in an indirect way, God's pain is our comfort.

—*GOD CAME NEAR*

*Y*ou might hear the news from a policeman: "I'm sorry. He didn't survive the accident."

You might return a friend's call, only to be told, "The surgeon brought bad news."

Too many spouses have heard these words from grim-faced soldiers: "We regret to inform you . . ."

In such moments, spring becomes winter, blue turns to gray, birds go silent, and the chill of sorrow settles in. It's cold in the valley of the shadow of death.

David's messenger isn't a policeman, friend, or soldier. He is a breathless Amalekite with torn clothing and hair full of dirt who stumbles into Camp Ziklag with the news: "The people have fled from the battle, many of the people are fallen and dead, and Saul and Jonathan his son are dead also" (2 Sam. 1:4 NKJV).

David knows the Hebrews are fighting the Philistines. He knows Saul and Jonathan are in for the battle of their lives. He's been awaiting the outcome. When the messenger presents David with Saul's crown and bracelet, David has undeniable proof—Saul and Jonathan are dead.

Jonathan. Closer than a brother. He had saved David's life and sworn to protect his children.

Saul. God's chosen. God's anointed. Yes, he had hounded David. He had badgered David. But he was still God's anointed.

God's chosen king—dead.

David's best friend—dead.

Leaving David to face yet another giant—the giant of grief.

We, like David, have two choices: flee or face the giant.

We've felt his heavy hand on our shoulders. Not in Ziklag but in emergency rooms, in children's hospitals, at car wrecks, and on battlefields. And we, like David, have two choices: flee or face the giant.

Many opt to flee grief. Captain Woodrow Call urged young Newt to do so. In the movie *Lonesome Dove*, Call and Newt are part of a 1880s Texas-to-Montana cattle drive. When a swimming swarm of water moccasins ends the life of Newt's best friend, Call offers bereavement counsel, western style. At the burial, in the shade of elms and the presence of cowboys, he advises, "Walk away from it, son. That's the only way to handle death. Walk away from it."

What else can you do? The grave stirs such unspeakable hurt and unanswerable questions, we're tempted to turn and walk. Change the subject, avoid the issue. Work hard. Drink harder. Stay busy. Stay distant. Head north to Montana and don't look back.

Yet we pay a high price when we do. Bereavement comes from the word *reave*. Look up *reave* in the dictionary, and you'll read "to take away by force, plunder, rob." Death robs you. The grave plunders moments and memories not yet shared: birthdays, vacations, lazy walks, talks over tea. You are bereaved because you've been robbed.

Normal is no more and never will be again. . . .

Just when you think the beast of grief is gone, you hear a song she loved or smell the cologne he wore or pass a restaurant where the two of you used to eat. The giant keeps showing up.

And the giant of grief keeps stirring up. Stirring up . . .

Anxiety. "Am I next?"

Guilt. "Why did I tell him . . ." "Why didn't I say to her . . ."

Wistfulness. You see intact couples and long for your mate. You see parents with kids and yearn for your child.

The giant stirs up insomnia, loss of appetite, forgetfulness, thoughts of suicide. Grief is not a mental illness, but it sure feels like one sometimes.

Captain Call didn't understand this.

Your friends may not understand this.

You may not understand this. But please try. Understand the gravity of your loss. You didn't lose at Monopoly or misplace your keys. You can't walk away from this. At some point, within minutes or months, you need to do what David did. Face your grief.

—*FACING YOUR GIANTS*

*W*e speak of a short life, but compared to eternity, who has a long one? A person's days on earth may appear as a drop in the ocean. Yours and mine may seem like a thimbleful. But compared to the Pacific of eternity, even the years of Methuselah filled no more than a glass. James was not speaking just to the young when he said, "Your life is like a mist. You can see it for a short time, but then it goes away" (James 4:14 NCV).

In God's plan every life is long enough and every death is

timely. And though you and I might wish for a longer life, God knows better.

And–this is important–though you and I may wish a longer life for our loved ones, they don't. Ironically, the first to accept God's decision of death is the one who dies.

While we are shaking heads in disbelief, they are lifting hands in worship. While we are mourning at a grave, they are marveling at heaven. While we are questioning God, they are praising God.

—*TRAVELING LIGHT*

We don't know how long Jesus wept. We don't know how long David wept. But we know how long we weep, and the time seems so truncated. Egyptians dress in black for six months. Some Muslims wear mourning clothes for a year. Orthodox Jews offer prayers for a deceased parent every day for eleven months. . . .

And today? Am I the only one who senses that we hurry our hurts?

Grief takes time. Give yourself some. "Sages invest themselves in hurt and grieving" (Eccl. 7:4 MSG). *Lament* may be a foreign verb in our world but not in Scripture's. Seventy percent of the psalms are poems of sorrow. Why, the Old Testament includes a book of lamentations. The son of David wrote, "Sorrow is better than laughter, for sadness has a refining influence on us" (Eccl. 7:3 NLT).

Grief takes time. Give yourself some.

We spelunk life's deepest issues in the cave of sorrow. Why am I here? Where am I headed? Cemetery strolls stir hard yet vital questions. David indulged the full force of his remorse: "I am worn out from sobbing. Every night tears drench my bed; my pillow is wet from weeping" (Ps. 6:6 NLT).

And then later: "I am dying from grief; my years are shortened by sadness. Misery has drained my strength; I am wasting away from within" (Ps. 31:10 NLT).

Are you angry with God? Tell him. Disgusted with God? Let him know. Weary of telling people you feel fine when you don't? Tell the truth. . . .

David called the nation to mourning. He rendered weeping a public policy. He refused to gloss over or soft-pedal death. He faced it, fought it, challenged it. But he didn't deny it. As his son Solomon explained, "There is . . . a time to mourn" (Eccl. 3:1, 4 NIV).

Give yourself some.

—*Facing Your Giants*

Compassion

Love for the Least

*S*ome of you have the master touch of the Physician himself. You use your hands to pray over the sick and minister to the weak. If you aren't touching them personally, your hands are writing letters, dialing phones, baking pies. You have learned the power of a touch.

But others of us tend to forget. Our hearts are good; it's just that our memories are bad. We forget how significant one touch can be. We fear saying the wrong thing or using the wrong tone or acting the wrong way. So rather than do it incorrectly, we do nothing at all.

Aren't we glad Jesus didn't make the same mistake? If your fear of doing the wrong thing prevents you from doing anything, keep in mind the perspective of the lepers of the world. They aren't picky. They aren't finicky. They're just lonely. They are yearning for a godly touch.

Jesus touched the untouchables of the world. Will you do the same?

—*Just Like Jesus*

*G*od calls us to change the way we look at people. Not to see them as Gentiles or Jews, insiders or outsiders, liberals or conservatives. Not to label. To label is to libel. "We have stopped evaluating others by what the world thinks about them" (2 Cor. 5:16 NLT).

Let's view people differently; let's view them as we do ourselves. Blemished, perhaps. Unfinished, for certain. Yet, once rescued and restored, we may shed light, like the two stained-glass windows in my office.

My brother found them on a junkyard heap. Some church had discarded them. Dee, a handy carpenter, reclaimed them. He repainted the chipped wood, repaired the worn frame. He sealed some of the cracks in the colored glass. The windows aren't perfect. But if suspended where the sun can pass through, they cascade multicolored light into the room.

In our lifetimes, you and I are going to come across some discarded people. Tossed out. Sometimes tossed out by a church. And we get to choose. Neglect or rescue? Label them or love them? We know Jesus' choice. Just look at what he did with us.

—*Outlive Your Life*

It's a wonderful day indeed when we stop working for God and begin working with God.

—*JUST LIKE JESUS*

*Y*ou are so proud of the new gloves you just bought. Your old set was worn and threadbare, defenseless against winter's bite. So you shopped until you found just the right pair. How many did you examine? Dozens. And how many did you try on? Nearly the same number. After all, what good are gloves if you don't like them or they don't fit?

Ah, but then you found these. The clerk did you a favor. She reached under the counter and produced a set still wrapped in plastic. You paid the price and walked out the door, unsealing the bag. And now, walking down the avenue on a chilly morning, you prepare to wear your brand-new gloves.

You step to the side of the foot traffic, tear open the plastic cover, and plunge your hand into the woolen warmth, only to be stopped. You can't get your fingers into the fingers! The five entry-ways are stitched together. Mistake of the factory? Oversight of the store? Who knows? One thing is certain: your fingers won't fill the glove. A closed fist will, but an extended hand won't.

No problem, you say to yourself. *I'll make do.* You fist your way into the palm and park there, your fingers folded, the glove fingers flopping. Not exactly what you had in mind, but, hey, when it comes to warmth, you can't complain. Folded fingers stay nice and toasty. Frostbite is no concern.

Function, however, is. Ever tried to pick up a newspaper with your fingers folded inside a glove? Not easy. Neither is tying your shoes. Your hands feel like horse hoofs. Wave at someone, and he thinks you are shaking your fist. And forget grabbing a pencil or dialing a cell phone. Floppy wool has no grip.

You want extended fingers, stretched and strong. Why? You have leaves to rake. A steering wheel to grip. A neighbor's hand to shake. Simply put, you have things to do.

So does God. Babies need hugs. Children need good-night tucks. AIDS orphans need homes. Stressed-out executives need hope. God has work to do. And he uses our hands to do it.

What the hand is to the glove, the Spirit is to the Christian. "Behold, I stand at the door and knock; if anyone hears My voice and opens the door, I will *come in* to him" (Rev. 3:20 NASB). God gets into us. At times, imperceptibly. Other times, disruptively. God gets his fingers into our lives, inch by inch reclaiming the territory that is rightfully his.

Your tongue. He claims it for his message.

Your feet. He requisitions them for his purpose.

Your mind? He made it and intends to use it for his glory.

God gets his fingers into our lives, inch by inch reclaiming the territory that is rightfully his.

Your eyes, face, and hands? Through them he will weep, smile, and touch.

As a glove responds to the strength of the hand, so you will respond to the leading of Christ to the point where you say, "I myself no longer live, but Christ lives in me" (Gal. 2:20 NLT).

—*Come Thirsty*

*G*od's cure for the common life includes a strong dose of servanthood. Timely reminder. As you celebrate your unique design, be careful. Don't so focus on what you love to do that you neglect what needs to be done.

A 3:00 a.m. diaper change fits in very few sweet spots. . . . Visiting your sick neighbor might not come naturally to you. Still, the sick need to be encouraged, garages need sweeping, and diapers need changing.

The world needs servants. People like Jesus, who "did not come to be served, but to serve" (Matthew 20:28 NKJV). He chose remote Nazareth over center-stage Jerusalem, his dad's carpentry shop over a marble-columned palace, and three decades of anonymity over a life of popularity.

Jesus came to serve. He selected prayer over sleep, the wilderness over the Jordan, irascible apostles over obedient angels. I'd have gone with the angels. Given the choice, I would have built my apostle team out of cherubim and seraphim or Gabriel and Michael, eyewitnesses of Red Sea rescues and Mount Carmel falling fires. I'd choose the angels.

Not Jesus. He picked the people. Peter, Andrew, John, and Matthew. When they feared the storm, he stilled it. When they had no coin for taxes, he supplied it. And when they had no wine for the wedding or food for the multitude, he made both.

He came to serve.

—*CURE FOR THE COMMON LIFE*

*P*eople are watching the way we act more than they are listening to what we say.

—*A GENTLE THUNDER*

*W*hat is your kindness quotient? When was the last time you did something kind for someone in your family—e.g., got a blanket, cleaned off the table, prepared the coffee—without being asked?

Think about your school or workplace. Which person is the most overlooked or avoided? A shy student? A grumpy employee? Maybe he doesn't speak the language. Maybe she doesn't fit in. Are you kind to this person?

Kind hearts are quietly kind. They let the car cut into traffic and the young mom with three kids move up in the checkout line. They pick up the neighbor's trash can that rolled into the street. And they are especially kind at church. They understand that perhaps the neediest person they'll meet all week is the one standing in the foyer or sitting on the row behind them in worship. Paul writes: "When we have the opportunity to help anyone, we should do it. But we should give special attention to those who are in the family of believers" (Gal. 6:10 NCV).

And, here is a challenge—what about your enemies? How kind are you to those who want what you want or take what you have?

A friend of mine witnessed a humorous act of kindness at an auction. The purpose of the gathering was to raise money for a school. Someone had donated a purebred puppy that melted the heart and opened the checkbooks of many guests. Two in particular.

They sat on opposite sides of the banquet room, a man and a woman. As the bidding continued, these two surfaced as the most determined. Others dropped off, but not this duo. Back and forth they went until they'd one-upped the bid to several thousand dollars. This was no longer about a puppy. This was about victory. This was the Wimbledon finals, and neither player was backing off the net. (Don't you know the school president was drooling?)

Kind hearts are quietly kind.

Finally the fellow gave in and didn't return the bid. "Going once, going twice, going three times. Sold!" The place erupted, and the lady was presented with her tail-wagging trophy. Her face softened, then reddened. Maybe she'd forgotten where she was. Never intended to go twelve rounds at a formal dinner. Certainly never intended for the world to see her pit-bull side.

So you know what she did? As the applause subsided, she walked across the room and presented the puppy to the competition.

Suppose you did that with your competition. With your enemy. With the boss who fired you or the wife who left you. Suppose you surprised them with kindness? Not easy? No, it's not. But mercy is the deepest gesture of kindness. Paul equates the two. "Be kind to one another, tenderhearted, forgiving one another, even as God in Christ forgave you" (Eph. 4:32 NKJV).

—A Love Worth Giving

$\mathcal{T}$he ultimate solution to poverty is found in the compassion of God's people. Scripture endorses not forced communism but Spirit-led volunteerism among God's people.

—Outlive Your Life

At 7:51 a.m., January 12, 2007, a young musician took his position against a wall in a Washington, DC, metro station. He wore jeans, a long-sleeved T-shirt, and a Washington Nationals' baseball cap. He opened a violin case, removed his instrument, threw a few dollars and pocket change into the case as seed money, and began to play.

He played for the next forty-three minutes. He performed six classical pieces. During that time, 1,097 people passed by. They tossed money to the total of $32.17. Of the 1,097 people, seven, only seven, paused longer than 60 seconds. And of the seven, one, only one, recognized the violinist Joshua Bell.

Three days prior to this metro appearance staged by the *Washington Post*, Bell filled Boston's symphony hall, where the cheap tickets went for $100 a seat. Two weeks after the experiment he played for a standing-room-only audience in Bethesda, Maryland. Joshua Bell's talents can command $1000 a minute. That day, in the subway station, he barely earned enough to buy a cheap pair of shoes.

You can't fault the instrument. He played a Stradivarius built in the golden period of Stradivari's career. It's worth $3.5 million. You can't fault the music. Bell successfully played a piece from Johann Sebastian Bach that Bell called "one of the greatest achievements of any man in history."

But scarcely anyone noticed. No one expected majesty in such a context. Shoeshine stand to one side, kiosk to the other. People buying magazines, newspapers, chocolate bars, and Lotto tickets. And who had time? This was a workday. This was the Washington workforce. Government workers mainly, on their way to budget meetings and management sessions. Who had time to notice beauty in the midst of busyness? Most did not.

Most of us will someday realize that we didn't either. From the perspective of heaven, we'll look back on these days, these busy, cluttered days, and realize, *That was Jesus playing the violin. That was Jesus wearing the ragged clothes. That was Jesus in the orphanage . . . in the jail . . . in the cardboard shanty. The person needing my help was Jesus.*

There are many reasons to help needy people.

"Benevolence is good for the world."

"We all float on the same ocean. When the tide rises, it benefits everyone."

"To deliver someone from poverty is to unleash their potential as a researcher, educator, or doctor."

"As we reduce poverty and disease we reduce war and atrocities. Healthy, happy people don't hurt each other."

Compassion has a dozen advocates.

But for the Christian, none is higher than this: when we love those in need, we are loving Jesus. It is a mystery beyond science, a truth beyond statistics. But it is a message that Jesus made crystal clear: when we love them, we love him.

—*OUTLIVE YOUR LIFE*

When we love those in need, we are loving Jesus.

Creation

A World Wrapped in Splendor

*W*hy do you stare at sunsets and ponder the summer night sky? Why do you search for a rainbow in the mist or gaze at the Grand Canyon? Why do you allow the Pacific surf to mesmerize and Niagara to hypnotize? How do we explain our fascination with such sights?

Beauty? Yes. But doesn't the beauty point to a beautiful Someone? Doesn't the immensity of the ocean suggest an immense Creator? Doesn't the rhythm of migrating cranes and beluga whales hint of a brilliant mind? And isn't that what we desire? A beautiful Maker? An immense Creator? A God so mighty that he can commission the birds and command the fish?

—*It's Not About Me*

"*In* the beginning God *created* the heavens and the earth" (Gen. 1:1 NIV).

That's what it says. "God *created* the heavens and the earth." It doesn't say, "God *made* the heavens and the earth." Nor does it say that he "xeroxed" the heavens and the earth. Or built or developed or mass produced. No, the word is *created*.

And that one word says a lot. Creating is something far different than constructing. The difference is pretty obvious. Constructing something engages only the hands while creating something engages the heart and the soul.

You've probably noticed this in your own life. Think about something you've created. A painting perhaps. Or a song. Those lines of poetry you never showed to anyone. Or even the doghouse in the backyard.

How do you feel toward that creation? Good? I hope so. Proud? Even protective? You should. Part of you lives in that project. When you create something you are putting yourself into it. It's far greater than an ordinary assignment or task; it's an expression of you!

Now, imagine God's creativity. Of all we don't know about the creation, there is one thing we do know–he did it with a smile. He must've had a blast. Painting the stripes on the zebra, hanging the stars in the sky, putting the gold in the sunset. What creativity! Stretching the neck of the giraffe, putting the flutter in the mockingbird's wings, planting the giggle in the hyena.

Of all we don't know about the creation, there is one thing we do know—he did it with a smile.

What a time he had. Like a whistling carpenter in his workshop, he loved every bit of it. He poured himself into the work. So intent was his creativity that he took a day off at the end of the week just to rest.

And then, as a finale to a brilliant performance, he made man. With his typical creative flair, he began with a useless mound of dirt and ended up with an invaluable species called a human. A human who had the unique honor to bear the stamp, "In His Image."

At this point in the story one would be tempted to jump and clap. "Bravo!" "Encore!" "Unmatchable!" "Beautiful!"

But the applause would be premature. The Divine Artist has yet to unveil his greatest creation.

As the story unfolds, a devil of a snake feeds man a line and an apple, and gullible Adam swallows them both. This one act of rebellion sets in motion a dramatic and erratic courtship between God and man. Though the characters and scenes change, the scenario repeats itself endlessly. God, still the compassionate Creator, woos his creation. Man, the creation, alternately reaches out in repentance and runs in rebellion.

It is within this simple script that God's creativity flourishes. If you thought he was imaginative with the sea and the stars, just wait until you read what he does to get his creation to listen to him!

For example:

A ninety-year-old woman gets pregnant.

A woman turns to salt.

A flood blankets the earth.

A bush burns (but doesn't burn up!).

The Red Sea splits in two.

The walls of Jericho fall.

The sky rains fire.

A donkey speaks.

Talk about special effects! But these acts, be they ever ingenious, still couldn't compare with what was to come.

Nearing the climax of the story, God, motivated by love and directed by divinity, surprised everyone. He became a man. In an untouchable mystery, he disguised himself as a carpenter and lived in a dusty Judaean village. Determined to prove his love for his creation, he walked incognito through his own world. His callused hands touched wounds and his compassionate words touched hearts. He became one of us.

—*No Wonder They Call Him the Savior*

*G*od, motivated by love and directed by divinity, surprised everyone. He became a man.

$\mathcal{W}$e are without excuse because God has revealed himself to us through his creation.

The psalmist wrote: "The heavens declare the glory of God, and the skies announce what his hands have made. Day after day they tell the story; night after night they tell it again. They have no speech or words; they have no voice to be heard. But their message goes out through all the world; their words go everywhere on earth" (Ps. 19:1-4 NCV).

Every star is an announcement. Each leaf a reminder. The glaciers are megaphones, the seasons are chapters, the clouds are banners. Nature is a song of many parts but one theme and one verse: *God is* . . .

Creation is God's first missionary. There are those who never held a Bible or heard a scripture. There are those who die before a translator puts God's Word in their tongue. There are millions who lived in ancient times before Christ or live in distant lands far from Christians. There are the simple-minded who are incapable of understanding the gospel. What does the future hold for the person who never hears of God?

Again, Paul's answer is clear. The human heart can know God through the handiwork of nature. If that is all one ever sees, that is enough. One need only respond to what he is given. And if he is given only the testimony of creation, then he has enough.

—In the Grip of Grace

Creation is God's first missionary.

*W*hy did he do it? A shack would have sufficed, but he gave us a mansion. Did he have to give the birds a song and the mountains a peak? Was he required to put stripes on the zebra and the hump on the camel? Would we have known the difference had he made the sunsets gray instead of orange? Why do stars have twinkles and the waves snowy crests? Why dash the cardinal in red and drape the beluga whale in white? Why wrap creation in such splendor? Why go to such trouble to give such gifts?

Why do you? You do the same. I've seen you searching for a gift. I've seen you stalking the malls and walking the aisles. I'm not talking about the obligatory gifts. I'm not describing the last-minute purchase of drugstore perfume on the way to the birthday party. Forget blue-light specials and discount purchases; I'm talking about that extra-special person and that extra-special gift. I'm talking about stashing away a few dollars a month out of the grocery money to buy him some lizard-skin boots; staring at a thousand rings to find her the best diamond; staying up all night Christmas Eve, assembling the new bicycle. Why do you do it? You do it so the eyes will pop. You do it so the heart will stop. You do it so the jaw will drop. You do it to hear those words of disbelief, "You did this for *me*?"

That's why you do it. And that is why God did it. Next time a sunrise steals your breath or a meadow of flowers leaves you speechless, remain that way. Say nothing and listen as heaven whispers, "Do you like it? I did it just for you."

I'm about to tell you something you may find hard to believe. You're about to hear an opinion that may stretch your imagination. You don't have to agree with me, but I would like you to consider it with me. You don't have to buy it, but at least think about it. Here it is: *If you were the only person on earth, the earth would look exactly the same.* The Himalayas would still have their drama and the Caribbean would still have its charm. The sun would still nestle behind the Rockies in the evenings and spray light on the desert in the mornings. If you were the sole pilgrim on this globe, God would not diminish its beauty one degree.

Because he did it all for you . . . and he's waiting for you to discover his gift. He's waiting for you to stumble into the den, rub the sleep from your eyes, and see the bright red bike he assembled, just for you. He's waiting for your eyes to pop and your heart to stop. He's waiting for the moment between the dropping of the jaw and the leap of the heart. For in that silence he leans forward and whispers: *I did it just for you.*

Sometimes, out of his great wisdom, our Father in heaven gives us a piece of heaven just to show he cares.

Find such love hard to believe? That's okay. . . . Just because we can't imagine God's giving us sunsets, don't think God doesn't do it. God's thoughts are higher than ours. God's ways are greater than ours. And sometimes, out of his great wisdom, our Father in heaven gives us a piece of heaven just to show he cares.

—*THE GREAT HOUSE OF GOD*

He splashed orange in the sunrise
and cast the sky in blue.
And if you love to see geese as they gather,
chances are you'll see that too.
Did he have to make the squirrel's tail furry?
Was he obliged to make the birds sing?
And the funny way that chickens scurry
or the majesty of thunder when it rings?
Why give a flower fragrance? Why give food its taste?
Could it be
he loves to see
that look upon your face?
—*HE CHOSE THE NAILS*

*L*et's go to the Garden and see the seed that both blessed and cursed. Let's see why God gave man . . . the choice.

Behind it all was a choice. A deliberate decision. An informed move. He didn't have to do it. But he chose to. He knew the price. He saw the implications. He was aware of the consequences.

We don't know when he decided to do it. We can't know. Not just because we weren't there. Because time was not there. *When* did not exist. Nor did *tomorrow* or *yesterday* or *next time*. For there was no time.

We don't know when he thought about making the choice. But we do know that he made it. He didn't have to do it. He chose to.

He chose to create.

"In the beginning God created . . ." (Gen. 1:1 NIV).

With one decision, history began. Existence became measurable.

Out of nothing came light.

Out of light came day.

Then came sky . . . and earth.

And on this earth? A mighty hand went to work.

Canyons were carved. Oceans were dug. Mountains erupted out of flatlands. Stars were flung. A universe sparkled.

Our sun became just one of millions. Our galaxy became just one of thousands. Planets invisibly tethered to suns roared through space at breakneck speeds. Stars blazed with heat that could melt our planet in seconds.

The hand behind it was mighty. He is mighty.

And with this might, he created. As naturally as a bird sings and a fish swims, he created. Just as an artist can't not paint and a runner can't not run, he couldn't not create. He was the Creator. Through and through, he was the Creator. A tireless dreamer and designer.

From the palette of the Ageless Artist came inimitable splendors. Before there was a person to see it, his creation was pregnant with wonder. Flowers didn't just grow; they blossomed. Chicks weren't just born; they hatched. Salmon didn't just swim; they leaped.

Mundaneness found no home in his universe.

He must have loved it. Creators relish creating. I'm sure his commands were delightful! "Hippo, you won't walk . . . you'll waddle!" "Hyena, a bark is too plain. Let me show you how to laugh!" "Look, raccoon, I've made you a mask!" "Come here, giraffe, let's stretch that neck a bit." And on and on he went. Giving the clouds their puff. Giving the oceans their blue. Giving the trees their sway. Giving the frogs their leap and croak. The mighty wed with the creative, and creation was born.

He was mighty. He was creative.

And he was love. Even greater than his might and deeper than his creativity was one all-consuming characteristic:

Love.

Water must be wet. A fire must be hot. You can't take the wet out of water and still have water. You can't take the heat out of fire and still have fire.

*B*efore there was a person to see it, his creation was pregnant with wonder.

In the same way, you can't take the love out of this One who lived before time and still have him exist. For he was . . . and is . . . Love.

Probe deep within him. Explore every corner. Search every angle. Love is all you find. Go to the beginning of every decision he has made, and you'll find it. Go to the end of every story he has told, and you'll see it.

Love.

No bitterness. No evil. No cruelty. Just love. Flawless love. Passionate love. Vast and pure love. He is love.

As a result, an elephant has a trunk with which to drink. A kitten has a mother from which to nurse. A bird has a nest in which to sleep. The same God who was mighty enough to carve out the canyon is tender enough to put hair on the legs of the Matterhorn fly to keep it warm. The same force that provides symmetry to the planets guides the baby kangaroo to its mother's pouch before the mother knows it is born.

And because of who he was, he did what he did.

He created a paradise. A sinless sanctuary. A haven before fear. A home before there was a human dweller. No time. No death. No hurt. A gift built by God for his ultimate creation. And when he was through, he knew "it was very good" (Gen. 1:31 NIV).

But it wasn't enough.

His greatest work hadn't been completed. One final masterpiece was needed before he would stop.

And because of who he was, he did what he did. . . . A gift built by God for his ultimate creation.

Look to the canyons to see the Creator's splendor. Touch the flowers and see his delicacy. Listen to the thunder and hear his power. But gaze on this—the zenith—and witness all three . . . and more.

Imagine with me what may have taken place on that day.

He placed one scoop of clay upon another until a form lay lifeless on the ground.

All of the Garden's inhabitants paused to witness the event. Hawks hovered. Giraffes stretched. Trees bowed. Butterflies paused on petals and watched.

"You will love me, nature," God said. "I made you that way. You will obey me, universe. For you were designed to do so. You will reflect my glory, skies, for that is how you were created. But this one will be like me. This one will be able to choose."

All were silent as the Creator reached into himself and removed something yet unseen. A seed. "It's called 'choice.' The seed of choice."

Creation stood in silence and gazed upon the lifeless form.

An angel spoke, "But what if he . . ."

"What if he chooses not to love?" the Creator finished. "Come, I will show you."

Unbound by today, God and the angel walked into the realm of tomorrow.

"There, see the fruit of the seed of choice, both the sweet and the bitter."

The angel gasped at what he saw. Spontaneous love. Voluntary devotion. Chosen tenderness. Never had he seen anything like these. He felt the love of the Adams. He heard the joy of Eve and her daughters. He saw the food and the burdens shared. He absorbed the kindness and marveled at the warmth.

"Heaven has never seen such beauty, my Lord. Truly, this is your greatest creation."

"Ah, but you've only seen the sweet. Now witness the bitter."

A stench enveloped the pair. The angel turned in horror and proclaimed, "What is it?"

The Creator spoke only one word: *selfishness*.

The angel stood speechless as they passed through centuries of repugnance. Never had he seen such filth. Rotten hearts. Ruptured promises. Forgotten loyalties. Children of the creation wandering blindly in lonely labyrinths.

"This is the result of choice?" the angel asked.

"Yes."

"They will forget you?"

"Yes."

"They will reject you?"

"Yes."

"They will never come back?"

"Some will. Most won't."

"What will it take to make them listen?"

The Creator walked on in time, further and further into the

future until he stood by a tree. A tree that would be fashioned into a cradle. Even then he could smell the hay that would surround him.

With another step into the future, he paused before another tree. It stood alone, a stubborn ruler of a bald hill. The trunk was thick, and the wood was strong. Soon it would be cut. Soon it would be trimmed. Soon it would be mounted on the stony brow of another hill. And soon he would be hung on it.

He felt the wood rub against a back he did not yet wear.

"Will you go down there?" the angel asked.

"I will."

"Is there no other way?"

"There is not."

"Wouldn't it be easier not to plant the seed? Wouldn't it be easier not to give the choice?"

"It would," the Creator spoke slowly. "But to remove the choice is to remove the love."

He looked around the hill and foresaw a scene. Three figures hung on three crosses. Arms spread. Heads fallen forward. They moaned with the wind.

Men clad in soldiers' garb sat on the ground near the trio. They played games in the dirt and laughed.

Men clad in religion stood off to one side. They smiled. Arrogant, cocky. They had protected God, they thought, by killing this false one.

But to remove the choice is
to remove the love.

Women clad in sorrow huddled at the foot of the hill. Speechless. Faces tear streaked. Eyes downward. One put her arm around another and tried to lead her away. She wouldn't leave. "I will stay," she said softly. "I will stay."

All heaven stood to fight. All nature rose to rescue. All eternity poised to protect. But the Creator gave no command.

"It must be done . . ." he said, and withdrew.

But as he stepped back in time, he heard the cry that he would someday scream: "My God, my God, why have you forsaken me?" (Mark 15:34 NIV).

He wrenched at tomorrow's agony.

The angel spoke again. "It would be less painful . . ."

The Creator interrupted softly. "But it wouldn't be love."

They stepped into the Garden again. The Maker looked earnestly at the clay creation. A monsoon of love swelled up within him. He had died for the creation before he had made him. God's form bent over the sculptured face and breathed. Dust stirred on the lips of the new one. The chest rose, cracking the red mud. The cheeks fleshened. A finger moved. And an eye opened.

But more incredible than the moving of the flesh was the stirring of the spirit. Those who could see the unseen gasped.

Perhaps it was the wind who said it first. Perhaps what the star saw that moment is what has made it blink ever since. Maybe it was left to an angel to whisper it:

"It looks like . . . it appears so much like . . . it is him!"

The angel wasn't speaking of the face, the features, or the body. He was looking inside–at the soul.

"It's eternal!" gasped another.

Within the man, God had placed a divine seed. A seed of his self. The God of might had created earth's mightiest. The Creator had created, not a creature, but another creator. And the One who had chosen to love had created one who could love in return.

Now it's our choice.

—*In the Eye of the Storm*

The One who had chosen to love had created one who could love in return.

The Cross

A Triumph of Tenderness

The cross.

It rests on the time line of history like a compelling diamond. Its tragedy summons all sufferers. Its absurdity attracts all cynics. Its hope lures all searchers.

And according to Paul, the cross is what counts.

My, what a piece of wood! History has idolized it and despised it, gold-plated it and burned it, worn and trashed it. History has done everything to it but ignore it.

That's the one option that the cross does not offer.

No one can ignore it! You can't ignore a piece of lumber that suspends the greatest claim in history. A crucified carpenter claiming that he is God on earth? Divine? Eternal? The death slayer?

No wonder Paul called it "the core of the gospel." Its bottom line is sobering: if the account is true, it is history's hinge. Period. If not, it is history's hoax.

That's why the cross is what matters.
—*No Wonder They Call Him the Savior*

The diadem of pain,
which sliced your gentle face,
three spikes piercing flesh and wood
to hold you in your place.
The need for blood I understand.
Your sacrifice I embrace.
But the bitter sponge, the cutting spear,
the spit upon your face?
Did it have to be a cross?
Did not a kinder death exist
than six hours hanging between life and death,
all spurred by a betrayer's kiss?
"Oh, Father," you pose,
heart-stilled at what could be,
"I'm sorry to ask, but I long to know,
did you do this for me?"
—*He Chose the Nails*

*L*ike a master painter God reserved his masterpiece until the end. All the earlier acts of love had been leading to this one. The angels hushed and the heavens paused to witness the finale. God unveils the canvas and the ultimate act of creative compassion is revealed.

God on a cross.

The Creator being sacrificed for the creation. God convincing man once and for all that forgiveness still follows failure.

I wonder if, while on the cross, the Creator allowed his thoughts to wander back to the beginning. One wonders if he allowed the myriad of faces and acts to parade in his memory. Did he reminisce about the creation of the sky and sea? Did he relive the conversations with Abraham and Moses? Did he remember the plagues and the promises, the wilderness and the wanderings? We don't know.

We do know, however, what he said.

"It is finished."

The mission was finished. All that the master painter needed to do was done and was done in splendor. His creation could now come home.

"It is finished!" he cried.

And the great Creator went home.

(He's not resting, though. Word has it that his tireless hands are preparing a city so glorious that even the angels get goose bumps upon seeing it. Considering what he has done so far, that is one creation I plan to see.)

—*No Wonder They Call Him the Savior*

*N*ails didn't hold God to a cross. Love did.

—*When God Whispers Your Name*

*S*ix hours, one Friday.

To the casual observer the six hours are mundane. A shepherd with his sheep, a housewife with her thoughts, a doctor with his patients. But to the handful of awestruck witnesses, the most maddening of miracles is occurring.

God is on a cross. The creator of the universe is being executed.

Spit and blood are caked to his cheeks, and his lips are cracked and swollen. Thorns rip his scalp. His lungs scream with pain. His legs knot with cramps. Taut nerves threaten to snap as pain twangs her morbid melody. Yet, death is not ready. And there is no one to save him, for he is sacrificing himself.

It is no normal six hours. . . . it is no normal Friday.

Far worse than the breaking of his body is the shredding of his heart.

His own countrymen clamored for his death.

His own disciple planted the kiss of betrayal.

His own friends ran for cover.

And now his own father is beginning to turn his back on him, leaving him alone.

A witness could not help but ask: Jesus, do you give no thought to saving yourself? What keeps you there? What holds you to the cross? Nails don't hold gods to trees. What makes you stay? . . .

Six hours. One Friday.

Let me ask you a question: What do you do with that day in history? What do you do with its claims?

If it really happened . . . if God did commandeer his own crucifixion . . . if he did turn his back on his own son . . . if he did storm Satan's gate, then those six hours that Friday were packed with tragic triumph. If that was God on that cross, then the hill called Skull is granite studded with stakes to which you can anchor.

Those six hours were no normal six hours. They were the most critical hours in history. For during those six hours on that Friday, God embedded in the earth three anchor points sturdy enough to withstand any hurricane.

Anchor point Nº 1–*My life is not futile.* This rock secures the hull of your heart. Its sole function is to give you something that you can grip when facing the surging tides of futility and relativism. It's a firm grasp on the conviction that there is truth. Someone is in control and you have a purpose.

The One who has the right to condemn you provided the way to acquit you. You make mistakes. God doesn't. And he made you.

Anchor point № 2–*My failures are not fatal*. It's not that he loves what you did, but he loves who you are. You are his. The One who has the right to condemn you provided the way to acquit you. You make mistakes. God doesn't. And he made you.

Anchor point № 3–*My death is not final*. There is one more stone to which you should tie. It's large. It's round. And it's heavy. It blocked the door of a grave. It wasn't big enough, though. The tomb that it sealed was the tomb of a transient. He only went in to prove he could come out. And on the way out he took the stone with him and turned it into an anchor point. He dropped it deep into the uncharted waters of death. Tie to his rock and the typhoon of the tomb becomes a spring breeze on Easter Sunday.

There they are. Three anchor points. The anchor points of the cross.

—*Six Hours One Friday*

*T*here was something about the crucifixion that made every witness either step toward it or away from it. It simultaneously compelled and repelled.

And today, two thousand years later, the same is true. It's the watershed. It's the Continental Divide. It's Normandy. And you are either on one side or the other. A choice is demanded. We can do what we want with the cross. We can examine its history. We can study its theology. We can reflect upon its prophecies. Yet the one thing we can't do is walk away in neutral. No fence sitting is permitted. The cross, in its absurd splendor, doesn't allow that. That is one luxury that God, in his awful mercy, doesn't permit.

On which side are you?

—NO WONDER THEY CALL HIM THE SAVIOR

*T*he sinless One took on the face of a sinner so that we sinners could take on the face of a saint.

—HE CHOSE THE NAILS

*O*ur Master lived a three-dimensional life. He had as clear a view of the future as he did of the present and the past.

This is why the ropes used to tie his hands and the soldiers used to lead him to the cross were unnecessary. They were incidental. Had they not been there, had there been no trial, no Pilate and no crowd, the very same crucifixion would have occurred. Had Jesus been forced to nail himself to the cross, he would have done it. For it was not the soldiers who killed him, nor the screams of the mob. It was his devotion to us.

So call it what you wish: An act of grace. A plan of redemption.

A martyr's sacrifice. But whatever you call it, don't call it an accident. It was anything but that.

—*GOD CAME NEAR*

*O*h, the hands of Jesus. Hands of incarnation at his birth. Hands of liberation as he healed. Hands of inspiration as he taught. Hands of dedication as he served. And hands of salvation as he died.

The crowd at the cross concluded that the purpose of the pounding was to skewer the hands of Christ to a beam. But they were only half-right. We can't fault them for missing the other half. They couldn't see it. But Jesus could. And heaven could. And we can.

Through the eyes of Scripture we see what others missed but what Jesus saw. "He canceled the record that contained the charges against us. He took it and destroyed it by nailing it to Christ's cross" (Col. 2:14 NLT).

Between his hand and the wood there was a list. A long list. A list of our mistakes: our lusts and lies and greedy moments and prodigal years. A list of our sins.

Dangling from the cross is an itemized catalog of your sins. The bad decisions from last year. The bad attitudes from last week. There, in broad daylight for all of heaven to see, is a list of your mistakes.

God has done with us what I am doing with our house. He has penned a list of our faults. The list God has made, however, cannot be read. The words can't be deciphered. The mistakes are covered. The sins are hidden. Those at the top are hidden by his hand; those down the list are covered by his blood. Your sins are "blotted out" by Jesus (see KJV). "He has forgiven you all your sins: Christ has utterly wiped out the damning evidence of broken laws and commandments which always hung over our heads, and has completely annulled it by nailing it over his own head on the cross" (Col. 2:14 PHILLIPS).

This is why he refused to close his fist. He saw the list! What kept him from resisting? This warrant, this tabulation of your failures. He knew the price of those sins was death. He knew the source of those sins was you, and since he couldn't bear the thought of eternity without you, he chose the nails.

The hand squeezing the handle was not a Roman infantryman.

The force behind the hammer was not an angry mob.

The verdict behind the death was not decided by jealous Jews.

Jesus himself chose the nails.

So the hands of Jesus opened up. Had the soldier hesitated, Jesus himself would have swung the mallet. He knew how; he was no stranger to the driving of nails. As a carpenter he knew what it took. And as a Savior he knew what it meant. He knew that the purpose of the nail was to place your sins where they could be hidden by his sacrifice and covered by his blood.

He knew the price of those sins was death. He knew the source of those sins was you, and since he couldn't bear the thought of eternity without you, he chose the nails.

So Jesus himself swung the hammer.

The same hand that stilled the seas stills your guilt.

The same hand that cleansed the Temple cleanses your heart.

The hand is the hand of God.

The nail is the nail of God.

And as the hands of Jesus opened for the nail, the doors of heaven opened for you.

—*HE CHOSE THE NAILS*

*P*aul said, "The cross of our Lord Jesus Christ is my only reason for bragging" (Gal. 6:14 NCV). Do you feel a need for affirmation? Does your self-esteem need attention? You don't need to drop names or show off. You need only pause at the base of the cross and be reminded of this: The maker of the stars would rather die for you than live without you. And that is a fact. So if you need to brag, brag about that.

—*TRAVELING LIGHT*

$\mathcal{A}$ boy went into a pet shop, looking for a puppy. The store owner showed him a litter in a box. The boy looked at the puppies. He picked each one up, examined it, and put it back into the box.

After several minutes, he walked back to the owner and said, "I picked one out. How much will it cost?"

The man gave him the price, and the boy promised to be back in a few days with the money. "Don't take too long," the owner cautioned. "Puppies like these sell quickly."

The boy turned and smiled knowingly, "I'm not worried," he said. "Mine will still be here."

The boy went to work–weeding, washing windows, cleaning yards. He worked hard and saved his money. When he had enough for the puppy, he returned to the store.

He walked up to the counter and laid down a pocketful of wadded bills. The store owner sorted and counted the cash. After verifying the amount, he smiled at the boy and said, "All right, son, you can go get your puppy."

The boy reached into the back of the box, pulled out a skinny dog with a limp leg, and started to leave.

The owner stopped him.

"Don't take that puppy," he objected. "He's crippled. He can't play. He'll never run with you. He can't fetch. Get one of the healthy pups."

"No thank you, sir," the boy replied. "This is exactly the kind of dog I've been looking for."

As the boy turned to leave, the store owner started to speak but remained silent. Suddenly he understood. For extending from the bottom of the boy's trousers was a brace—a brace for his crippled leg.

Why did the boy want the dog? Because he knew how it felt. And he knew it was very special.

What did Jesus know that enabled him to do what he did? He knew how the people felt, and he knew that they were special.

I hope you never forget that.

Jesus knows how you feel. You're under the gun at work? Jesus knows how you feel. You've got more to do than is humanly possible? So did he. You've got children who make a "piranha hour" out of your dinner hour? Jesus knows what that's like. People take more from you than they give? Jesus understands. Your teenagers won't listen? Your students won't try? Your employees give you blank stares when you assign tasks? Believe me, friend, Jesus knows how you feel.

When you struggle, he listens.
When you yearn, he responds.
When you question, he hears.

You are precious to him. So precious that he became like you so that you would come to him.

When you struggle, he listens. When you yearn, he responds. When you question, he hears. He has been there. You've heard that before, but you need to hear it again. . . .

He understands you with the compassion of the crippled boy. . . .

And, like the boy, he paid a great price to take you home.

—*In the Eye of the Storm*

*W*hen Christ is great, our fears are not.

—*Fearless*

*T*he way to deal with discouragement? The cure for disappointment? Go back to the story. Read it again and again. Be reminded that you aren't the first person to weep. And you aren't the first person to be helped.

Read the story and remember, their story is yours!

The challenge too great? Read the story. That's you crossing the Red Sea with Moses.

Too many worries? Read the story. That's you receiving heavenly food with the Israelites.

Your wounds too deep? Read the story. That's you, Joseph, forgiving your brothers for betraying you.

Your enemies too mighty? Read the story. That's you marching with Jehoshaphat into a battle already won.

Your disappointments too heavy? Read the story of the Emmaus-bound disciples. The Savior they thought was dead now walked beside them. He entered their house and sat at their table. And something happened in their hearts. "It felt like a fire burning in us when Jesus talked to us on the road and explained the Scriptures to us" (Luke 24:32 NCV).

Next time you're disappointed, don't panic. . . . Don't give up. Just be patient and let God remind you he's still in control. It ain't over till it's over.

—*HE STILL MOVES STONES*

You have a ticket to heaven no thief can take,
an eternal home no divorce can break.
Every sin of your life has been cast to the sea.
Every mistake you've made is nailed to the tree.
You're blood-bought and heaven-made.
A child of God—forever saved.
So be grateful, joyful—for isn't it true?
What you don't have is much less than what you do.

—*A LOVE WORTH GIVING*

*S*eek first the kingdom of wealth, and you'll worry over every dollar. Seek first the kingdom of health, and you'll sweat every blemish and bump. Seek first the kingdom of popularity, and you'll relive every conflict. Seek first the kingdom of safety, and you'll jump at every crack of the twig. But seek first his kingdom, and you will find it. On that, we can depend and never worry.

—*Fearless*

A storm on the Sea of Galilee was akin to a sumo wrestler's belly flop on a kiddy pool. The northern valley acted like a wind tunnel, compressing and hosing squalls onto the lake. Waves as tall as ten feet were common.

The account begins at nightfall. Jesus is on the mountain in prayer, and the disciples are in the boat in fear. They are "far away from land . . . fighting heavy waves" (Matt. 14:24 NLT). When does Christ come to them? At three o'clock in the morning (v. 25 NLT)! If "evening" began at six o'clock and Christ came at three in the morning, the disciples were alone in the storm for nine hours! Nine tempestuous hours. Long enough for more than one disciple to ask, "Where is Jesus? He knows we are in the boat. For heaven's sake, it was his idea. Is God anywhere near?"

And from within the storm comes an unmistakable voice: "I am."

Wet robe, soaked hair. Waves slapping his waist and rain stinging his face. Jesus speaks to them at once. "Courage! I am! Don't be afraid!" (v. 27).[1]

That wording sounds odd, doesn't it? If you've read the story, you're accustomed to a different shout from Christ. Something like, "Take courage! It is I" (NIV), or "It's all right. . . . I am here!" (NLT), or "Courage, it's me" (MSG).

A literal translation of his announcement results in "Courage! I am! Don't be afraid." Translators tinker with his words for obvious reasons. "I am" sounds truncated. "I am here" or "It is I" feels more complete. But what Jesus shouted in the storm was simply the magisterial: "I am."

The words ring like the cymbal clash in the *1842 Overture*. We've heard them before.

Speaking from a burning bush to a knee-knocking Moses, God announced, "I AM WHO I AM" (Exod. 3:14 NASB).

Double-dog daring his enemies to prove him otherwise, Jesus declared, "Before Abraham was born, I am" (John 8:58 NASB).

Determined to say it often enough and loud enough to get our attention, Christ chorused:

- "I am the bread of life." (John 6:48 NASB)
- "I am the Light of the world." (John 8:12 NASB)

- "I am the gate; whoever enters through me will be saved." (John 10:9 NIV)
- "I am the good shepherd." (John 10:11 NASB)
- "I am God's Son." (John 10:36 NCV)
- "I am the resurrection and the life." (John 11:25 NASB)
- "I am the way, and the truth, and the life." (John 14:6 NASB)
- "I am the true vine." (John 15:1 NASB)

The present-tense Christ. He never says, "I was." We do. We do because *we were.* We were younger, faster, prettier. Prone to be people of the past tense, we reminisce. Not God. Unwavering in strength, he need never say, "I was." Heaven has no rearview mirrors.

Or crystal balls. Our "I am" God never yearns, "Someday I will be."

Again, we do. Dream-fueled, we reach for horizons. "Someday I will . . ." Not God. Can water be wetter? Could wind be windless? Can God be more God? No. He does not change. He is the "I am" God. "Jesus Christ is the same yesterday, today, and forever" (Heb. 13:8 NLT).

From the center of the storm, the unwavering Jesus shouts, "I am." Tall in the Trade Tower wreckage. Bold against the Galilean waves. ICU, battlefield, boardroom, prison cell, or maternity ward—whatever your storm, "I am."

—NEXT DOOR SAVIOR

Can God be more God? No. He does not change.

It's not too late to seek your Father's heart. Your God is a good God. . . . He lavished you with strengths in this life and a promise of the next. Go out on a limb; he won't let you fall. Take a big risk; he won't let you fail. He invites you to dream of the day you feel his hand on your shoulder and his eyes on your face. "Well done," he will say, "good and faithful servant."

—*Cure for the Common Life*

The Bible says that "in everything God works for the good of those who love him" (Rom. 8:28 NCV). . . . Do this simple exercise. Remove the word *everything*, and replace it with the symbol of your tragedy. . . .

How would Romans 8:28 read in your life?

In *hospital stays* God works for the good.

In *divorce papers* God works for the good.

In *a prison term* God works for the good. . . .

As hard as it may be to believe, you could be only a Saturday away from a resurrection. You could be only hours from that precious prayer of a changed heart, "God, did you do this for me?"

—*He Chose the Nails*

*W*hat you and I might rate as an absolute disaster, God may rate as a pimple-level problem that will pass. He views your life the way you view a movie after you've read the book. When something bad happens, you feel the air sucked out of the theater. Everyone else gasps at the crisis on the screen. Not you. Why? You've read the book. You know how the good guy gets out of the tight spot. God views your life with the same confidence. He's not only read your story . . . he wrote it.

—*COME THIRSTY*

"*E*verything that was written in the past was written to teach us," Paul penned. "The Scriptures give us patience and encouragement so that we can have hope" (Rom. 15:4 NCV).

These are not just Sunday school stories. Not romantic fables. Not somewhere-over-the-rainbow illusions. They are historic moments in which a real God met real pain so we could answer the question, "Where is God when I hurt?"

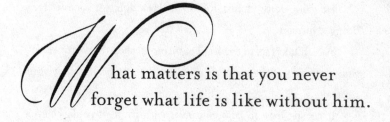

What matters is that you never forget what life is like without him.

How does God react to dashed hopes? Read the story of Jairus. How does the Father feel about those who are ill? Stand with him at the pool of Bethesda. Do you long for God to speak to your lonely heart? Then listen as he speaks to the Emmaus-bound disciples. What is God's word for the shameful? Watch as his finger draws in the dirt of the Jerusalem courtyard.

He's not doing it just for them. He's doing it for me. He's doing it for you.

Which takes us to the final painting in the gallery–yours. . . . Stand in front of the canvases that bear your name and draw your portrait.

It doesn't have to be on a canvas with paint. It could be on a paper with pencil, on a computer with words, in a sculpture with clay, in a song with lyrics. It doesn't matter how you do it, but I urge you to do it. Record your drama. Retell your saga. Plot your journey.

Begin with "before." What was it like before you knew him? Do you remember? Could be decades ago. Perhaps it was yesterday. Maybe you know him well. Maybe you've just met him. Again, that doesn't matter. What matters is that you never forget what life is like without him.

Remembering can hurt. Parts of our past are not pleasant to revisit. But the recollection is necessary. "Look at what you were when God called you," Paul instructed (1 Cor. 1:26 NCV). We, the adopted, can't forget what life was like as orphans. We, the liberated, should revisit the prison. We, the found, can't forget the despair of being lost.

Amnesia fosters arrogance. We can't afford to forget. We need to remember.

And we need to share our story. Not with everyone but with someone. There is someone who is like you were. And he or she needs to know what God can do. Your honest portrayal of your past may be the courage for another's future.

But don't just portray the past, depict the present. Describe his touch. Display the difference he has made in your life. This task has its challenges, too. Whereas painting the "before" can be painful, painting the "present" can be unclear. He's not finished with you yet!

Ah, but look how far you've come! I don't even know you, but I know you've come a long way. . . . God has begun a work in your heart. And what God begins, God completes. "God began doing a good work in you, and I am sure he will continue it until it is finished when Jesus Christ comes again" (Phil. 4:6 NCV).

So chronicle what Christ has done. If he has brought peace, sketch a dove. If joy, splash a rainbow on a wall. If courage, sing a song about mountain-movers. And when you're finished, don't hide it away. Put it where you can see it. Put it where you can be reminded, daily, of the Father's tender power.

And when we all get home, we'll make a gallery.

*Y*our honest portrayal of your past may be the courage for another's future.

That's my idea. I know it's crazy, but what if, when we all get home, we make a gallery? I don't know if they allow this kind of stuff in heaven. But something tells me the Father won't mind. After all, there's plenty of space and lots of time.

And what an icebreaker! What a way to make friends! Can you envision it? There's Jonah with a life-size whale. Moses in front of a blazing bush. David is giving slingshot lessons. Gideon is letting people touch the fleece–*the* fleece–and Abraham is describing a painting entitled, "The Night with a Thousand Stars."

You can sit with Zacchaeus in his tree. A young boy shows you a basket of five loaves and two fishes. Martha welcomes you in her kitchen. The centurion invites you to touch the cross.

Martin Luther is there with the Book of Romans. Susannah Wesley tells how she prayed for her sons–Charles and John. Dwight Moody tells of the day he left the shoe store to preach. And John Newton volunteers to sing "Amazing Grace" with an angelic backup.

Some are famous, most are not . . . but all are heroes. A soldier lets you sit in a foxhole modeled after the one he was in when he met Christ. A housewife shows you her tear-stained New Testament. Beside a Nigerian is the missionary who taught him. And behind the Brazilian is a drawing of the river in which he was baptized.

And somewhere in the midst of this arena of hope is your story. Person after person comes. They listen as if they have all the time in the world. (And they do!) They treat you as if you are royalty. (For you are!) Solomon asks you questions. Job compliments your stamina. Joshua lauds your courage. And when they all applaud, you applaud too. For in heaven, everyone knows that all praise goes to one source.

And speaking of the source, he's represented in the heavenly gallery as well. Turn and look. High above the others. In the most prominent place. Exactly in the middle. There is one display elevated high on a platform above the others. Visible from any point in the gallery is a boulder. It's round. It's heavy. It used to seal the opening of a tomb.

But not anymore. Ask Mary and Mary. Ask Peter. Ask Lazarus. Ask anyone in the gallery. They'll tell you. Stones were never a match for God.

Will there be such a gallery in heaven? Who knows? But I do know there used to be a stone in front of a tomb. And I do know it was moved. And I also know that there are stones in your path. Stones that trip and stones that trap. Stones too big for you. . . .

He comes into your world. He comes to do what you can't. He comes to move the stones you can't budge.

Stones are no match for God. Not then and not now. He still moves stones.

—*HE STILL MOVES STONES*

He comes into your world.
He comes to do what you can't.

Evangelism

Hope for Searching Hearts

$\mathcal{A}$ woman in a small Arkansas community was a single mom with a frail baby. Her neighbor would stop by every few days and keep the child so she could shop. After some weeks her neighbor shared more than time; she shared her faith, and the woman did what Matthew did. She followed Christ.

The friends of the young mother objected. "Do you know what those people teach?" they contested.

"Here is what I know," she told them. "They held my baby."

I think Jesus likes that kind of answer, don't you? (Thanks to Landon Saunders for sharing this story with me.)

—*Next Door Savior*

*Y*ou've heard the voice whispering your name, haven't you? You've felt the nudge to go and sensed the urge to speak. Hasn't it occurred to you?

You invite a couple over for coffee. Nothing heroic, just a nice evening with old friends. But from the moment they enter, you can feel the tension. Colder than glaciers, they are. You can tell something is wrong. Typically you're not one to inquire, but you feel a concern that won't be silent. So you ask.

You are in a business meeting where one of your coworkers gets raked over the coals. Everyone else is thinking, *I'm glad that wasn't me.* But the Holy Spirit is leading you to think, *How hard this must be.* So after the meeting you approach the employee and express your concern.

You notice the fellow on the other side of the church auditorium. He looks a bit out of place, what with his strange clothing and all. You learn that he is from Africa, in town on business. The next Sunday he is back. And the third Sunday he is present. You introduce yourself. He tells you how he is fascinated by the faith and how he wants to learn more. Rather than offer to teach him, you simply urge him to read the Bible.

Later in the week you regret not being more direct. You call the office where he is consulting and learn that he is leaving today for home. You know in your heart you can't let him leave. So you rush to the airport and find him awaiting his flight with a Bible open on his lap.

 o you understand what you are reading?" you inquire.

"Do you understand what you are reading?" you inquire.

"How can I unless someone explains it to me?"

And so you, like Philip, explain. And he, like the Ethiopian, believes. Baptism is requested, and baptism is offered. He catches a later flight, and you catch a glimpse of what it means to be led by the Spirit.

"How can I unless someone explains it to me?"

Were there lights? You just lit one. Were there voices? You just were one. Was there a miracle? You just witnessed one. Who knows? If the Bible were being written today, that might be your name in the eighth chapter of Acts.

—*When God Whispers Your Name*

*L*ong ago or maybe not so long ago, there was a tribe in a dark, cold cavern.

The cave dwellers would huddle together and cry against the chill. . . . It was all they did. It was all they knew to do. The sounds in the cave were mournful, but the people didn't know it, for they had never known joy. The spirit in the cave was death, but the people didn't know it, for they had never known life.

But then, one day, they heard a different voice. "I have heard your cries," it announced. "I have felt your chill and seen your darkness. I have come to help."

The cave people grew quiet. They had never heard this voice. Hope sounded strange to their ears. "How can we know you have come to help?"

"Trust me," he answered. "I have what you need."

The cave people peered through the darkness at the figure of the stranger. He was stacking something, then stooping and stacking more.

"What are you doing?" one cried, nervous.

The stranger didn't answer.

"What are you making?" one shouted even louder.

Still no response.

"Tell us!" demanded a third.

The visitor stood and spoke in the direction of the voices. "I have what you need." With that he turned to the pile at his feet and lit it. Wood ignited, flames erupted, and light filled the cavern.

The cave people turned away in fear. "Put it out!" they cried. "It hurts to see it."

"Light always hurts before it helps," he answered. "Step closer. The pain will soon pass."

"Not I," declared a voice.

"Nor I," agreed a second.

"Only a fool would risk exposing his eyes to such light."

The stranger stood next to the fire. "Would you prefer the darkness? Would you prefer the cold? Don't consult your fears. Take a step of faith."

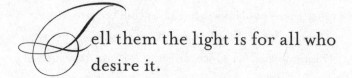ell them the light is for all who desire it.

For a long time no one spoke. The people hovered in groups covering their eyes. The fire builder stood next to the fire. "It's warm here," he invited.

"He's right," one from behind him announced. "It's warmer." The stranger turned and saw a figure slowly stepping toward the fire. "I can open my eyes now," she proclaimed. "I can see."

"Come closer," invited the fire builder.

She did. She stepped into the ring of light. "It's so warm!" She extended her hands and sighed as her chill began to pass.

"Come, everyone! Feel the warmth," she invited.

"Silence, woman!" cried one of the cave dwellers. "Dare you lead us into your folly? Leave us. Leave us, and take your light with you."

She turned to the stranger. "Why won't they come?"

"They choose the chill, for though it's cold, it's what they know. They'd rather be cold than change."

"And live in the dark?"

"And live in the dark."

The now-warm woman stood silent, looking first at the dark, then at the man.

"Will you leave the fire?" he asked.

She paused then answered, "I cannot. I cannot bear the cold." Then she spoke again. "But nor can I bear the thought of my people in darkness."

"You don't have to," he responded, reaching into the fire and removing a stick. "Carry this to your people. Tell them the light is here, and the light is warm. Tell them the light is for all who desire it."

And so she took the small flame and stepped into the shadows.

—*A GENTLE THUNDER*

*I*f God's goal is the salvation of the world, then my goal should be the same. The details will differ from person to person, but the big picture is identical for all of us. "We're Christ's representatives. God uses us to persuade men and women" (2 Cor. 5:20 MSG). Regardless of what you don't know about your future, one thing is certain: you are intended to contribute to the good plan of God, to tell others about the God who loves them and longs to bring them home.

—*JUST LIKE JESUS*

*D*ear friend,

I'm writing to say thanks. I wish I could thank you personally, but I don't know where you are. I wish I could call you, but I don't know your name. If I knew your appearance, I'd look for you, but your face is fuzzy in my memory. But I'll never forget what you did.

There you were, leaning against your pickup in the West Texas oil field. An engineer of some sort. A supervisor on the job. Your khakis and clean shirt set you apart from us roustabouts. In the oil field pecking order, we were at the bottom. You were the boss. We were the workers. You read the blueprints. We dug the ditches. You inspected the pipe. We laid it. You ate with the bosses in the shed. We ate with each other in the shade.

Except that day.

I remember wondering why you did it.

We weren't much to look at. What wasn't sweaty was oily. Faces burnt from the sun, skin black from the grease. Didn't bother me, though. I was there only for the summer. A high-school boy, earning good money laying pipe. For me, it was a summer job. For the others, it was a way of life. Most were illegal immigrants from Mexico. Others were drifters, bouncing across the prairie as rootless as tumbleweeds.

We weren't much to listen to, either. Our language was sandpaper coarse. After lunch we'd light the cigarettes and begin the jokes. Someone always had a deck of cards with lacy-clad girls on the back. For thirty minutes in the heat of the day, the oil patch became Las Vegas–replete with foul language, dirty stories, blackjack, and barstools that doubled as lunch pails.

In the middle of such a game, you approached us. I thought you had a job for us that couldn't wait another few minutes. Like the others, I groaned when I saw you coming.

You were nervous. You shifted your weight from one leg to the other as you began to speak.

"Uh, fellows," you started.

We turned and looked up at you.

"I, uh, I just wanted, uh, to invite . . ."

You were way out of your comfort zone. I had no idea what you might be about to say, but I knew that it had nothing to do with work.

"I just wanted to tell you that, uh, our church is having a service tonight and, uh . . ."

What? I couldn't believe it. *He's talking church? Out here? With us?*

"I wanted to invite any of you to come along."

Silence. Screaming silence. The same silence you'd hear if a nun asked a madam if she could use the brothel for a mass. The same silence you'd hear if an IRS representative invited the Mafia to a seminar on tax integrity.

Several guys stared at the dirt. A few shot glances at the others. Snickers rose just inches from the surface.

"Well, that's it. Uh, if any of you want to go . . . uh, let me know."

After you turned and left, we turned and laughed. We called you *reverend*, *preacher*, and *the pope*. We poked fun at each other, daring one another to go. You became the butt of the day's jokes.

I'm sure you knew that. I'm sure you went back to your truck knowing the only good you'd done was to make a good fool out of yourself. If that's what you thought, then you were wrong.

That's the reason for this letter.

Something told him that if he would plant the seed, God would grant the crop.

I thought of you this week. I thought of you when I read about someone else who took a risk at lunch. I thought of you when I read the story of the little boy who gave his lunch to Jesus (John 6:1–14).

His lunch wasn't much. In fact, it wasn't anything compared to what was needed for more than five thousand people.

He probably wrestled with the silliness of it all. What was one lunch for so many? He probably asked himself if it was even worth the effort.

How far could one lunch go?

I think that's why he didn't give the lunch to the crowd. Instead he gave it to Jesus. Something told him that if he would plant the seed, God would grant the crop.

So he did.

He summoned his courage, got up off the grass, and walked into the circle of grown-ups. He was as out of place in that cluster as you were in ours. He must have been nervous. No one likes to appear silly.

Someone probably snickered at him too.

If they didn't snicker, they shook their heads. "The little fellow doesn't know any better."

If they didn't shake their heads, they rolled their eyes. "Here we have a hunger crisis, and this little boy thinks that a sack lunch will solve it."

But it wasn't the men's heads or eyes that the boy saw; he saw only Jesus.

*B*ut Jesus said to give . . . so you gave.

You must have seen Jesus, too, when you made your decision. Most people would have considered us to be unlikely deacon material. Most would have saved their seeds for softer soil. And they'd have been almost right. But Jesus said to give . . . so you gave.

As I think about it, you and the little boy have a lot in common:

- You both used your lunch to help others.
- You both chose faith over logic.
- You both brought a smile to your Father's face.

There's one difference, though. The boy got to see what Jesus did with his gift, and you didn't. That's why I'm writing. I want you to know that at least one of the seeds fell into a fertile crevice.

Some five years later, a college sophomore was struggling with a decision. He had drifted from the faith given to him by his parents. He wanted to come back. He wanted to come home. But the price was high. His friends might laugh. His habits would have to change. His reputation would have to be overcome.

Could he do it? Did he have the courage?

That's when I thought of you. As I sat in my dorm room late one night, looking for the guts to do what I knew was right, I thought of you.

I thought of how your love for God had been greater than your love for your reputation.

I thought of how your obedience had been greater than your common sense.

I remembered how you had cared more about making disciples than about making a good first impression.

I remembered how you had cared more about making disciples than about making a good first impression. And when I thought of you, your memory became my motivation.

So I came home.

I've told your story dozens of times to thousands of people. Each time the reaction is the same: The audience becomes a sea of smiles, and heads bob in understanding. Some smile because they think of the clean-shirted engineers in their lives. They remember the neighbor who brought the cake, the aunt who wrote the letter, the teacher who listened . . .

Others smile because they have done what you did. And they, too, wonder if their lunchtime loyalty was worth the effort.

You wondered that. What you did that day wasn't much. And I'm sure you walked away that day thinking that your efforts had been wasted.

They weren't.

So I'm writing to say thanks. Thanks for the example. Thanks for the courage. Thanks for giving your lunch to God. He did something with it; it became the Bread of Life for me.

Gratefully,

Max

P.S. If by some remarkable coincidence you read this and remember that day, please give me a call. I owe you lunch.

—*IN THE EYE OF THE STORM*

"*If* I can just touch his clothes," she thinks, "I will be healed" (Mark 5:28 NCV).

Risky decision. To touch him, she will have to touch the people. If one of them recognizes her . . . hello rebuke, good-bye cure. But what choice does she have? She has no money, no clout, no friends, no solutions. All she has is a crazy hunch that Jesus can help and a high hope that he will.

Maybe that's all you have: a crazy hunch and a high hope. You have nothing to give. But you are hurting. And all you have to offer him is your hurt.

Maybe that has kept you from coming to God. Oh, you've taken a step or two in his direction. But then you saw the other people around him. They seemed so clean, so neat, so trim and fit in their faith. And when you saw them, they blocked your view of him. So you stepped back.

If that describes you, note carefully, only one person was commended that day for having faith. It wasn't a wealthy giver. It wasn't a loyal follower. It wasn't an acclaimed teacher. It was a shame-struck, penniless outcast who clutched onto her hunch that he could and her hope that he would.

Which, by the way, isn't a bad definition of faith: *A conviction that he can and a hope that he will.* Sounds similar to the definition of faith given by the Bible. "Without faith no one can please God. Anyone who comes to God must believe that he is real and that he rewards those who truly want to find him" (Heb. 11:6 NCV).

Not too complicated is it? Faith is the belief that God is real and that God is good. Faith is not a mystical experience or a midnight vision or a voice in the forest . . . it is a choice to believe that the one who made it all hasn't left it all and that he still sends light into shadows and responds to gestures of faith.

There was no guarantee, of course. She hoped he'd respond . . . she longed for it . . . but she didn't know if he would. All she knew was that he was there and that he was good. That's faith.

Faith is not the belief that God will do what you want. Faith is the belief that God will do what is right.

—HE STILL MOVES STONES

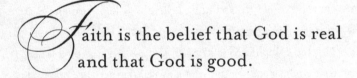

Faith is the belief that God is real and that God is good.

*F*eed your fears, and your faith will starve.
Feed your faith, and your fears will.

—*FEARLESS*

*F*aith in the future begets power in the present.

—*WHEN GOD WHISPERS YOUR NAME*

*W*hether he was born paralyzed or became paralyzed—the end result was the same: total dependence on others. Someone had to wash his face and bathe his body. He couldn't blow his nose or go on a walk. When he ran, it was in his dreams, and his dreams would always awaken to a body that couldn't roll over and couldn't go back to sleep for all the hurt the night dream had brought.

"What he needs is a new body," any man in half his mind would say. What he needs is a God in heaven to restore what tragedy has robbed: arms that swing, hands that grip, and feet that dance.

When people looked at him, they didn't see the man; they saw a body in need of a miracle. That's not what Jesus saw, but that's what the people saw. And that's certainly what his friends saw. So they did what any of us would do for a friend. They tried to get him some help.

Word was out that a carpenter-turned-teacher-turned-wonder-worker was in town. And as the word got out, the people came. They came from every hole and hovel in Israel. They came like soldiers returning from battle–bandaged, crippled, sightless. The old with prune faces and toothless mouths. The young with deaf babies and broken hearts. Fathers with sons who couldn't speak. Wives with wombs that wouldn't bear fruit. The world, it seemed, had come to see if he was real or right or both.

By the time his friends arrived at the place, the house was full. People jammed the doorways. Kids sat in the windows. Others peeked over shoulders. How would this small band of friends ever attract Jesus' attention? They had to make a choice: Do we go in or give up?

What would have happened had the friends given up? What if they had shrugged their shoulders and mumbled something about the crowd being big and dinner getting cold and turned and left? After all, they had done a good deed in coming this far. Who could fault them for turning back? You can only do so much for somebody. But these friends hadn't done enough.

One said that he had an idea. The four huddled over the paralytic and listened to the plan to climb to the top of the house, cut through the roof, and lower their friend down with their sashes.

*Faith does the unexpected.
And faith gets God's attention.*

It was risky–they could fall. It was dangerous–*he* could fall. It was unorthodox–de-roofing is antisocial. It was intrusive–Jesus was busy. But it was their only chance to see Jesus. So they climbed to the roof.

Faith does those things. Faith does the unexpected. And faith gets God's attention. Look what Mark says: "When Jesus saw the faith of these people, he said to the paralyzed man, 'Young man, your sins are forgiven'" (Mark 2:5 NCV).

Finally, someone took him at his word! Four men had enough hope in him and love for their friend that they took a chance. The stretcher above was a sign from above–somebody believes! Someone was willing to risk embarrassment and injury for just a few moments with the Galilean. . . .

Jesus was moved by the scene of faith. So he applauds–if not with his hands, at least with his heart. And not only does he applaud, he blesses. And we witness a divine "loveburst."

The friends want him to heal their friend. But Jesus won't settle for a simple healing of the body–he wants to heal the soul. He leapfrogs the physical and deals with the spiritual. To heal the body is temporal; to heal the soul is eternal.

The request of the friends is valid–but timid. The expectations of the crowd are high–but not high enough. They expect Jesus to say, "I heal you." Instead he says, "I forgive you."

They expect him to treat the body, for that is what they see.

Jesus won't settle for a simple healing of the body—he wants to heal the soul.

He chooses to treat not only the body but also the spiritual, for that is what he sees.

They want Jesus to give the man a new body so he can walk. Jesus gives grace so the man can live.

Remarkable. Sometimes God is so touched by what he sees that he gives us what we need and not simply that for which we ask.

It's a good thing. For who would have ever thought to ask God for what he gives? Which of us would have dared to say: "God, would you please hang yourself on a tool of torture as a substitution for every mistake I have ever committed?" And then have the audacity to add: "And after you forgive me, could you prepare me a place in your house to live forever?"

And if that wasn't enough: "And would you please live within me and protect me and guide me and bless me with more than I could ever deserve?"

Honestly, would we have the chutzpah to ask for that? No, we, like the friends, would have only asked for the small stuff.

We would ask for little things like a long life and a healthy body and a good job. Grand requests from our perspective, but from God's it's like taking the moped when he offers the limo.

So, knowing the paralytic didn't know enough to ask for what he needed, Jesus gave it anyway: "Young man, your sins are forgiven" (Mark 2:5 NCV).

The Pharisees start to grumble. That's not kosher. Even a tenderfoot Jew knows, "Only God can forgive sins" (v. 7 NCV).

Their mumbling spawns one of Christ's greatest questions: "Which is easier: to tell this paralyzed man, 'Your sins are forgiven,' or to tell him, 'Stand up. Take your mat and walk'?" (v. 9 NCV).

You answer the question. Which is easier for Jesus? To forgive a soul or heal a body? Which caused Jesus less pain—providing this man with health or providing this man with heaven?

To heal the man's body took a simple command; to forgive the man's sins took Jesus' blood. The first was done in the house of friends; the second on a hill with thieves. One took a word; the other took his body. One took a moment; the other took his life.

Which was easier?

So strong was his love for this crew of faith that he went beyond their appeal and went straight to the cross.

—*HE STILL MOVES STONES*

I sit a few feet from a man on death row. Jewish by birth. Tentmaker by trade. Apostle by calling. His days are marked. I'm curious about what bolsters this man as he nears his execution. So I ask some questions.

Do you have family, Paul? *I have none.*

What about your health? *My body is beaten and tired.*

What do you own? *I have my parchments. My pen. A cloak.*

And your reputation? *Well, it's not much. I'm a heretic to some, a maverick to others.*

Do you have friends? *I do, but even some of them have turned back.*

Any awards? *Not on earth.*

Then what do you have, Paul? No belongings. No family. Criticized by some. Mocked by others. What do you have, Paul? What do you have that matters?

I sit back quietly and watch. Paul rolls his hand into a fist. He looks at it. I look at it. What is he holding? What does he have?

He extends his hand so I can see. As I lean forward, he opens his fingers. I peer at his palm. It's empty.

I have my faith. It's all I have. But it's all I need. I have kept the faith.

Paul leans back against the wall of his cell and smiles. And I lean back against another and stare into the face of a man who has learned that there is more to life than meets the eye.

For that's what faith is. Faith is trusting what the eye can't see.

Eyes see the prowling lion. Faith sees Daniel's angel.

Eyes see storms. Faith sees Noah's rainbow.

Eyes see giants. Faith sees Canaan.

Your eyes see your faults. Your faith sees your Savior.

Your eyes see your guilt. Your faith sees his blood.

Your eyes see your grave. Your faith sees a city whose builder and maker is God.

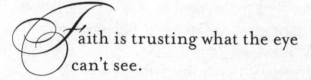Faith is trusting what the eye can't see.

Your eyes look in the mirror and see a sinner, a failure, a promise-breaker. But by faith you look in the mirror and see a robed prodigal bearing the ring of grace on your finger and the kiss of your Father on your face.

—*WHEN GOD WHISPERS YOUR NAME*

*D*o something that demonstrates faith. For faith with no effort is no faith at all. *God will respond.* He has never rejected a genuine gesture of faith. Never.

God honors radical, risk-taking faith.

—*HE STILL MOVES STONES*

*H*ow would you fill in this blank?

A person is made right with God through _____

_____.

Simple statement. Yet don't let its brevity fool you. How you complete it is critical; it reflects the nature of your faith.

A person is made right with God through . . .

Being good. A person is made right with God through goodness. Pay your taxes. Give sandwiches to the poor. Don't drive too fast or drink too much or drink at all. Christian conduct—that's the secret.

Suffering. There's the answer. That's how to be made right

with God–suffer. Sleep on dirt floors. Stalk through dank jungles. Malaria. Poverty. Cold days. Nightlong vigils. Vows of chastity. Shaved heads, bare feet. The greater the pain, the greater the saint.

No, no, no. The way to be made right with God? Doctrine. Dead-center interpretation of the truth. Air-tight theology that explains every mystery. The Millennium simplified. Inspiration clarified. The role of women defined once and for all. God has to save us–we know more than he does.

How are we made right with God? All of the above are tried. All are taught. All are demonstrated. But none are from God.

In fact, that is the problem. None are from God. All are from people. Think about it. Who is the major force in the above examples? Humankind or God? Who does the saving, you or him?

If we are saved by good works, we don't need God–weekly reminders of the do's and don'ts will get us to heaven. If we are saved by suffering, we certainly don't need God. All we need is a whip and a chain and the gospel of guilt. If we are saved by doctrine then, for heaven's sake, let's study! We don't need God. We need a lexicon. Weigh the issues. Explore the options. Decipher the truth.

But be careful, student. For if you are saved by having exact doctrine, then one mistake would be fatal. That goes for those who believe we are made right with God through deeds. I hope the temptation is never greater than the strength. If it is, a bad fall could be a bad omen. And those who think we are saved by suffering, take caution as well, for you never know how much suffering is required.

$\mathcal{B}$e careful . . . if you are saving
yourself, you never know for sure
about anything.

In fact, if you are saving yourself, you never know for sure about anything. You never know if you've hurt enough, wept enough, or learned enough. Such is the result of computerized religion: fear, insecurity, instability. And, most ironically, arrogance.

That's right—arrogance. The insecure boast the most. Those who are trying to save themselves promote themselves. Those saved by works display works. Those saved by suffering unveil scars. Those saved by emotion flash their feelings. And those saved by doctrine—you got it. They wear their doctrine on their sleeves. . . .

Dare you stand before God and ask him to save you because of your suffering or your sacrifice or your tears or your study?

Nor do I.

Nor did Paul. It took him decades to discover what he wrote in only one sentence.

"A person is made right with God through faith" (Rom. 3:28 NCV).

Not through good works, suffering, or study. All those may be the result of salvation but they are not the cause of it.

How will you escape God's judgment? Only one way. Through faith in God's sacrifice. It's not what you do; it's what he did.

—*AND THE ANGELS WERE SILENT*

Family

A Priceless Treasure

*M*y daughters are too old for this now, but when they were young—crib-size and diaper-laden—I would come home, shout their names, and watch them run to me with extended arms and squealing voices. For the next few moments we would speak the language of love. We'd roll on the floor, gobble bellies, and tickle tummies and laugh and play.

We delighted in each other's presence. They made no requests of me, with the exception of "Let's play, Daddy." And I made no demands of them, except, "Don't hit Daddy with the hammer."

My kids let me love them.

—*Just Like Jesus*

Parents, we can't protect children from every threat in life, but we can take them to the Source of life. We can entrust our kids to Christ.

—*FEARLESS*

Crankcase oil coursed my dad's veins. He repaired oil-field engines for a living and rebuilt car engines for fun. He worked in grease and bolts like sculptors work in clay; they were his media of choice. Dad loved machines.

But God gave him a mechanical moron, a son who couldn't differentiate between a differential and a brake disc. My dad tried to teach me. I tried to learn. Honestly, I did. But more than once I actually dozed off under the car on which we were working. Machines anesthetized me. But books fascinated me. I biked to the library a thousand times. What does a mechanic do with a son who loves books?

He gives him a library card. Buys him a few volumes for Christmas. Places a lamp by his bed so he can read at night. Pays tuition so his son can study college literature in high school. My dad did that. You know what he didn't do? Never once did he say, "Why can't you be a mechanic like your dad and granddad?" Maybe he understood my bent. Or maybe he didn't want me to die of hunger. . . .

Study your kids while you can. The greatest gift you can give your children is not your riches, but revealing to them their own.

—*CURE FOR THE COMMON LIFE*

*T*he love of a parent for a child is a mighty force. Consider the couple with their newborn child. The infant offers his parents absolutely nothing. No money. No skill. No words of wisdom. If he had pockets, they would be empty. To see an infant lying in a bassinet is to see utter helplessness. What is there to love?

Whatever it is, Mom and Dad find it. Just look at Mom's face as she nurses her baby. Just watch Dad's eyes as he cradles the child. And just try to harm or speak evil of the infant. If you do, you'll encounter a mighty strength, for the love of a parent is a mighty force.

—*HE CHOSE THE NAILS*

*I*t was her singing that did it. At first I didn't notice. Had no reason to. The circumstances were commonplace. A daddy picking up his six-year-old from a Brownie troop meeting. Sara loves Brownies; she loves the awards she earns and the uniform she wears. She'd climbed in the car and shown me her new badge and freshly baked cookie. I'd turned onto the road, turned on her favorite music, and turned my attention to more sophisticated matters of schedules and obligations.

But only steps into the maze of thought I stepped back out. Sara was singing. Singing about God. Singing to God. Head back, chin up, and lungs full, she filled the car with music. Heaven's harps paused to listen.

Is that my daughter? She sounds older. She looks older, taller, even prettier. Did I sleep through something? What happened to the chubby cheeks? What happened to the little face and pudgy fingers? She is becoming a young lady. Blonde hair down to her shoulders. Feet dangling over the seat. Somewhere in the night a page had turned and, well, look at her!

If you're a parent you know what I mean. Just yesterday diapers, today the car keys? Suddenly your child is halfway to the dormitory, and you're running out of chances to show your love, so you speak.

That's what I did. The song stopped and Sara stopped, and I ejected the tape and put my hand on her shoulder and said, "Sara, you're something special." She turned and smiled tolerantly. "Someday some hairy-legged boy is going to steal your heart and sweep you into the next century. But right now, you belong to me."

She tilted her head, looked away for a minute, then looked back and asked, "Daddy, why are you acting so weird?"

I suppose such words would sound strange to a six-year-old.

The love of a parent falls awkwardly on the ears of a child. My burst of emotion was beyond her. But that didn't keep me from speaking.

—*IN THE GRIP OF GRACE*

*N*o one told me that newborns make nighttime noises. All night long. They gurgle; they pant. They whimper; they whine. They smack their lips and sigh. They keep Daddy awake. At least Jenna kept me awake. I wanted Denalyn to sleep. Thanks to a medication mix-up, her post-C-section rest was scant. So for our first night home with our first child, I volunteered to serve as first responder. We wrapped our eight pounds and four ounces of beauty in a soft pink blanket, placed her in the bassinet, and set it next to my side of the bed. Denalyn fell quickly into a sound slumber. Jenna followed her mom's example. And Dad? This dad didn't know what to make of the baby noises.

When Jenna's breathing slowed, I leaned my ear onto her mouth to see if she was alive. When her breathing hurried, I looked up "infant hyperventilation" in the family medical encyclopedia. When she burbled and panted, so did I. After a couple of hours I realized, *I have no clue how to behave!* I lifted Jenna out of her bed, carried her into the living room of our apartment, and sat in a rocker. That's when a tsunami of sobriety washed over me.

"We're in charge of a human being."

I don't care how tough you are. You may be a Navy SEAL who specializes in high-altitude skydiving behind enemy lines. You might spend each day making million-dollar, split-second stock market decisions. Doesn't matter. Every parent melts the moment he or she feels the full force of parenthood.

I did.

How did I get myself into this? I retraced my steps. First came love, then came marriage, then the *discussions* of a baby carriage. Of course I was open to the idea. Especially when I considered my role in launching the effort. Somehow during the nine-month expansion project, the reality of fatherhood didn't dawn on me. Women are nodding and smiling. "Never underestimate the density of a man," you say. True. But moms have an advantage: thirty-six weeks of reminders elbowing around inside them. Our kick in the gut comes later. But it does come. And for me it came in the midnight quiet of an apartment living room in downtown Rio de Janeiro, Brazil, as I held a human being in my arms.

—*FEARLESS*

How's your marriage?

Consider it your Testore cello. This finely constructed, seldom-seen instrument has reached the category of rare and is fast earning the status of priceless. Few musicians are privileged to play a Testore; even fewer are able to own one.

I happen to know a man who does. He, gulp, loaned it to me for a sermon. Wanting to illustrate the fragile sanctity of marriage, I asked him to place the nearly-three-centuries-old instrument on the stage, and I explained its worth to the church.

How do you think I treated the relic? Did I twirl it, flip it, and pluck the strings? No way. The cello is far too valuable for my clumsy fingers. Besides, its owner loaned it to me. I dared not dishonor his treasure.

On your wedding day, God loaned you his work of art: an intricately crafted, precisely formed masterpiece. He entrusted you with a one-of-a-kind creation. Value her. Honor him. Having been blessed with a Testore, why fiddle around with anyone else?

David missed this. He collected wives as trophies. He saw spouses as a means to his pleasure, not a part of God's plan. Don't make his mistake.

Be fiercely loyal to one spouse. *Fiercely* loyal. Don't even look twice at someone else. No flirting. No teasing. No loitering at her desk or lingering in his office. Who cares if you come across as rude or a prude? You've made a promise. Keep it.

And, as you do, nourish the children God gives.

How are things with your kids?

*G*od loaned you his work of art . . . He entrusted you with a one-of-a-kind creation. Value her. Honor him.

Quiet heroes dot the landscape of our society. They don't wear ribbons or kiss trophies; they wear spit-up and kiss boo-boos. They don't make the headlines, but they do sew the hemlines and check the outlines and stand on the sidelines. You won't find their names on the Nobel Prize short list, but you will find their names on the homeroom, carpool, and Bible teacher lists.

They are parents, both by blood and deed, name and calendar. Heroes. News programs don't call them. But that's okay. Because their kids do . . . They call them Mom. They call them Dad. And these moms and dads, more valuable than all the executives and lawmakers west of the Mississippi, quietly hold the world together.

Be numbered among them. Read books to your kids. Play ball while you can and they want you to. Make it your aim to watch every game they play, read every story they write, hear every recital in which they perform.

Children spell love with four letters: T-I-M-E. Not just quality time, but hang time, downtime, anytime, all the time. Your children are not your hobby; they are your calling.

Your spouse is not your trophy but your treasure.

Don't pay the price David paid. Can we flip ahead a few chapters to his final hours? To see the ultimate cost of a neglected family, look at the way our hero dies.

David is hours from the grave. A chill has set in that blankets can't remove. Servants decide he needs a person to warm him, someone to hold him tight as he takes his final breaths.

Do they turn to one of his wives? No. Do they call on one of his children? No. They seek "for a lovely young woman throughout all the territory of Israel . . . and she cared for the king, and served him; but the king did not know her" (1 Kings 1:3–4 NKJV).

I suspect that David would have traded all his conquered crowns for the tender arms of a wife. But it was too late. He died in the care of a stranger because he made strangers out of his family.

But it's not too late for you.

Make your wife the object of your highest devotion. Make your husband the recipient of your deepest passion. Love the one who wears your ring.

And cherish the children who share your name.

Succeed at home first.

—*FACING YOUR GIANTS*

*T*here are times when we . . . are called to love, expecting nothing in return.

—*HE STILL MOVES STONES*

*H*ave you ever noticed the way a groom looks at his bride during the wedding? I have. Perhaps it's my vantage point. As the minister of the wedding, I'm positioned next to the groom. Side by side we stand, he about to enter the marriage, I about to perform it. By the time we reach the altar, I've been with him for some time backstage as he tugged his collar and mopped his brow. His buddies reminded him that it's not too late to escape, and there's always a half-serious look in his eyes that he might. As the minister, I'm the one to give him the signal when it's our turn to step out of the wings up to the altar. He follows me into the chapel like a criminal walking to the gallows. But all that changes when she appears. And the look on his face is my favorite scene in the wedding.

Most miss it. Most miss it because they are looking at her. But when other eyes are on the bride, I sneak a peek at the groom. If the light is just so and the angle just right, I can see a tiny reflection in his eyes. Her reflection. And the sight of her reminds him why he is here. His jaw relaxes and his forced smile softens. He forgets he's wearing a tux. He forgets his sweat-soaked shirt. He forgets the bet he made that he wouldn't puke. When he sees her, any thought of escape becomes a joke again. For it's written all over his face, "Who could bear to live without this bride?"

—*WHEN CHRIST COMES*

*H*ealthy marriages have a sense of "remaining." The husband remains in the wife, and she remains in him. There is a tenderness, an honesty, an ongoing communication. The same is true in our relationship with God. Sometimes we go to him with our joys, and sometimes we go with our hurts, but we always go. And as we go, the more we go, the more we become like him. Paul says we are being changed from "glory to glory" (2 Cor. 3:18 KJV).

People who live long lives together eventually begin to sound alike, to talk alike, even to think alike. As we walk with God, we take on his thoughts, his principles, his attitudes. We take on his heart.

And just as in marriage, communion with God is no burden. Indeed, it is a delight. "How lovely is your dwelling place, O LORD Almighty! My soul yearns, even faints, for the courts of the LORD; my heart and my flesh cry out for the living God" (Ps. 84:1–2 NIV). The level of communication is so sweet nothing compares with it.

—JUST LIKE JESUS

*D*oes Jesus have anything to say about dealing with difficult relatives? Is there an example of Jesus bringing peace to a painful family? Yes, there is.

His own.

It may surprise you to know that Jesus had a difficult family. It may surprise you to know that Jesus had a family at all! You may not be aware that Jesus had brothers and sisters. He did. Quoting

Jesus' hometown critics, Mark wrote, "{Jesus} is just the carpenter, the son of Mary and the brother of James, Joseph, Judas, and Simon. And his sisters are here with us" (Mark 6:3 NCV).

And it may surprise you to know that his family was less than perfect. They were. If your family doesn't appreciate you, take heart, neither did Jesus'. "A prophet is honored everywhere except in his hometown and with his own people and in his own home" (Mark 6:4 NCV).

I wonder what he meant when he said those last five words. He went to the synagogue where he was asked to speak. The people were proud that this hometown boy had done well—until they heard what he said. He referred to himself as the Messiah, the one to fulfill prophecy.

Their response? "Isn't this Joseph's son?" Translation? This is no Messiah! He's just like us! He's the plumber's kid from down the street. He's the accountant on the third floor. He's the construction worker who used to date my sister. God doesn't speak through familiar people.

One minute he was a hero, the next a heretic. Look what happens next. "They got up, forced Jesus out of town, and took him to the edge of the cliff on which the town was built. They planned to throw him off the edge, but Jesus walked through the crowd and went on his way" (Luke 4:29–30 NCV).

*I*f your family doesn't appreciate you, take heart, neither did Jesus'.

What an ugly moment! Jesus' neighborhood friends tried to kill him. But even uglier than what we see is what we don't see. Notice what is missing from this verse. Note what words should be there but aren't. "They planned to throw him over the cliff, but Jesus' brothers came and stood up for him."

We'd like to read that, but we can't because it doesn't say that. That's not what happened. When Jesus was in trouble, his brothers were invisible.

They weren't always invisible, however. There was a time when they spoke. There was a time when they were seen with him in public. Not because they were proud of him but because they were ashamed of him. "His family . . . went to get him because they thought he was out of his mind" (Mark 3:21 NCV).

Jesus' siblings thought their brother was a lunatic. They weren't proud—they were embarrassed!

"He's off the deep end, Mom. You should hear what people are saying about him."

"People say he's loony."

"Yeah, somebody asked me why we don't do something about him."

"It's a good thing Dad isn't around to see what Jesus is doing."

Hurtful words spoken by those closest to Jesus.

Here are some more:

So Jesus' brothers said to him, "You should leave here and go to Judea so your followers there can see the miracles you do. Anyone who wants to be well known does not hide what he does. If you are doing these things, show yourself to the world." (John 7:3–5 NCV) (Even Jesus' brothers did not believe in him.)

Listen to the sarcasm in those words! They drip with ridicule. How does Jesus put up with these guys? How can you believe in yourself when those who know you best don't? How can you move forward when your family wants to pull you back? When you and your family have two different agendas, what do you do?

Jesus gives us some answers.

It's worth noting that he didn't try to control his family's behavior, nor did he let their behavior control his. He didn't demand that they agree with him. He didn't sulk when they insulted him. He didn't make it his mission to try to please them.

Each of us has a fantasy that our family will be like the Waltons, an expectation that our dearest friends will be our next of kin. Jesus didn't have that expectation. Look how he defined his family: "My true brother and sister and mother are those who do what God wants" (Mark 3:35 NCV).

*I*f Jesus himself couldn't force his family to share his convictions, what makes you think you can force yours?

When Jesus' brothers didn't share his convictions, he didn't try to force them. He recognized that his spiritual family could provide what his physical family didn't. If Jesus himself couldn't force his family to share his convictions, what makes you think you can force yours?

We can't control the way our family responds to us. When it comes to the behavior of others toward us, our hands are tied. We have to move beyond the naive expectation that if we do good, people will treat us right. The fact is they may and they may not—we cannot control how people respond to us.

If your father is a jerk, you could be the world's best daughter, and he still won't tell you so.

If your aunt doesn't like your career, you could change jobs a dozen times and still never satisfy her.

If your sister is always complaining about what you got and she didn't, you could give her everything, and she still may not change.

As long as you think you can control people's behavior toward you, you are held in bondage by their opinions. If you think you can control their opinion and their opinion isn't positive, then guess who you have to blame? Yourself.

It's a game with unfair rules and fatal finishes. Jesus didn't play it, nor should you.

We don't know if Joseph affirmed his son Jesus in his ministry—but we know God did: "This is my Son, whom I love, and I am very pleased with him" (Matt. 3:17 NCV).

I can't assure you that your family will ever give you the blessing you seek, but I know God will. Let God give you what your family doesn't. If your earthly father doesn't affirm you, then let your heavenly Father take his place.

How do you do that? By emotionally accepting God as your father. You see, it's one thing to accept him as Lord, another to recognize him as Savior–but it's another matter entirely to accept him as Father.

To recognize God as Lord is to acknowledge that he is sovereign and supreme in the universe. To accept him as Savior is to accept his gift of salvation offered on the cross. To regard him as Father is to go a step further. Ideally, a father is the one in your life who provides and protects. That is exactly what God has done.

He has provided for your needs (Matt. 6:25-34). He has protected you from harm (Ps. 139:5). He has adopted you (Eph. 1:5). And he has given you his name (1 John 3:1).

God has proven himself as a faithful father. Now it falls to us to be trusting children. Let God give you what your family doesn't. Let him fill the void others have left. Rely upon him for your affirmation and encouragement. Look at Paul's words: "You are God's child, and *God will give you the blessing he promised*, because you are his child" (Gal. 4:7 NCV).

A father is the one in your life who provides and protects. That is exactly what God has done.

Having your family's approval is desirable but not necessary for happiness and not always possible. Jesus did not let the difficult dynamic of his family overshadow his call from God. And because he didn't, this chapter has a happy ending.

What happened to Jesus' family?

Mine with me a golden nugget hidden in a vein of the Book of Acts. "Then {the disciples} went back to Jerusalem from the Mount of Olives. . . . They all continued praying together with some women, *including Mary the mother of Jesus, and Jesus' brothers*" (Acts 1:12, 14 NCV).

What a change! The ones who mocked him now worship him. The ones who pitied him now pray for him. What if Jesus had disowned them? Or worse still, what if he'd suffocated his family with his demand for change?

He didn't. He instead gave them space, time, and grace. And because he did, they changed. How much did they change? One brother became an apostle (Gal. 1:19) and others became missionaries (1 Cor. 9:5).

So don't lose heart. God still changes families.

—HE STILL MOVES STONES

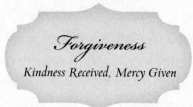

Forgiveness

Kindness Received, Mercy Given

$\mathcal{C}$hrist lived the life we could not live and took the punishment we could not take to offer the hope we cannot resist. His sacrifice begs us to ask this question: if he so loved us, can we not love each other? Having been forgiven, can we not forgive? Having feasted at the table of grace, can we not share a few crumbs? "My dear, dear friends, if God loved us like this, we certainly ought to love each other" (1 John 4:11 MSG).

—*FACING YOUR GIANTS*

$\mathcal{S}$tanding before ten thousand eyes is Abraham Lincoln. An uncomfortable Abraham Lincoln. His discomfort comes not from the thought of delivering his first inaugural address but from the ambitious efforts of well-meaning tailors. He's unaccustomed to such attire–formal black dress coat, silk vest, black trousers, and a glossy top hat. He holds a huge ebony cane with a golden head the size of an egg.

He approaches the platform with hat in one hand and cane in the other. He doesn't know what to do with either one. In the nervous silence that comes after the applause and before the speech, he searches for a spot to place them. He finally leans the cane in a corner of the railing, but he still doesn't know what to do with the hat. He could lay it on the podium, but it would take up too much room. Perhaps the floor . . . no, too dirty.

Just then, and not a moment too soon, a man steps forward and takes the hat, returns to his seat, and listens intently to Lincoln's speech.

Who is he? Lincoln's dearest friend. The president said of him, "He and I are about the best friends in the world."

He was one of the strongest supporters of the early stages of Lincoln's presidency. He was given the honor of escorting Mrs. Lincoln in the inaugural grand ball. As the storm of the Civil War began to boil, many of Lincoln's friends left, but not this one. He amplified his loyalty by touring the South as Lincoln's peace ambassador. He begged Southerners not to secede and Northerners to rally behind the president.

His efforts were great, but the wave of anger was greater. The country did divide, and civil war bloodied the nation. Lincoln's friend never lived to see it. He died three months after Lincoln's inauguration. Wearied by his travels, he succumbed to a fever, and Lincoln was left to face the war alone.

Upon hearing the news of his friend's death, Lincoln wept openly and ordered the White House flag to be flown at half-staff. Some feel Lincoln's friend would have been chosen as his running mate in 1864 and would thus have become president following the assassination of the Great Emancipator.

No one will ever know about that. But we do know that Lincoln had one true friend. And we can only imagine the number of times the memory of him brought warmth to a cold Oval Office. He was a model of friendship.

He was also a model of forgiveness.

This friend could just as easily have been an enemy. Long before he and Lincoln were allies, they were competitors—politicians pursuing the same office. And unfortunately, their debates are better known than their friendship. The debates between Abraham Lincoln and his dear friend, Stephen A. Douglas.

But on Lincoln's finest day, Douglas set aside their differences and held the hat of the president. . . . Douglas heard a higher call. . . . He was present at the party.

Wise are we if we do the same. Wise are we if we rise above our hurts. For if we do, we'll be present at the Father's final celebration. A party to end all parties. A party where no pouters will be permitted.

Why don't you come and join the fun?

—*HE STILL MOVES STONES*

*T*here was once a person in our world who brought Denalyn and me a lot of stress. She would call in the middle of the night. She was demanding and ruthless. She screamed at us in public. When she wanted something she wanted it immediately and she wanted it exclusively from us.

But we never asked her to leave us alone. We never told her to bug someone else. We never tried to get even.

After all, she was only a few months old.

It was easy for us to forgive our infant daughter's behavior because we knew she didn't know better.

Now, there is a world of difference between an innocent child and a deliberate Judas. But there is still a point to my story and it is this: The way to handle a person's behavior is to understand the cause of it. One way to deal with a person's peculiarities is to try to understand why they are peculiar.

Jesus knew Judas had been seduced by a powerful foe. He was aware of the wiles of Satan's whispers (he had just heard them himself). He knew how hard it was for Judas to do what was right.

He didn't justify what Judas did. He didn't minimize the deed. Nor did he release Judas from his choice. But he did look eye to eye with his betrayer and try to understand.

One way to deal with a person's
peculiarities is to try to
understand why they are peculiar.

As long as you hate your enemy, a jail door is closed and a prisoner is taken. But when you try to understand and release your foe from your hatred, then the prisoner is released and that prisoner is you.

—*And the Angels Were Silent*

*W*ant to learn to forgive? Then consider how you've been forgiven. "Be kind and compassionate to one another, forgiving each other, just as in Christ God forgave you" (Eph. 4:32 NIV).

—*A Love Worth Giving*

*W*hy did the disciples come back? What made them return? Rumors of the resurrection? That had to be part of it. . . .

But it was more than just rumors of an empty tomb that brought them back. There was something in their hearts that wouldn't let them live with their betrayal. For as responsible as their excuses were, they weren't good enough to erase the bottom line of the story: they had betrayed their Master. When Jesus needed them they had scampered. And now they were having to deal with the shame.

Seeking forgiveness but not knowing where to look for it, they came back. They gravitated to that same upper room that contained the sweet memories of broken bread and symbolic wine. The simple fact that they returned says something about their leader. It says something about Jesus that those who knew him best could not stand to be in his disfavor. For the original twelve there were only two options—surrender or suicide. Yet it also says something about Jesus: those who knew him best knew that although they had done exactly what they had promised they wouldn't, they could still find forgiveness.

So they came back. Each with a scrapbook full of memories and a thin thread of hope. Each knowing that it is all over, but in his heart hoping that the impossible will happen once more. "If I had just one more chance."

There they sat. What little conversation there is focuses on the rumors of an empty tomb. Someone sighs. Someone locks the door. Someone shuffles his feet.

And just when the gloom gets good and thick, just when their wishful thinking is falling victim to logic, just when someone says, "How I'd give my immortal soul to see him one more time," a familiar face walks through the wall.

It also says something about Jesus: those who knew him best knew that although they had done exactly what they had promised they wouldn't, they could still find forgiveness.

My, what an ending. Or, better said, what a beginning! Don't miss the promise unveiled in this story. For those of us who, like the apostles, have turned and run when we should have stood and fought, this passage is pregnant with hope. A repentant heart is all he demands. Come out of the shadows! Be done with your hiding! A repentant heart is enough to summon the Son of God himself to walk through our walls of guilt and shame. He who forgave his followers stands ready to forgive the rest of us. All we have to do is come back.

No wonder they call him the Savior.

—*No Wonder They Call Him the Savior*

*D*uring World War I, a German soldier plunged into an out-of-the-way shell hole. There he found a wounded enemy. The fallen soldier was soaked with blood and only minutes from death. Touched by the plight of the man, the German soldier offered him water. Through this small kindness a bond was developed. The dying man pointed to his shirt pocket; the German soldier took from it a wallet and removed some family pictures. He held them so the wounded man could gaze at his loved ones one final time. With bullets raging over them and war all around them, these two enemies were, but for a few moments, friends.

What happened in that shell hole? Did all evil cease? Were

all wrongs made right? No. What happened was simply this: Two enemies saw each other as humans in need of help. This is forgiveness. Forgiveness begins by rising above the war, looking beyond the uniform, and choosing to see the other, not as a foe or even as a friend but simply as a fellow fighter longing to make it home safely.

—*IN THE GRIP OF GRACE*

*W*e will never be cleansed until we confess we are dirty. We will never be pure until we admit we are filthy. And we will never be able to wash the feet of those who have hurt us until we allow Jesus, the one we have hurt, to wash ours.

You see, that is the secret of forgiveness. You will never forgive anyone more than God has already forgiven you. Only by letting him wash your feet can you have strength to wash those of another.

Still hard to imagine? Is it still hard to consider the thought of forgiving the one who hurt you?

If so, go one more time to the room. Watch Jesus as he goes from disciple to disciple. Can you see him? Can you hear the water splash? Can you hear him shuffle on the floor to the next person? Good. Keep that image.

John 13:12 says, "When he had finished washing their feet . . ." (NCV)

Please note; he *finished* washing their feet. That means he left no one out. Why is that important? Because that also means he washed the feet of Judas. Jesus washed the feet of his betrayer. He gave his traitor equal attention. In just a few hours Judas's feet would guide the Roman guard to Jesus. But at this moment they are caressed by Christ.

That's not to say it was easy for Jesus.

That's not to say it is easy for you.

That is to say that God will never call you to do what he hasn't already done.

—*A GENTLE THUNDER*

God's Love

Never Failing, Never Ending

$\mathcal{G}$od will not let you go. He has handcuffed himself to you in love. And he owns the only key. You need not win his love. You already have it. And since you can't win it, you can't lose it.

—3:16: The Numbers of Hope

$\mathcal{T}$he big news of the Bible is not that you love God but that God loves you; not that you can know God but that God already knows you! He tattooed your name on the palm of his hand. His thoughts of you outnumber the sand on the shore. You never leave his mind, escape his sight, flee his thoughts. He sees the worst of you and loves you still. Your sins of tomorrow and failings of the future will not surprise him; he sees them now. Every day and deed of your life has passed before his eyes and been calculated in his decision. He knows you better than you know you and has reached his verdict: he loves you still. No discovery will disillusion him; no rebellion will dissuade him. He loves you with an everlasting love.

—*COME THIRSTY*

*S*everal hundred feet beneath my chair is a lake, an underground cavern of crystalline water known as Edwards Aquifer. We South Texans know much about this aquifer. We know its length (175 miles). We know its layout (west to east except under San Antonio, where it runs north to south). We know the water is pure. Fresh. It irrigates farms and waters lawns and fills pools and quenches thirst. We know much about the aquifer.

But for all the facts we do know, there is an essential one we don't. We don't know its size. The depth of the cavern? A mystery. Number of gallons? Unmeasured. No one knows the amount of water the aquifer contains.

Watch the nightly weather report, and you'd think otherwise. Meteorologists give regular updates on the aquifer level. You get the impression that the amount of water is calculated. "The truth is," a friend told me, "no one knows how much water is down there."

We know the impact of God's love. But the volume? No person has ever measured it.

Could this be? I decided to find out. I called a water conservationist. "That's right," he affirmed. "We estimate. We don't try to measure. But the exact quantity? No one knows." Remarkable. We use it, depend upon it, would perish without it . . . but measure it? We can't.

Bring to mind another unmeasured pool? It might. Not a pool of water but a pool of love. God's love. Aquifer fresh. Pure as April snow. One swallow slackens the thirsty throat and softens the crusty heart. Immerse a life in God's love, and watch it emerge cleansed and changed. We know the impact of God's love.

But the volume? No person has ever measured it.

Moral meteorologists, worried we might exhaust the supply, suggest otherwise. "Don't drink too deeply," they caution, recommending rationed portions. Some people, after all, drink more than their share. Terrorist and traitors and wife beaters–let such scoundrels start drinking, and they may take too much.

But who has plumbed the depths of God's love? Only God has. "Want to see the size of my love?" he invites. "Ascend the winding path outside Jerusalem. Follow the dots of bloody dirt until you crest the hill. Before looking up, pause and hear me whisper, 'This is how much I love you.'"

—*IT'S NOT ABOUT ME*

There are many questions about the Bible that we won't be able to answer until we get home. Many knotholes and snapshots. Many times we will muse, "I wonder . . ."

But in our wonderings, there is one question we never need to ask. Does God care? Do we matter to God? Does he still love his children?

Through the small face of the stable-born baby, he says yes.

Yes, your sins are forgiven.

Yes, your name is written in heaven.

Yes, death has been defeated.

And yes, God has entered your world.

Immanuel. God is with us.

—He Still Moves Stones

*L*ove never fails.

Governments will fail, but God's love will last. Crowns are temporary, but love is eternal. Your money will run out, but his love never will.

How could God have a love like this? No one has unfailing love. No person can love with perfection. You're right. No person can. But God is not a person. Unlike our love, his never fails. His love is immensely different from ours.

Our love depends on the receiver of the love. Let a thousand people pass before us, and we will not feel the same about each. Our love will be regulated by their appearance, by their personalities. Even when we find a few people we like, our feelings will fluctuate. How they treat us will affect how we love them. The receiver regulates our love.

Not so with the love of God. We have no thermostatic impact on his love for us. The love of God is born from within him, not from what he finds in us. His love is uncaused and spontaneous. . . .

Does he love us because of our goodness? Because of our kindness? Because of our great faith? No, he loves us because of *his* goodness, kindness, and great faith. John says it like this: "This is love: not that we loved God, but that he loved us" (4 John 4:10 NIV).

Doesn't this thought comfort you? God's love does not hinge on yours. The abundance of your love does not increase his. The lack of your love does not diminish his. Your goodness does not enhance his love, nor does your weakness dilute it. What Moses said to Israel is what God says to us:

> The LORD did not choose you and lavish his love on you because you were larger or greater than other nations, for you were the smallest of all nations! It was simply because the LORD loves you. (Deut. 7:7–8 NLT)

God loves you simply because he has chosen to do so.
He loves you when you don't feel lovely.

The love of God is born from within him, not from what he finds in us.

He loves you when no one else loves you. Others may abandon you, divorce you, and ignore you, but God will love you. Always. No matter what.

—*A Love Worth Giving*

*H*e loves each one of us like there was only one of us to love.

—*When God Whispers Your Name*

*G*od loves you just the way you are, but he refuses to leave you that way. More than anything, he wants you to be just like Jesus.

—*Just Like Jesus*

*W*e love to be with the ones we love.

May I remind you? So does God. He loves to be with the ones he loves. How else do you explain what he did? Between him and us there was a distance—a great span. And he couldn't bear it. He couldn't stand it. So he did something about it.

Before coming to the earth, "Christ himself was like God in everything. . . . But he gave up his place with God and made himself nothing. He was born as a man and became like a servant" (Phil. 2:6-7 NCV).

*B*etween [God] and us there was a distance—a great span. And he couldn't bear it. He couldn't stand it. So he did something about it.

Why? Why did Jesus travel so far?

I was asking myself that question when I spotted the squirrels outside my window. A family of black-tailed squirrels has made its home amid the roots of the tree north of my office. We've been neighbors for three years now. They watch me peck the keyboard. I watch them store their nuts and climb the trunk. We're mutually amused. I could watch them all day. Sometimes I do.

But I've never considered becoming one of them. The squirrel world holds no appeal to me. Who wants to sleep next to a hairy rodent with beady eyes? (No comments from you wives who feel you already do.) Give up the Rocky Mountains, bass fishing, weddings, and laughter for a hole in the ground and a diet of dirty nuts? Count me out.

But count Jesus in. What a world he left. Our classiest mansion would be a tree trunk to him. Earth's finest cuisine would be walnuts on heaven's table. And the idea of becoming a squirrel with claws and tiny teeth and a furry tail? It's nothing compared to God becoming a one-celled embryo and entering the womb of Mary.

But he did. The God of the universe kicked against the wall of a womb, was born into the poverty of a peasant, and spent his first night in the feed trough of a cow. "The Word became flesh and lived among us" (John 1:14 NRSV). The God of the universe left the glory of heaven and moved into the neighborhood.

Our neighborhood! Who could have imagined he would do such a thing.

Why? He loves to be with the ones he loves.

—*NEXT DOOR SAVIOR*

*G*rab hold of this verse and let it lower you down: "God is love" (1 John 4:16 NLT).

One word into the passage reveals the supreme surprise of God's love–it has nothing to do with you. Others love you because of you, because your dimples dip when you smile or your rhetoric charms when you flirt. Some people love you because of you. Not God. He loves you because he is he. He loves you because he decides to. Self-generated, uncaused, and spontaneous, his constant-level love depends on his choice to give it. "The LORD did not set his affection on you and choose you because you were more numerous than other peoples, for you were the fewest of all peoples. But it was because the LORD loved you" (Deut. 7:7–8 NIV).

You don't influence God's love. You can't impact the treeness of a tree, the skyness of the sky, or the rockness of a rock. Nor can you affect the love of God. If you could, John would have used more ink: "God is *occasional* love" or "*sporadic* love" or "*fair-weather* love." If your actions altered his devotion, then God would not be love; indeed, he would be human, for this is human love.

And you've had enough of human love. Haven't you? Enough guys wooing you with Elvis-impersonator sincerity. Enough tabloids telling you that true love is just a diet away. Enough helium-filled expectations of bosses and parents and pastors. Enough mornings smelling like the mistakes you made while searching for love the night before.

Don't you need a fountain of love that won't run dry? You'll find one on a stone-cropped hill outside Jerusalem's walls where Jesus hangs, cross-nailed and thorn-crowned. When you feel unloved, ascend this mount. Meditate long and hard on heaven's love for you.

—*COME THIRSTY*

*G*od's love is not human. His love is not normal. His love sees your sin and loves you still. Does he approve of your error? No. Do you need to repent? Yes. But do you repent for his sake or yours? Yours. His ego needs no apology. His love needs no bolstering.

And he could not love you more than he does right now.

—*A GENTLE THUNDER*

*W*hen we read John 3:16, we simply (and happily) read, "For God so loved the world" (NKJV).

How wide is God's love? Wide enough for the whole world.
Are you included in the world? Then you are included in God's love.

—*HE CHOSE THE NAILS*

*O*ur finest love is a preschool watercolor to God's Rembrandt, a
vacant-lot dandelion next to his garden rose. His love stands sequoia
strong; out best attempts bend like weeping willows.

. . . Look at the round belly of the pregnant peasant girl in
Bethlehem. God's in there; the same God who can balance the universe on the tip of his finger floats in Mary's womb. Why? Love.

Peek through the Nazareth workshop window. See the lanky
lad sweeping the sawdust from the floor? He once blew stardust
into the night sky. Why swap the heavens for a carpentry shop? One
answer: love.

Love explains why he came.

Love explains how he endured.

—*3:16: THE NUMBERS OF HOPE*

Grace

A Gift Beyond All Expectations

$\mathscr{L}$isten. You have not been sprinkled with forgiveness. You have not been spattered with grace. You have not been dusted with kindness. You have been immersed in it. You are submerged in mercy. You are a minnow in the ocean of his mercy. Let it change you!

—*A Love Worth Giving*

"$\mathscr{C}$hrist accepted you, so you should accept each other, which will bring glory to God" (Rom. 15:7 NCV).

Is God asking us to do anything more than what he has already done? Hasn't he gone a long way in accepting us? If God can tolerate my mistakes, can't I tolerate the mistakes of others? If God allows me, with my foibles and failures, to call him Father, shouldn't I extend the same grace to others? In fact, who can offer grace except those secure in the grip of grace?

—*IN THE GRIP OF GRACE*

"*L*emonade, 5¢"

The *e* is larger than the *L*. The *m* is uppercased; all the other letters are lowered. The last two letters, *de*, curve downward because the artist ran out of room on the poster board.

Norman Rockwell would have loved it.

Two girls sit on the sidewalk in little chairs behind a little table. The six-year-old is the cashier. She monitors a plastic bowl of change. The four-year-old is the waitress. She handles the ice. Pours the drinks. Stacks and restacks the paper cups.

Behind them, seated on the grass, is Dad. He leans against an oak tree and smiles as he witnesses his daughters' inauguration into capitalism.

Business has been steady. The Saturday-afternoon stream of patrons has nearly emptied the pitcher. The bottom of the cashier's bowl is covered with thirty-five cents of change. With the exception of a few spills, the service has been exceptional. No complaints. Many compliments.

Part of the success, though, has been due to the marketing strategy.

Our street doesn't get much traffic, so we did a little advertising.

As my daughters painted the sign, I called several families in the neighborhood and invited them to the grand opening of our lemonade stand. So all of our clients, thus far, had been partial.

I was proud of myself. I leaned back against the tree. Closed my eyes. Turned up the radio I had brought. And listened to the baseball game.

Then I heard an unfamiliar voice.

"I'll have a cup of lemonade, please."

I opened my eyes. It was a customer. A real customer. An unsolicited neighbor who had driven by, seen the sign, stopped, and ordered a drink.

Uh-oh, I thought. Our service was about to be tested.

Andrea, the four-year-old, grabbed a cup that had already been used.

"Get a clean cup," I whispered.

"Oh," she giggled, and got a clean cup.

She opened the ice bucket, looked in, and then looked back at me. "Daddy, we are out of ice."

The patron overheard her. "That's OK. I'll take it warm."

She picked up the pitcher and poured. Syrupy sugar oozed out of the pitcher. "Daddy, there's just a little bit."

Our customer spoke again. "That's fine. I don't want much."

"I hope you like it sweet," I said under my breath.

She handed the cup to the man, and he handed her a dollar. She gave it to Jenna.

Jenna turned to me. "Daddy, what do I do?" (We weren't used to such big bills.)

I stuck my hands in my pockets; they were empty.

"Uh, we don't have any . . ." I began.

"No problem," he said, smiling. "Just keep the change."

I smiled sheepishly. He thanked the girls. Told them they were doing a great job. Climbed back into his car. And drove off.

Quite a transaction, I thought. *We give him a warm, partially filled cup of lemonade syrup, and he gives us a compliment and a payment twenty times too much.*

I had set out to teach the girls about free enterprise. They ended up with a lesson on grace.

—*IN THE EYE OF THE STORM*

*G*od's trust makes us eager to do right. Such is the genius of grace. The law can show us where we do wrong, but it can't make us eager to do right. Grace can.

—*IN THE GRIP OF GRACE*

*G*od gives no sponge baths. He washes us from head to toe. Paul reflected on his conversion and wrote: "He gave us a good bath, and we came out of it new people, washed inside and out by the Holy Spirit" (Titus 3:5 MSG). Your sins stand no chance against the fire hydrant of God's grace.

—*NEXT DOOR SAVIOR*

*W*hat do you do if you don't have any money? What do you do if you have nothing to deposit but an honest apology and good intentions? You pray that some wealthy soul will make a huge deposit in your account. If you're talking about your financial debt, that's not likely to happen. If you're talking about your spiritual debt, however, it already has.

Your Father has covered your shortfall. . . .

Though you've spent a lifetime writing insufficient checks, God has stamped these words on your statement: My Grace Is Sufficient for You.

—*THE GREAT HOUSE OF GOD*

*S*ometimes I give away money at the end of a sermon. Not to pay the listeners (though some may feel they've earned it) but to make a point. I offer a dollar to anyone who will accept it. Free money. A gift. I invite anyone who wants the cash to come and take it.

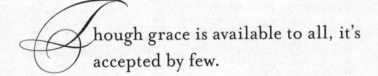 hough grace is available to all, it's accepted by few.

The response is predictable. A pause. Some shuffling of feet. A wife elbows her husband, and he shakes his head. A teen starts to stand and then remembers her reputation. A five-year-old starts walking down the aisle, and his mother pulls him back. Finally some courageous (or impoverished) soul stands up and says, "I'll take it!" The dollar is given, and the application begins.

"Why didn't you take my offer?" I ask the rest. Some say they were too embarrassed. The pain wasn't worth the gain. Others feared a catch, a trick. And then there are those whose wallets are fat. What's a buck to someone who has hundreds?

Then the obvious follow-up question. "Why don't people accept Christ's free gift?" The answers are similar. Some are too embarrassed. To accept forgiveness is to admit sin, a step we are slow to take. Others fear a trick, a catch. Surely there is some fine print in the Bible. Others think, *Who needs forgiveness when you're as good as I am?*

The point makes itself. Though grace is available to all, it's accepted by few. Many choose to sit and wait while only a few choose to stand and trust.

Usually that is the end of it. The lesson is over, I'm a dollar poorer, one person is a dollar richer, and all of us are a bit wiser. Something happened a couple of weeks back, however, that added a new dimension to the exercise. Myrtle was the one who said yes to the dollar. I'd made the offer and was waiting for a taker when she yelled, "I'll take it!" Up she popped and down she came and I gave her the dollar. She took her seat, I made my point, and we all went home.

I ran into her a few days later and kidded her about making money off my sermons. "Do you still have the dollar?" I asked.

"No."

"Did you spend it?"

"No, I gave it away," she answered. "When I returned to my seat a youngster asked me if he could have it, and I said, 'Sure, it was a gift to me; it's a gift to you.'"

My, isn't that something? As simply as she received, she gave. As easily as it came, it went. The boy didn't beg, and she didn't struggle. How could she, who had been given a gift, not give a gift in return? She was caught in the grip of grace. . . .

Can one who has been given a free gift not share that gift with others? I suppose. But let him remember Myrtle. Let him remember that he, like she, received a free gift. Let him remember that all of life is a gift of grace. And let him remember that the call of grace is to live a gracious life.

For that is how grace works.

—*In the Grip of Grace*

I've never been surprised by God's judgment, but I'm still stunned by his grace.

—*When God Whispers Your Name*

*W*hat is it, then, that God wants us to do? What is the work he seeks? Just believe. Believe the One he sent. "The work God wants you to do is this: Believe the One he sent" (John 6:29 NCV).

Someone is reading this and shaking his or her head and asking, "Are you saying it is possible to go to heaven with no good works?" The answer is no. Good works are a requirement. Someone else is reading and asking, "Are you saying it is possible to go to heaven without good character?" My answer again is no. Good character is also required. In order to enter heaven one must have good works and good character.

But, alas, there is the problem. You have neither.

Oh, you've done some nice things in your life. But you do not have enough good works to go to heaven regardless of your sacrifice. No matter how noble your gifts, they are not enough to get you into heaven.

Nor do you have enough character to go to heaven. Please don't be offended. (Then, again, be offended, if necessary.) You're probably a very decent person. But decency isn't enough. Those who see God are not the decent; they are the holy. "Anyone whose life is not holy will never see the Lord" (Heb. 12:14 NCV).

You may be decent. You may pay taxes and kiss your kids and sleep with a clean conscience. But apart from Christ you aren't holy. So how can you go to heaven?

The cross was heavy, the blood was real, and the price was extravagant.

Only believe.

Accept the work already done, the work of Jesus on the cross.

Only believe.

Accept the goodness of Jesus Christ. Abandon your own works and accept his. Abandon your own decency and accept his. Stand before God in his name, not yours. "Anyone who believes and is baptized will be saved, but anyone who does not believe will be punished" (Mark 16:16 NCV).

It's that simple? It's that simple. It's that easy? There was nothing easy at all about it. The cross was heavy, the blood was real, and the price was extravagant. It would have bankrupted you or me, so he paid it for us. Call it simple. Call it a gift. But don't call it easy.

Call it what it is. Call it grace.

—*A Gentle Thunder*

*W*e must not see grace as a provision made after the law had failed. Grace was offered *before* the law was revealed. Indeed, grace was offered before man was created! "You were bought, not with something that ruins like gold or silver, but with the precious blood of Christ, who was like a pure and perfect lamb. Christ was chosen before the world was made, but he was shown to the world in these last times for your sake" (1 Pet. 1:18–20 NCV).

Why would God offer grace before we needed it? Glad you asked. Let's return one final time to the charge card my father gave me. Did I mention that I went several months without needing it? But when I needed it, I *really* needed it. You see, I wanted to visit a friend on another campus. Actually, the friend was a girl in another city, six hours away. On an impulse I skipped class one Friday morning and headed out. Not knowing whether my parents would approve, I didn't ask their permission. Because I left in a hurry, I forgot to take any money. I made the trip without their knowledge and with an empty wallet.

Everything went fine until I rear-ended a car on the return trip. Using a crowbar, I pried the fender off my front wheel so the car could limp to a gas station. I can still envision the outdoor phone where I stood in the autumn chill. My father, who assumed I was on campus, took my collect call and heard my tale. My story wasn't much to boast about. I'd made a trip without his knowledge, without any money, and wrecked his car.

"Well," he said after a long pause, "these things happen. That's why I gave you the card. I hope you learned a lesson."

Did I learn a lesson? I certainly did. I learned that my father's forgiveness predated my mistake. He had given me the card before my wreck in the event that I would have one. He had provided for my blunder before I blundered. Need I tell you that God has done the same? Please understand; Dad didn't want me to wreck the car. He didn't give me the card *so* that I would wreck the car. But he knew his son. And he knew his son would some-day need grace.

Please understand; God doesn't want us to sin. He didn't give us grace *so* we would sin. But he knows his children. "He made their hearts and understands everything they do" (Ps. 33:15 NCV). "He knows how we were made" (Ps. 103:14 NCV). And he knew that we would someday need his grace.

—*In the Grip of Grace*

*S*eparating you and God is not 350 feet of ocean water but an insurmountable flood of imperfection and sin. Do you think that by virtue of your moral muscle you can push this vessel to the surface? Do you think your baptism and Sunday attendance will be enough to save you?

Legalists do. They miss the gravity of the problem. By offer-ing to help, they not only make light of sin, they mock God.

Who would look at the cross of Christ and say, "Great work, Jesus. Sorry you couldn't finish it, but I'll take up the slack"?

Dare we question the crowning work of God? Dare we think heaven needs our help in saving us? We're stuck on the bottom of the ocean. We can't see the light of day! Legalism discounts God and in the process makes a mess out of us.

To anyone attempting to earn heaven, Paul asks, "How is it

that you are turning back to those weak and miserable principles? Do you wish to be enslaved by them all over again? . . . What has happened to all your joy?" (Gal. 4:9, 15 NIV).

Legalism is joyless because legalism is endless. There is always another class to attend, person to teach, mouth to feed. Inmates incarcerated in self-salvation find work but never joy. How could they? They never know when they are finished. Legalism leaches joy.

Grace, however, dispenses peace.

—IT'S NOT ABOUT ME

Heaven

The Happiness That Lies Ahead

I'll be home soon. My plane is nearing San Antonio. I can feel the nose of the jet dipping downward. I can see the flight attendants getting ready. Denalyn is somewhere in the parking lot, parking the car and hustling the girls toward the terminal.

I'll be home soon. The plane will land. I'll walk down that ramp and hear my name and see their faces. I'll be home soon.

You'll be home soon, too. You may not have noticed it, but you are closer to home than ever before. Each moment is a step taken. Each breath is a page turned. Each day is a mile marked, a mountain climbed. You are closer to home than you've ever been.

Before you know it, your appointed arrival time will come; you'll descend the ramp and enter the City.

You'll see faces that are waiting for you. You'll hear your name spoken by those who love you. And, maybe, just maybe—in the back, behind the crowds—the One who would rather die than live

without you will remove his pierced hands from his heavenly robe
and . . . applaud.

—*THE APPLAUSE OF HEAVEN*

*O*ne thing's for sure. When we get to heaven, we'll be surprised
at some of the folks we see. And some of them will be surprised
to see us.

—*WHEN GOD WHISPERS YOUR NAME*

*T*here is a story told in Brazil about a missionary who discovered a tribe of Indians in a remote part of the jungle. They lived
near a large river. The tribe was friendly and in need of medical
attention. A contagious disease was ravaging the population and
people were dying daily. An infirmary was located in another part
of the jungle and the missionary determined that the only hope
for the tribe was to go to the hospital for treatment and inocula-
tions. In order to reach the hospital, however, the Indians would
have to cross the river—a feat they were unwilling to perform.

The river, they believed, was inhabited by evil spirits. To enter
the water meant certain death. The missionary set about the difficult task of overcoming the superstition of the tribe.

It was necessary for him to enter the river, to submerge himself in the water of death before people would believe that death had been conquered.

He explained how he had crossed the river and arrived unharmed. No luck. He led the people to the bank and placed his hand in the water. The people still wouldn't believe him. He walked out into the river and splashed water on his face. The people watched closely yet were still hesitant. Finally he turned and dove into the water. He swam beneath the surface until he emerged on the other side.

Having proven that the power of the river was a farce, the missionary punched a triumphant fist into the air. He had entered the water and escaped. The Indians broke into cheers and followed him across.

Jesus saw people enslaved by their fear of a cheap power. He explained that the river of death was nothing to fear. The people wouldn't believe him. He touched a boy and called him back to life. The followers were still unconvinced. He whispered life into the dead body of a girl. The people were still cynical. He let a dead man spend four days in a grave and then called him out. Is that enough? Apparently not. For it was necessary for him to enter the river, to submerge himself in the water of death before people would believe that death had been conquered.

But after he did, after he came out on the other side of death's river, it was time to sing . . . it was time to celebrate.

—*Six Hours One Friday*

*D*read of death ends when you know heaven is your true home. In all my air travels I've never seen one passenger weep when the plane landed. Never. No one clings to the armrests and begs, "Don't make me leave. Don't make me leave. Let me stay and eat more peanuts." We're willing to exit because the plane has no permanent mailing address. Nor does this world. "But we are citizens of heaven, where the Lord Jesus Christ lives. And we are eagerly waiting for him to return as our Savior" (Phil. 3:20 NLT).

—*COME THIRSTY*

*U*nhappiness on earth cultivates a hunger for heaven. By gracing us with a deep dissatisfaction, God holds our attention. The only tragedy, then, is to be satisfied prematurely. To settle for earth. To be content in a strange land. To intermarry with the Babylonians and forget Jerusalem.

We are not happy here because we are not at home here. We are not happy here because we are not supposed to be happy here. We are "like foreigners and strangers in this world" (1 Pet. 2:11 NCV).

Take a fish and place him on the beach. (With appreciation to Landon Saunders for this idea.)

Watch his gills gasp and scales dry. Is he happy? No! How do you make him happy? Do you cover him with a mountain of cash? Do you get him a beach chair and sunglasses? Do you bring him a

Playfish magazine and martini? Do you wardrobe him in double-breasted fins and people-skinned shoes?

Of course not. Then how do you make him happy? You put him back in his element. You put him back in the water. He will never be happy on the beach simply because he was not made for the beach.

And you will never be completely happy on earth simply because you were not made for earth. Oh, you will have your moments of joy. You will catch glimpses of light. You will know moments or even days of peace. But they simply do not compare with the happiness that lies ahead.

—*WHEN GOD WHISPERS YOUR NAME*

*B*y calling us home, God is doing what any father would do. He is providing a better place to rest. A place he has "prepared for us." Heaven is not mass-produced; it is tailor-made.

Sometime ago I indulged and ordered two shirts from a tailor. I selected the cloth. The tailor measured my body. And several weeks later, I received two shirts made especially for me. There is a big difference between these two shirts and the other shirts in my closet. The tailored shirts were made with me in mind. The other shirts were made for any hundred thousand or so males my size. But not these two. They were made just for me.

As a result, they fit! They don't bulge. They don't choke. They are just right. Such is the promise of heaven. It was made with us in mind. Elsewhere Jesus invites us to "receive the kingdom God has prepared for you since the world was made" (Matt. 25:34 NCV).

The problem with this world is that it doesn't fit. Oh, it will do for now, but it isn't tailor-made. We were made to live with God, but on earth we live by faith. We were made to live forever, but on this earth we live but for a moment. We were made to live holy lives, but this world is stained by sin.

This world wears like a borrowed shirt. Heaven, however, will fit like one tailor-made.

—*A Gentle Thunder*

"*No* one has ever imagined what God has prepared for those who love him" (1 Cor. 2:9 NCV).

What a breathtaking verse! Do you see what it says? *Heaven is beyond our imagination.* We cannot envision it. At our most creative moment, at our deepest thought, at our highest level, we still cannot fathom eternity.

Try this. Imagine a perfect world. Whatever that means to you, imagine it. Does that mean peace? Then envision absolute tranquility. Does a perfect world imply joy? Then create your highest happiness. Will a perfect world have love? If so, ponder a place where love has no bounds. Whatever heaven means to you, imagine it. Get it firmly fixed in your mind. Delight in it. Dream about it. Long for it.

And then smile as the Father reminds you, *No one has ever imagined what God has prepared for those who love him.*

Anything you imagine is inadequate. Anything anyone imagines is inadequate. No one has come close. No one. Think of all the songs about heaven. All the artists' portrayals. All the lessons preached, poems written, and chapters drafted.

When it comes to describing heaven, we are all happy failures.

—*WHEN GOD WHISPERS YOUR NAME*

The 1989 Armenian earthquake needed only four minutes to flatten the nation and kill thirty thousand people. Moments after the deadly tremor ceased, a father raced to an elementary school to save his son. When he arrived, he saw that the building had been leveled. Looking at the mass of stones and rubble, he remembered a promise he had made to his child: "No matter what happens, I'll always be there for you." Driven by his own promise, he found the area closest to his son's room and began to pull back the rocks. Other parents arrived and began sobbing for their children. "It's too late," they told the man. "You know they are dead. You can't help." Even a police officer encouraged him to give up.

But the father refused. For eight hours, then sixteen, then

thirty-two, thirty-six hours he dug. His hands were raw and his energy gone, but he refused to quit. Finally, after thirty-eight wrenching hours, he pulled back a boulder and heard his son's voice. He called his boy's name, "Arman! Arman!" And a voice answered him, "Dad, it's me!" Then the boy added these priceless words, "I told the other kids not to worry. I told them if you were alive, you'd save me, and when you saved me, they'd be saved, too. Because you promised, 'No matter what, I'll always be there for you.'"[2]

God has made the same promise to us. "I will come back . . . ," he assures us. Yes, the rocks will tumble. Yes, the ground will shake. But the child of God needn't fear—for the Father has promised to take us to be with him. . . .

Because we can accept the resurrection story, it is safe to accept the rest of the story.

Because of the resurrection, everything changes.

Death changes. It used to be the end; now it is the beginning.

The cemetery changes. People once went there to say goodbye; now they go to say, "We'll be together again."

Even the coffin changes. The casket is no longer a box where we hide bodies, but rather a cocoon in which the body is kept until God sets it free to fly.

And someday, according to Christ, he will set us free. He will come back. "I will come back and take you to be with me" (John 14:3 NCV). And to prove that he was serious about his promise, the stone was rolled and his body was raised.

*B*ut the child of God needn't fear—for the Father has promised to take us to be with him.

For he knows that someday this world will shake again. In the blink of an eye, as fast as the lightning flashes from the east to the west, he will come back. And everyone will see him—you will, I will. Bodies will push back the dirt and break the surface of the sea. The earth will tremble, the sky will roar, and those who do not know him will shudder. But in that hour you will not fear because you know him.

For you, like the boy in Armenia, have heard the promise of your Father. You know that he has moved the stone—not the stone of the Armenian earthquake, but the stone of the Arimathean's grave. And in the moment he removed the stone, he also removed all reason for doubt. And we, like the boy, can believe the words of our Father: "I will come back and take you to be with me so that you may be where I am" (John 14:3 NCV).

—*When Christ Comes*

$\mathcal{H}$eaven is a perfect place of perfected people with our perfect Lord.

—*3:16: The Numbers of Hope*

$\mathcal{W}$hen my daughters were younger, we enjoyed many fun afternoons in the swimming pool. Just like all of us, they had to overcome their fears in order to swim. One of the final fears they had to face was the fear of the deep. It's one thing to swim on the surface; it's another to plunge down to the bottom. I mean, who knows what kind of dragons and serpents dwell in the depths of an eight-foot pool? You and I know there is no evil to fear, but a six-year-old doesn't. A child feels the same way about the deep that you and I feel about death. We aren't sure what awaits us down there.

I didn't want my daughters to be afraid of the deep end, so with each I played Shamu the whale. My daughter would be the trainer. I would be Shamu. She would pinch her nose and put her arm around my neck, then down we would go. Deep, deep, deep until we could touch the bottom of the pool. Then up we would explode, breaking the surface. After several plunges they realized they had nothing to fear. They feared no evil. Why? Because I was with them.

And when God calls us into the deep valley of death, he will be with us. Dare we think that he would abandon us in the moment of death? Would a father force his child to swim the deep alone? Would the shepherd require his sheep to journey to the highlands alone? Of course not. Would God require his child to journey to eternity alone? Absolutely not! He is with you!

—*TRAVELING LIGHT*

What prevents people from being rightly related to God? Sin. And if heaven promises a right relationship with God, what is missing in heaven? You got it, baby. Sin. Heaven will be sin free. Both death and sin will be things of the past.

Is this a big deal? I think so. Earlier we tried to imagine a world with no death; let's do the same with sin. Can you imagine a world minus sin? Have you done anything recently because of sin?

At the very least, you've complained. You've worried. You've grumbled. You've hoarded when you should have shared. You've turned away when you should have helped. You've second-guessed, and you've covered up. But you won't do that in heaven.

Because of sin, you've snapped at the ones you love and argued with the ones you cherish. You have felt ashamed, guilty, bitter. You have ulcers, sleepless nights, cloudy days, and a pain in the neck. But you won't have those in heaven.

Because of sin, the young are abused and the elderly forgotten. Because of sin, God is cursed and drugs are worshiped. Because of sin, the poor have less and the affluent want more. Because of sin, babies have no daddies and husbands have no wives. But in heaven, sin will have no power; in fact, sin will have no presence. There will be no sin.

Sin has sired a thousand heartaches and broken a million promises. Your addiction can be traced back to sin. Your mistrust can be traced back to sin. Bigotry, robbery, adultery–all because of sin. But in heaven, all of this will end.

Can you imagine a world without sin?
If so, you can imagine heaven.

Can you imagine a world without sin? If so, you can imagine heaven.

—*WHEN CHRIST COMES*

*T*his is not our forever house. It will serve for the time being. But there is nothing like the moment we enter his door.

Molly can tell you. After a month in our house she ran away. I came home one night to find the place unusually quiet. Molly was gone.

She'd slipped out unnoticed. The search began immediately. Within an hour we knew that she was far, far from home. Now, if you don't like pets, what I'm about to say is going to sound strange. If you do like pets, you will understand.

You'll understand why we walked up and down the street, calling her name. You'll understand why I drove around the neighborhood at 10:30 P.M. You'll understand why I put up a poster in the convenience store and convened the family for a prayer. (Honestly, I did.) You'll understand why I sent e-mails to the staff, asking for prayers, and to her breeder, asking for advice. And you'll understand why we were ready to toss the confetti and party when she showed up.

Here is what happened. The next morning Denalyn was on her way home from taking the girls to school when she saw the trash truck. She asked the workers to keep an eye out for Molly and then hurried home to host a moms' prayer group. Soon after the ladies arrived, the trash truck pulled into our driveway; a worker opened the door and out bounded our dog. She had been found.

When Denalyn called to tell me the news, I could barely hear her voice. It was Mardi Gras in the kitchen. The ladies were celebrating the return of Molly.

This story pops with symbolism. The master leaving his house, searching for the lost. Victories in the midst of prayer. Great things coming out of trash. But most of all: the celebration at the coming home. That's something else you have in common with Molly—a party at your homecoming. . . .

Those you love will shout. Those you know will applaud. But all the noise will cease when {God} cups your chin and says, "Welcome home."

—*3:16: THE NUMBERS OF HOPE*

This is not our forever house. It will serve for the time being. But there is nothing like the moment we enter his door.

*W*hat will happen when you see Jesus?

You will see unblemished purity and unbending strength. You will feel his unending presence and know his unbridled protection. And—all that he is, you will be, for you will be like Jesus. Wasn't that the promise of John? "We know that when Christ comes again, we will be like him, because we will see him as he really is" (1 John 3:2 NCV).

Since you'll be pure as snow, you will never sin again.

Since you will be as strong as bronze, you will never stumble again.

Since you'll dwell near the river, you will never feel lonely again.

Since the work of the priest will have been finished, you will never doubt again.

When Christ comes, you will dwell in the light of God. And you will see him as he really is.

—*WHEN CHRIST COMES*

*O*f all the blessings of heaven, one of the greatest will be you! You will be God's magnum opus, his work of art. The angels will gasp. God's work will be completed. At last, you will have a heart like his.

You will love with a perfect love.

You will worship with a radiant face.

You'll hear each word God speaks.

Your heart will be pure, your words will be like jewels, your thoughts will be like treasures.

You will be just like Jesus. You will, at long last, have a heart like his. Envision the heart of Jesus, and you'll be envisioning your own. Guiltless. Fearless. Thrilled and joyous. Tirelessly worshiping. Flawlessly discerning. As the mountain stream is pristine and endless, so will be your heart. You will be like him.

And if that were not enough, everyone else will be like him as well. . . . Heaven is populated by those who let God change them. Arguments will cease, for jealousy won't exist. Suspicions won't surface, for there will be no secrets. Every sin is gone. Every insecurity is forgotten. Every fear is past. Pure wheat. No weeds. Pure gold. No alloy. Pure love. No lust. Pure hope. No fear. No wonder the angels rejoice when one sinner repents; they know another work of art will soon grace the gallery of God. They know what heaven holds.

—*JUST LIKE JESUS*

*F*or all we don't know about the next life, this much is certain. The day Christ comes will be a day of reward. Those who went unknown on earth will be known in heaven. Those who never heard the cheers of men will hear the cheers of angels. Those who missed the blessing of a father will hear the blessing of their heavenly Father. The small will be great. The forgotten will be remembered. The unnoticed will be crowned and the faithful will be honored.

—*WHEN CHRIST COMES*

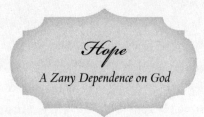

Hope

A Zany Dependence on God

"*Finally*, brethren, whatever things are true, whatever things are noble, whatever things are just, whatever things are pure, whatever things are lovely, whatever things are of good report, if there is any virtue and if there is anything praiseworthy–meditate on these things" (Phil. 4:8 NKJV).

This is more than a silver-lining attitude, more than seeing the cup as half-full rather than half-empty. This is an admission that unseen favorable forces populate and direct the affairs of humanity. When we see as God wants us to see, we see heaven's hand in the midst of sickness, . . . the Holy Spirit comforting a broken heart. We see, not what is seen, but what is unseen. We see with faith and not flesh, and since faith begets hope, we of all people are hope filled. For we know there is more to life than what meets the eye.

—*Every Day Deserves a Chance*

"Do not be anxious about anything, but in everything, by prayer and petition, with thanksgiving, present your requests to God" (Phil. 4:6 NIV).

Don't measure the size of the mountain; talk to the One who can move it. Instead of carrying the world on your shoulders, talk to the One who holds the universe on his. Hope is a look away.

Now, what were you looking at?

—*TRAVELING LIGHT*

*I*t's one of the most compelling narratives in all of Scripture. So fascinating is the scene, in fact, that Luke opted to record it in detail.

Two disciples are walking down the dusty road to the village of Emmaus. Their talk concerns the crucified Jesus. Their words come slowly, trudging in cadence with the dirge-like pace of their feet.

"I can hardly believe it. He's gone."

"What do we do now?"

"It's Peter's fault, he shouldn't have . . ."

Just then a stranger comes up from behind and says, "I'm sorry, but I couldn't help overhearing you. Who are you discussing?"

They stop and turn. Other travelers make their way around

them as the three stand in silence. Finally one of them asks, "Where have you been the last few days? Haven't you heard about Jesus of Nazareth?" And he continues to tell what has happened (Luke 24:13–24).

This scene fascinates me—two sincere disciples telling how the last nail has been driven in Israel's coffin. God, in disguise, listens patiently, his wounded hands buried deeply in his robe. He must have been touched at the faithfulness of this pair. Yet he also must have been a bit chagrined. He had just gone to hell and back to give heaven to earth, and these two were worried about the political situation of Israel.

"But we had hoped that he was the one who was going to redeem Israel."

But we had hoped . . . How often have you heard a phrase like that?

"We were hoping the doctor would release him."

"I had hoped to pass the exam."

"We had hoped the surgery would get all the tumor."

"I thought the job was in the bag."

Words painted gray with disappointment. What we wanted didn't come. What came, we didn't want. The result? Shattered hope. The foundation of our world trembles.

We trudge up the road to Emmaus dragging our sandals in the dust, wondering what we did to deserve such a plight. "What kind of God would let me down like this?"

Our problem is not so much that God doesn't give us what we hope for as it is that we don't know the right thing for which to hope.

And yet, so tear-filled are our eyes and so limited is our perspective that God could be the fellow walking next to us and we wouldn't know it.

You see, the problem with our two heavy-hearted friends was not a lack of faith, but a lack of vision. Their petitions were limited to what they could imagine–an earthly kingdom. Had God answered their prayer, had he granted their hope, the Seven-Day War would have started two thousand years earlier and Jesus would have spent the next forty years training his apostles to be cabinet members. You have to wonder if God's most merciful act is his refusal to answer some of our prayers.

We are not much different than burdened travelers, are we? We roll in the mud of self-pity in the very shadow of the cross. We piously ask for his will and then have the audacity to pout if everything doesn't go our way. If we would just remember the heavenly body that awaits us, we'd stop complaining that he hasn't healed this earthly one.

Our problem is not so much that God doesn't give us what we hope for as it is that we don't know the right thing for which to hope.

Hope is not what you expect; it is what you would never dream. It is a wild, improbable tale with a pinch-me-I'm-dreaming ending. It's Abraham adjusting his bifocals so he can see not his grandson, but his son. It's Moses standing in the promised land not with Aaron or Miriam at his side, but with Elijah and the transfigured Christ. It's Zechariah left speechless at the sight of his wife, Elizabeth, gray-headed and pregnant. And it is the two Emmaus-bound pilgrims reaching out to take a piece of bread only to see that the hands from which it is offered are pierced.

Hope is not a granted wish or a favor performed; no, it is far greater than that. It is a zany, unpredictable dependence on a God who loves to surprise us out of our socks and be there in the flesh to see our reaction.

—*GOD CAME NEAR*

*Y*ou and I live in a trashy world. Unwanted garbage comes our way on a regular basis. . . . Haven't you been handed a trash sack of mishaps and heartaches? Sure you have. May I ask, what are you going to do with it?

You have several options. You could hide it. You could take the trash bag and cram it under your coat or stick it under your dress and pretend it isn't there. But you and I know you won't fool anyone. Besides, sooner or later it will start to stink. Or you could disguise it. Paint it green, put it on the front lawn, and tell everybody it is a tree. Again, no one will be fooled, and pretty soon it's going to reek. So what will you do? If you follow the example of Christ, you will learn to see tough times differently. Remember, God loves you just the way you are, but he refuses to leave you that way. He wants you to have a hope-filled heart . . . just like Jesus. . . .

Wouldn't you love to have a hope-filled heart? Wouldn't you love to see the world through the eyes of Jesus? Where we see unanswered prayer, Jesus saw answered prayer. Where we see the absence of God, Jesus saw the plan of God. Note especially Matthew 26:53: "Surely you know I could ask my Father, and he would give me more than twelve armies of angels" (NCV). Of all the treasures Jesus saw in the trash, this is most significant. He saw his Father. He saw his Father's presence in the problem. Twelve armies of angels were within his sight.

Sure, Max, but Jesus was God. He could see the unseen. He had eyes for heaven and a vision for the supernatural. I can't see the way he saw.

Not yet maybe, but don't underestimate God's power. He can change the way you look at life.

—*JUST LIKE JESUS*

"*G*od will help you overflow with hope in him through the Holy Spirit's power within you" (Rom. 15:13 TLB).

Heaven's hope does for your world what the sunlight did for my grandmother's cellar. I owe my love of peach preserves to her. She canned her own and stored them in an underground cellar near her West Texas house. It was a deep hole with wooden steps, plywood walls, and a musty smell. As a youngster I used to climb in, close the door, and see how long I could last in the darkness. Not even a slit of light entered that underground hole. I would sit silently, listening to my breath and heartbeats, until I couldn't take it anymore and then would race up the stairs and throw open the door. Light would avalanche into the cellar. What a change! Moments before I couldn't see anything–all of a sudden I could see everything.

Just as light poured into the cellar, God's hope pours into your world. Upon the sick, he shines the ray of healing. To the bereaved, he gives the promise of reunion. For the dying, he lit the flame of resurrection. To the confused, he offers the light of Scripture.

God gives hope. So what if someone was born thinner or stronger, lighter or darker than you? Why count diplomas or compare résumés? What does it matter if they have a place at the head table? You have a place at God's table. And he is filling your cup to overflowing. . . .

Your cup overflows with joy. Overflows with grace. Shouldn't your heart overflow with gratitude?

The heart of the boy did. Not at first, mind you. Initially he was full of envy. But, in time, he was full of gratitude.

According to the fable, he lived with his father in a valley at the base of a large dam. Every day the father would go to work on the mountain behind their house and return home with a wheelbarrow full of dirt. "Pour the dirt in the sacks, Son," the father would say. "And stack them in front of the house."

*G*od's hope pours into your world. Upon the sick, he shines the ray of healing. To the bereaved, he gives the promise of reunion.

And though the boy would obey, he also complained. He was tired of dirt. He was weary of bags. Why didn't his father give him what other fathers gave their sons? They had toys and games; he had dirt. When he saw what the others had, he grew mad at them. "It's not fair," he said to himself.

And when he saw his father, he objected. "They have fun. I have dirt."

The father would smile and place his arm on the boy's shoulders and say, "Trust me, Son. I'm doing what is best."

But it was so hard for the boy to trust. Every day the father would bring the load. Every day the boy would fill bags. "Stack them as high as you can," the father would say as he went for more. And so the boy filled the bags and piled them high. So high he couldn't see over them.

"Work hard, Son," the father said one day. "We're running out of time." As the father spoke, he looked at the darkening sky. The boy stared at the clouds and turned to ask about them, but when he did, the thunder cracked and the sky opened. The rain poured so hard he could scarcely see his father through the water. "Keep stacking, Son!" And as he did, the boy heard a mighty crash.

The water of the river poured through the dam and toward the little village. In a moment the tide swept everything in its path, but the dike of dirt gave the boy and the father the time they needed. "Hurry, Son. Follow me."

They ran to the side of the mountain behind their house and

into a tunnel. In a matter of moments they exited the other side and scampered up the hill and came upon a new cottage.

"We'll be safe here," the father said to the boy.

Only then did the son realize what the father had done. He had burrowed an exit. Rather than give him what he wanted, the father gave his boy what he needed. He gave him a safe passage and a safe place.

Hasn't our Father given us the same? A strong wall of grace to protect us? A sure exit to deliver us? Of whom can we be envious? Who has more than we do? Rather than want what others have, shouldn't we wonder if they have what we do? Instead of being jealous of them, how about zealous for them? For heaven's sake, drop the rifles and hold out the cup. There is enough to go around.

One thing is certain. When the final storm comes and you are safe in your Father's house, you won't regret what he didn't give. You'll be stunned at what he did.

—*TRAVELING LIGHT*

*J*eremiah was depressed, as gloomy as a giraffe with a neck ache. Jerusalem was under siege, his nation under duress. His world collapsed like a sand castle in a typhoon. He faulted God for his horrible emotional distress. He also blamed God for his physical ailments. "{God} has made my flesh and my skin waste away, and broken my bones" (Lam. 3:4 RSV).

His body ached. His heart was sick. His faith was puny. . . . He realized how fast he was sinking, so he shifted his gaze. "But this I call to mind, and therefore I have hope: The steadfast love of the LORD never ceases, his mercies never come to an end; they are new every morning; great is thy faithfulness. 'The LORD is my portion,' says my soul, 'therefore I will hope in him'" (vv. 21–24 RSV).

"But this I call to mind . . ." Depressed, Jeremiah altered his thoughts, shifted his attention. He turned his eyes away from his stormy world and looked into the wonder of God. He quickly recited a quintet of promises. (I can envision him tapping these out on the five fingers of his hand.)

1. The steadfast love of the Lord never ceases.
2. His mercies never come to an end.
3. They are new every morning.
4. Great is thy faithfulness.
5. The Lord is my portion.

The storm didn't cease, but his discouragement did.

—*Fearless*

Jesus
Steadfast Savior

$\mathcal{W}$ant to know the coolest thing about {Christ's} coming?

Not that the One who played marbles with the stars gave it up to play marbles with marbles. Or that the One who hung the galaxies gave it up to hang doorjambs to the displeasure of a cranky client who wanted everything yesterday but couldn't pay for anything until tomorrow.

Not that he, in an instant, went from needing nothing to needing air, food, a tub of hot water and salts for his tired feet, and, more than anything, needing somebody—anybody—who was more concerned about where he would spend eternity than where he would spend Friday's paycheck.

Or that he resisted the urge to fry the two-bit, self-appointed hall monitors of holiness who dared suggest that he was doing the work of the devil.

Not that he kept his cool while the dozen best friends he ever had felt the heat and got out of the kitchen. Or that he gave no command to the angels who begged, "Just give the nod, Lord. One word and these demons will be deviled eggs."

Not that he refused to defend himself when blamed for every sin of every slut and sailor since Adam. Or that he stood silent as a million guilty verdicts echoed in the tribunal of heaven and the giver of light was left in the chill of a sinner's night.

Not even that after three days in a dark hole he stepped into the Easter sunrise with a smile and a swagger and a question for lowly Lucifer–"Is that your best punch?"

That was cool, incredibly cool.

But want to know the coolest thing about the One who gave up the crown of heaven for a crown of thorns?

He did it for you. Just for you.

—*He Chose the Nails*

*T*he noise and the bustle began earlier than usual in the village. As night gave way to dawn, people were already on the streets. Vendors were positioning themselves on the corners of the most heavily traveled avenues. Store owners were unlocking the doors to their shops. Children were awakened by the excited barking of the street dogs and the complaints of donkeys pulling carts.

The owner of the inn had awakened earlier than most in the town. After all, the inn was full, all the beds taken. Every available mat or blanket had been put to use. Soon all the customers would be stirring and there would be a lot of work to do.

One's imagination is kindled thinking about the conversation of the innkeeper and his family at the breakfast table. Did anyone mention the arrival of the young couple the night before? Did anyone ask about their welfare? Did anyone comment on the pregnancy of the girl on the donkey? Perhaps. Perhaps someone raised the subject. But, at best, it was raised, not discussed. There was nothing *that* novel about them. They were, possibly, one of several families turned away that night.

Besides, who had time to talk about them when there was so much excitement in the air? Augustus did the economy of Bethlehem a favor when he decreed that a census should be taken. Who could remember when such commerce had hit the village?

No, it is doubtful that anyone mentioned the couple's arrival or wondered about the condition of the girl. They were too busy. The day was upon them. The day's bread had to be made. The morning's chores had to be done. There was too much to do to imagine that the impossible had occurred.

God had entered the world as a baby.

Yet were someone to chance upon the sheep stable on the outskirts of Bethlehem that morning, what a peculiar scene they would behold.

There was too much to do to imagine that the impossible had occurred. God had entered the world as a baby.

The stable stinks like all stables do. The stench of urine, dung, and sheep reeks pungently in the air. The ground is hard, the hay scarce. Cobwebs cling to the ceiling and a mouse scurries across the dirt floor.

A more lowly place of birth could not exist.

Off to one side sit a group of shepherds. They sit silently on the floor; perhaps perplexed, perhaps in awe, no doubt in amazement. Their night watch had been interrupted by an explosion of light from heaven and a symphony of angels. God goes to those who have time to hear him—so on this cloudless night he went to simple shepherds.

Near the young mother sits the weary father. If anyone is dozing, he is. He can't remember the last time he sat down. And now that the excitement has subsided a bit, now that Mary and the baby are comfortable, he leans against the wall of the stable and feels his eyes grow heavy. He still hasn't figured it all out. The mystery of the event puzzles him. But he hasn't the energy to wrestle with the questions. What's important is that the baby is fine and that Mary is safe. As sleep comes he remembers the name the angel told him to use . . . Jesus. "We will call him Jesus."

Wide awake is Mary. My, how young she looks! Her head rests on the soft leather of Joseph's saddle. The pain has been eclipsed by wonder. She looks into the face of the baby. Her son. Her Lord. His Majesty. At this point in history, the human being who best understands who God is and what he is doing is a teenage girl in a smelly stable. She can't take her eyes off him. Somehow Mary knows she is holding God. *So this is he.* She remembers the words of the angel. "His kingdom will never end" (Luke 1:33 NIV).

He looks like anything but a king. His face is prunish and red. His cry, though strong and healthy, is still the helpless and piercing cry of a baby. And he is absolutely dependent upon Mary for his well-being.

Majesty in the midst of the mundane. Holiness in the filth of sheep manure and sweat. Divinity entering the world on the floor of a stable, through the womb of a teenager and in the presence of a carpenter.

She touches the face of the infant-God. *How long was your journey!*

This baby had overlooked the universe. These rags keeping him warm were the robes of eternity. His golden throne room had been abandoned in favor of a dirty sheep pen. And worshiping angels had been replaced with kind but bewildered shepherds.

Meanwhile, the city hums. The merchants are unaware that God has visited their planet. The innkeeper would never believe that he had just sent God into the cold. And the people would scoff at anyone who told them the Messiah lay in the arms of a teenager on the outskirts of their village. They were all too busy to consider the possibility.

*H*e looks like anything but a king. His face is prunish and red. His cry, though strong and healthy, is still the helpless and piercing cry of a baby.

Those who missed His Majesty's arrival that night missed it not because of evil acts or malice; no, they missed it because they simply weren't looking.

Little has changed in the last two thousand years, has it?

—*GOD CAME NEAR*

*W*hat do you do with a man who claims to be God, yet hates religion? What do you do with a man who calls himself the Savior, yet condemns systems? What do you do with a man who knows the place and time of his death, yet goes there anyway?

Pilate's question is yours. "What should I do with Jesus?" (Matt. 27:22 NCV).

You have two choices.

You can reject him. That is an option. You can, as have many, decide that the idea of God's becoming a carpenter is too bizarre—and walk away.

Or you can accept him. You can journey with him. You can listen for his voice amidst the hundreds of voices and follow him.

—*AND THE ANGELS WERE SILENT*

TWENTY-FIVE QUESTIONS FOR MARY

What was it like watching him pray?

How did he respond when he saw other kids giggling during the service at the synagogue?

When he saw a rainbow, did he ever mention a flood?

Did you ever feel awkward teaching him how he created the world?

When he saw a lamb being led to the slaughter, did he act differently?

Did you ever see him with a distant look on his face as if he were listening to someone you couldn't hear?

How did he act at funerals?

Did the thought ever occur to you that the God to whom you were praying was asleep under your own roof?

Did you ever try to count the stars with him . . . and succeed?

Did he ever come home with a black eye?

How did he act when he got his first haircut?

Did he have any friends by the name of Judas?

Did he do well in school?

Did you ever scold him?

Did he ever have to ask a question about Scripture?

What do you think he thought when he saw a prostitute offering to the highest bidder the body he made?

Did he ever get angry when someone was dishonest with him?

Did you ever catch him pensively looking at the flesh on his own arm while holding a clod of dirt?

Did he ever wake up afraid?

Who was his best friend?

When someone referred to Satan, how did he act?

Did you ever accidentally call him Father?

What did he and his cousin John talk about as kids?

Did his other brothers and sisters understand what was happening?

Did you ever think, *That's God eating my soup?*

—<small>GOD CAME NEAR</small>

$\mathcal{I}$ have a sketch of Jesus laughing. It hangs on the wall across from my desk.

It's quite a drawing. His head is back. His mouth is open. His eyes are sparkling. He isn't just grinning. He isn't just chuckling. He's roaring. He hasn't heard or seen one like that in quite a while. He's having trouble catching his breath.

It was given to me by an Episcopal priest who carries cigars in his pocket and collects portraits of Jesus smiling. "I give them to anyone who might be inclined to take God too seriously," he explained as he handed me the gift.

He pegged me well.

Can you honestly imagine Jesus bouncing children on his knee with a somber face?

I'm not one who easily envisions a smiling God. A weeping God, yes. An angry God, OK. A mighty God, you bet. But a chuckling God? It seems too . . . too . . . too unlike what God should do—and be. Which just shows how much I know—or don't know—about God.

What do I think he was doing when he stretched the neck of the giraffe? An exercise in engineering? What do I think he had in mind when he told the ostrich where to put his head? Spelunking? What do I think he was doing when he designed the mating call of an ape? Or the eight legs of the octopus? And what do I envision on his face when he saw Adam's first glance at Eve? A yawn?

Hardly.

As my vision improves, and I'm able to read without my stained glasses, I'm seeing that a sense of humor is perhaps the only way God has put up with us for so long.

Is that him with a smile as Moses does a double take at the burning bush that speaks?

Is he smiling again as Jonah lands on the beach, dripping gastric juices and smelling like whale breath?

Is that a twinkle in his eye as he watches the disciples feed thousands with one boy's lunch?

Do you think that his face is deadpan as he speaks about the man with a two-by-four in his eye who points out a speck in a friend's eye?

Can you honestly imagine Jesus bouncing children on his knee with a somber face?

No, I think that Jesus smiled. I think that he smiled a bit at people and a lot with people.

—*IN THE EYE OF THE STORM*

*J*esus could have been a "Joe." If Jesus came today, his name might have been John or Bob or Jim. Were he here today, it is doubtful he would distance himself with a lofty name like Reverend Holiness Angelic Divinity III. No, when God chose the name his son would carry, he chose a human name (Matt. 1:24).

He chose a name so typical that it would appear two or three times on any given class roll.

"The Word became flesh," John said, in other words (John 1:14 NKJV).

He was touchable, approachable, reachable. And, what's more, he was ordinary. If he were here today you probably wouldn't notice him as he walked through a shopping mall. He wouldn't turn heads by the clothes he wore or the jewelry he flashed.

"Just call me Jesus," you can almost hear him say.

He was the kind of fellow you'd invite to watch the

Rams-Giants game at your house. He'd wrestle on the floor with your kids, doze on your couch, and cook steaks on your grill. He'd laugh at your jokes and tell a few of his own. And when you spoke, he'd listen to you as if he had all the time in eternity.

And one thing's for sure, you'd invite him back.

It is worth noting that those who knew him best remembered him as Jesus. The titles Jesus Christ and Lord Jesus are seen only six times. Those who walked with him remembered him not with a title or designation, but with a name—Jesus.

Think about the implications. When God chose to reveal himself to mankind, what medium did he use? A book? No, that was secondary. A church? No. That was consequential. A moral code? No. To limit God's revelation to a cold list of do's and don'ts is as tragic as looking at a Colorado road map and saying that you'd seen the Rockies.

When God chose to reveal himself, he did so (surprise of surprises) through a human body. The tongue that called forth the dead was a human one. The hand that touched the leper had dirt under its nails. The feet upon which the woman wept were calloused and dusty. And his tears . . . oh, don't miss the tears . . . they came from a heart as broken as yours or mine ever has been.

"For we do not have a high priest who is unable to sympathize with our weaknesses" (Heb. 4:15 NIV).

*H*e was touchable, approachable, reachable . . . "Just call me Jesus," you can almost hear him say.

So people came to him. My, how they came to him! They came at night; they touched him as he walked down the street; they followed him around the sea; they invited him into their homes and placed their children at his feet. Why? Because he refused to be a statue in a cathedral or a priest in an elevated pulpit. He chose instead to be Jesus.

There is not a hint of one person who was afraid to draw near him. There were those who mocked him. There were those who were envious of him. There were those who misunderstood him. There were those who revered him. But there was not one person who considered him too holy, too divine, or too celestial to touch. *There was not one person who was reluctant to approach him for fear of being rejected.*

Remember that.

Remember that the next time you find yourself amazed at your own failures.

Or the next time acidic accusations burn holes in your soul.

Or the next time you see a cold cathedral or hear a lifeless liturgy.

Remember. It is man who creates the distance. It is Jesus who builds the bridge.

"Just call me Jesus."

—*GOD CAME NEAR*

His tears . . . oh, don't miss the tears . . . they came from a heart as broken as yours or mine ever has been.

*J*esus claims to be, not a *top* theologian, an *accomplished* theologian, or even the *Supreme* Theologian, but rather the *Only* Theologian. "No one truly knows the Father except the Son" (Luke 10:22 NLT). He does not say, "No one truly knows the Father *like* the Son" or "*in the fashion* of the Son." But rather, "No one truly knows the Father except the Son."

—*3:16: The Numbers of Hope*

*J*esus was not a godlike man, nor a manlike God. He was God-man.

Midwifed by a carpenter.

Bathed by a peasant girl.

The maker of the world with a bellybutton.

The author of the Torah being taught the Torah.

Heaven's human. And because he was, we are left with scratch-your-head, double-blink, what's-wrong-with-this-picture? moments like these:

Bordeaux instead of H_2O.

A cripple sponsoring the town dance.

A sack lunch satisfying five thousand tummies.

And most of all, a grave: guarded by soldiers, sealed by a rock, yet vacated by a three-days-dead man.

What do we do with such moments?

What do we do with such a *person*? We applaud men for doing good things. We enshrine God for doing great things. But when a man does God things?

One thing is certain, we can't ignore him.

Why would we want to? If these moments are factual, if the claim of Christ is actual, then he was, at once, man and God.

There he was, the single most significant person who ever lived. Forget MVP; he is the entire league. The head of the parade? Hardly. No one else shares the street. Who comes close? Humanity's best and brightest fade like dime-store rubies next to him.

Dismiss him? We can't.

Resist him? Equally difficult. Don't we need a God-man Savior? A just-God Jesus could make us but not understand us. A just-man Jesus could love us but never save us. But a God-man Jesus? Near enough to touch. Strong enough to trust. A next door Savior.

A Savior found by millions to be irresistible. Nothing compares to "the surpassing worth of knowing Christ Jesus my Lord" (Phil. 3:8 RSV). The reward of Christianity is Christ.

Do you journey to the Grand Canyon for the souvenir T-shirt or the snow globe with the snowflakes that fall when you shake it? No. The reward of the Grand Canyon is the Grand Canyon. The wide-eyed realization that you are part of something ancient, splendid, powerful, and greater than you.

The Fort Knox of faith is Christ. Fellowshipping with him. Walking with him. Pondering him. Exploring him.

The cache of Christianity is Christ. Not money in the bank or a car in the garage or a healthy body or a better self-image. Secondary and tertiary fruits perhaps. But the Fort Knox of faith is Christ. Fellowshipping with him. Walking with him. Pondering him. Exploring him. The heart-stopping realization that in him you are part of something ancient, endless, unstoppable, and unfathomable. And that he, who can dig the Grand Canyon with his pinkie, thinks you're worth his death on Roman timber. Christ is the reward of Christianity. Why else would Paul make him his supreme desire? "I want to know Christ" (Phil. 3:10 NCV).

Do you desire the same? My idea is simple. Let's look at some places he went and some people he touched. Join me on a quest for his "God-manness." You may be amazed.

More important, you may be changed. "We all, with unveiled face, beholding the glory of the Lord, are being changed into his likeness from one degree of glory to another; for this comes from the Lord who is the Spirit" (2 Cor. 3:18 RSV).

As we behold him, we become like him.

—*NEXT DOOR SAVIOR*

*B*eloved means "priceless" and "unique." There is none other like Christ. Not Moses. Not Elijah. Not Peter. Not Zoroaster, Buddha, or Muhammad. No one in heaven or on earth. Jesus, the Father declared, is not "a son" or even "the best of all sons." He is the "beloved Son."

—*FEARLESS*

*J*ust as his divinity is becoming unapproachable, just when his holiness is becoming untouchable, just when his perfection becomes inimitable, the phone rings and a voice whispers, "He was human. Don't forget. He had flesh."

Just at the right time we are reminded that the one to whom we pray knows our feelings. He knows temptation. He has felt discouraged. He has been hungry and sleepy and tired. He knows what we feel like when the alarm clock goes off. He knows what we feel like when our children want different things at the same time. He nods in understanding when we pray in anger. He is touched when we tell him there is more to do than can ever be done. He smiles when we confess our weariness.

But we are most indebted to John for choosing to include verse 28 of {John} chapter 19. It reads simply:

"I'm thirsty" (MSG).

That's not *the Christ* that's thirsty. That's the carpenter. And those are words of humanity in the midst of divinity.

He pioneered our salvation through the world that you and I face daily.

This phrase messes up your sermon outline. The other six statements are more "in character." They are cries we would expect: forgiving sinners, promising paradise, caring for his mother, even the cry "My God, my God, why have you forsaken me?" is one of power (Matt. 27:46 NIV).

But, "I thirst"?

Just when we had it all figured out. Just when the cross was all packaged and defined. Just when the manuscript was finished. Just when we had invented all those nice clean "ation" words like sanctification, justification, propitiation, and purification. Just when we put our big golden cross on our big golden steeple, he reminds us that "the Word became flesh" (John 1:14 NIV).

He wants us to remember that he, too, was human. He wants us to know that he, too, knew the drone of the humdrum and the weariness that comes with long days. He wants us to remember that our trailblazer didn't wear bulletproof vests or rubber gloves or an impenetrable suit of armor. No, he pioneered our salvation through the world that you and I face daily.

He is the King of kings, the Lord of lords, and the Word of Life. More than ever he is the Morning Star, the Horn of Salvation, and the Prince of Peace.

But there are some hours when we are restored by remembering that God became flesh and dwelt among us. Our Master knew what it meant to be a crucified carpenter who got thirsty.

—*No Wonder They Call Him the Savior*

*T*he longer we live in {Christ}, the greater he becomes in us. It's not that he changes but that we do; we see more of him. We see dimensions, aspects, and characteristics we never saw before, increasing and astonishing increments of his purity, power, and uniqueness. We discard boxes and old images of Christ like used tissues. We don't dare place Jesus on a political donkey or elephant. Arrogant certainty becomes meek curiosity. Define Jesus with a doctrine or confine him to an opinion? By no means. We'll sooner capture the Caribbean in a butterfly net than we'll capture Christ in a box.

In the end, we respond like the apostles. We, too, fall on our faces and worship.

—*FEARLESS*

Miracles

Mysteries of Majesty

We come to God humbly. No swagger, no boasts, no "all by myself" declarations. We flex no muscles and claim no achievements. We cup sullied hearts in hands and offer them to God as we would a crushed, scentless flower: "Can you bring life to this?"

And he does. *He* does. We don't. He works the miracle of salvation. He immerses us in mercy. He stitches together our shredded souls. He deposits his Spirit and implants heavenly gifts. Our big God blesses our small faith.

—*OUTLIVE YOUR LIFE*

*J*ohn the Baptist saw a dove and believed. James Whittaker saw a seagull and believed. Who's to say the one who sent the first didn't send the second?

James Whittaker was a member of the handpicked crew that flew the B-17 Flying Fortress captained by Eddie Rickenbacker. Anybody who remembers October of 1942 remembers the day Rickenbacker and his crew were reported lost at sea.

Somewhere over the Pacific, out of radio range, the plane ran out of fuel and crashed into the ocean. The nine men spent the next month floating in three rafts. They battled the heat, the storms, and the water. Sharks, some ten feet long, would ram their nine-foot boats. After only eight days their rations were eaten or destroyed by saltwater. It would take a miracle to survive.

One morning after their daily devotions, Rickenbacker leaned his head back against the raft and pulled his hat over his eyes. A bird landed on his head. He peered out from under his hat. Every eye was on him. He instinctively knew it was a seagull.

Rickenbacker caught it, and the crew ate it. The bird's intestines were used for bait to catch fish . . . and the crew survived to tell the story. A story about a stranded crew with no hope or help in sight. A story about prayers offered and prayers answered. A story about a visitor from an unknown land traveling a great distance to give his life as a sacrifice.

A story of salvation.

A story much like our own. Weren't we, like the crew, stranded? Weren't we, like the crew, praying? And weren't we, like the crew, rescued by a visitor we've never seen through a sacrifice we'll never forget?

Oh, the lengths to which God will go to get our attention and win our affection.

You may have heard the Rickenbacker story before. You may have even heard it from me. You may have read it in one of my books. Coreen Schwenk did. She was engaged to the only crew member who did not survive, young Sgt. Alex Kacymarcyck. As a result of a 1985 reunion of the crew, Mrs. Schwenk learned that the widow of James Whittaker lived only eighty miles from her house. The two women met and shared their stories.

After reading this story in my book *In the Eye of the Storm*, Mrs. Schwenk felt compelled to write to me. The real miracle, she informed me, was not a bird on the head of Eddie Rickenbacker but a change in the heart of James Whittaker. The greatest event of that day was not the rescue of a crew but the rescue of a soul.

James Whittaker was an unbeliever. The plane crash didn't change his unbelief. The days facing death didn't cause him to reconsider his destiny. In fact, Mrs. Whittaker said her husband grew irritated with John Bartak, a crew member who continually read his Bible privately and aloud.

But his protests didn't stop Bartak from reading. Nor did Whittaker's resistance stop the Word from penetrating his soul. Unknown to Whittaker, the soil of his heart was being plowed. For it was one morning after a Bible reading that the seagull landed on Captain Rickenbacker's head.

And at that moment Jim became a believer.

I chuckled when I read the letter. Not at the letter; I believe every word of it. Nor at James Whittaker. I have every reason to believe his conversion was real. But I had to chuckle at . . . please excuse me . . . I had to chuckle at God.

Isn't that just like him? Who would go to such extremes to save a soul? Such an effort to get a guy's attention. The rest of the world is occupied with Germany and Hitler. Every headline is reporting the actions of Roosevelt and Churchill. The globe is locked in a battle for freedom . . . and the Father is in the Pacific sending a missionary pigeon to save a soul. Oh, the lengths to which God will go to get our attention and win our affection.

—*A Gentle Thunder*

*F*ear creates a form of spiritual amnesia. It dulls our miracle memory. It makes us forget what Jesus has done and how good God is.

—*Fearless*

*S*omeone who witnesses God's daily display of majesty doesn't find the secret of Easter absurd. Someone who depends upon the mysteries of nature for his livelihood doesn't find it difficult to depend on an unseen God for his salvation.

"Nature," wrote Jonathan Edwards, "is God's greatest evangelist."

"Faith," wrote Paul, "does not rest in the wisdom of men, but in the power of God" (1 Cor. 2:5, author's paraphrase).

"God's testimony," wrote David, "makes wise the simple" (Ps. 19:7, author's paraphrase).

God's testimony. When was the last time you witnessed it? A stroll through knee-high grass in a green meadow. An hour listening to seagulls or looking at seashells on the beach. Or witnessing the shafts of sunlight brighten the snow on a crisp winter dawn. Miracles that almost match the magnitude of the empty tomb happen all around us; we only have to pay attention. . . .

There comes a time when we should lay down our pens and commentaries and step out of our offices and libraries. To really understand and believe in the miracle on the cross, we'd do well to witness God's miracles every day.

—*No Wonder They Call Him the Savior*

*F*rom where I write I can see several miracles.

White-crested waves slap the beach with rhythmic regularity. One after the other the rising swells of saltwater gain momentum, humping, rising, then standing to salute the beach before crashing onto the sand. How many billions of times has this simple mystery repeated itself since time began?

They remind us of the same truth: The unseen is now visible. The distant has drawn near.

In the distance lies a miracle of colors–twins of blue. The ocean-blue of the Atlantic encounters the pale blue of the sky, separated only by the horizon, stretched like a taut wire between two poles.

Also within my eyesight are the two bookends of life. A young mother pushes a baby in a carriage, both recent participants with God in the miracle of birth. They pass a snowy-haired, stooped old gentleman seated on a bench, a victim of life's thief–age. (I wonder if he is aware of the curtain closing on his life.)

Behind them are three boys kicking a soccer ball on the beach. With effortless skill they coordinate countless muscles and reflexes, engage and disengage perfectly designed joints . . . all to do one task–move a ball in the sand.

Miracles. Divine miracles.

These are miracles because they are mysteries. Scientifically explainable? Yes. Reproducible? To a degree.

But still they are mysteries. Events that stretch beyond our understanding and find their origins in another realm. They are every bit as divine as divided seas, walking cripples, and empty tombs.

And they are as much a reminder of God's presence as were the walking lame, fleeing demons, and silenced storms. They are miracles. They are signs. They are testimonies. They are instantaneous incarnations. They remind us of the same truth: The unseen is now visible. The distant has drawn near. His Majesty has come to be seen. And he is in the most common of earth's corners.

In fact, it is the normality, not the uniqueness of God's miracles that causes them to be so staggering. Rather than shocking the globe with an occasional demonstration of deity, God has opted to display his power daily. Proverbially. Pounding waves. Prism-cast colors. Birth, death, life. We are surrounded by miracles. God is throwing testimonies at us like fireworks, each one exploding, "God is! God is!"

The psalmist marveled at such holy handiwork. "Where can I go from your Spirit?" he questioned with delight. "Where can I flee from your presence? If I go up to the heavens, you are there; if I make my bed in the depths, you are there" (Ps. 139:7–8 NIV).

We wonder, with so many miraculous testimonies around us, how we could escape God. But somehow we do. We live in an art gallery of divine creativity and yet are content to gaze only at the carpet.

Or what is pathetically worse, we demand *more*. More signs. More proof. More hat tricks. As if God were some vaudeville magician we could summon for a dollar.

How have we grown so deaf? How have we grown so immune to awesomeness? Why are we so reluctant to be staggered or thunderstruck?

Perhaps the frequency of the miracles blinds us to their beauty. After all, what spice is there in springtime or a tree blossom? Don't the seasons come every year? Aren't there countless seashells just like this one?

We live in an art gallery of divine creativity and yet are content to gaze only at the carpet.

Bored, we say *ho hum* and replace the remarkable with the regular, the unbelievable with the anticipated. Science and statistics wave their unmagic wand across the face of life, squelching the *oohs* and *aahs* and replacing them with formulas and figures.

Would you like to see Jesus? Do you dare be an eyewitness of His Majesty? Then rediscover amazement.

The next time you hear a baby laugh or see an ocean wave, take note. Pause and listen as His Majesty whispers ever so gently, "I'm here."

—*GOD CAME NEAR*

*W*ant to see a miracle? Plant a word of love heartdeep in a person's life. Nurture it with a smile and a prayer, and watch what happens.

An employee gets a compliment. A wife receives a bouquet of flowers. A cake is baked and carried next door. A widow is hugged. A gas-station attendant is honored. A preacher is praised.

Sowing seeds of peace is like sowing beans. You don't know why it works; you just know it does. Seeds are planted, and topsoils of hurt are shoved away.

Don't forget the principle. Never underestimate the power of a seed.

God didn't. When his kingdom was ravaged and his people had forgotten his name, he planted his seed.

When the soil of the human heart had grown crusty, he planted his seed. When religion had become a ritual and the temple a trading post, he planted his seed.

Want to see a miracle? Watch him as he places the seed of his own self in the fertile womb of a Jewish girl.

Up it grew, "like a tender green shoot, sprouting from a root in dry and sterile ground" (Isa. 53:2 TLB).

The seed spent a lifetime pushing back the stones that tried to keep it underground. The seed made a ministry out of shoving away the rocks that cluttered his father's soil.

The stones of legalism that burdened backs.

The stones of oppression that broke bones.

The stones of prejudice that fenced out the needy.

But it was the final stone that proved to be the supreme test of the seed. The stone of death—rolled by humans and sealed by Satan in front of the tomb. For a moment it appeared the seed would be stuck in the earth. For a moment, it looked like this rock was too big to be budged.

But then, somewhere in the heart of the earth, the seed of God stirred, shoved, and sprouted. The ground trembled, and the rock of the tomb tumbled. And the flower of Easter blossomed.

Never underestimate the power of a seed.

—*THE APPLAUSE OF HEAVEN*

*J*ohn doesn't tell us everything Jesus did. But he tells us those acts that will lead us to faith. John selects seven miracles. He begins softly with the quiet miracle of water to wine and then crescendos to the public resurrection of Lazarus. Seven miracles are offered, and seven witnesses are examined, each one building on the testimony of the previous.

Let's see if we can feel their full impact.

Pretend you are in a courtroom, a nearly empty courtroom. Present are four people: a judge, a lawyer, an orphan, and a would-be guardian. The judge is God, Jesus is the one who seeks to be the guardian, and you are the orphan. You have no name, no inheritance, no home. The lawyer is proposing that you be placed in Jesus' care.

Who is the lawyer? A Galilean fisherman by the name of John.

He has presented the court with six witnesses. It is time for the seventh. But before calling him to the stand, the lawyer reviews the case. "We started this case with the wedding in Cana." He paces as he speaks, measuring each word. "They had no wine, none at all. But when Jesus spoke, water became wine. The best wine. Delicious wine. You heard the testimony of the wedding attendants. They saw it happen."

He pauses, then moves on. "Then we heard the words of the foreign official. His son was nearly dead."

*J*ust when he was about to give up hope, someone told him about a healer in Galilee.

You nod. You remember the man's testimony. Articulate, he had spoken of how he had called every doctor and tried every treatment, but nothing had helped his son. Just when he was about to give up hope, someone told him about a healer in Galilee.

Through his thickened accent the dignitary had explained, "I had no other choice. I went to him out of desperation. Look! Look what the teacher did for my son." The boy had stood, and you had stared. It was hard to believe such a healthy youngster had ever been near death.

You listen intently as John continues, "And, your honor, don't forget the crippled man near the pool. For thirty-eight years he had not walked. But then Jesus came and, well, the court saw him. Remember? We saw him walk into this room. We heard his story.

"And as if that was not enough, we also heard the testimony of the boy with the lunch. He was part of a crowd of thousands who had followed Jesus in order to hear him teach and to see him heal. Just when the little boy was about to open his lunch basket to eat, he was asked to bring it to Jesus. One minute it held a lunch; the next it held a feast."

John pauses again, letting the silence of the courtroom speak. No one can deny these testimonies. The judge listens. The lawyer listens. And you, the orphan, say nothing.

"Then there was the storm. Peter described it to us. The boat bouncing on the waves. Thunder. Lightning. Storms like that can kill. I know. I used to make a living on a boat! Peter's testimony about what happened was true. I was there. The Master walked on the water. And the moment he stepped into the boat, we were safe."

John pauses again. Sunlight squared by a window makes a box on the floor. John steps into the box. "Then, yesterday, you met a man who had never seen light. His world was dark. Black. He was blind. Blind from birth."

John pauses and dramatically states what the man born blind had said: "Jesus healed my eyes."

Six testimonies have been given. Six miracles have been verified. John gestures toward the table where sit the articles of evidence: The water jugs that held the wine. The signed affidavit of the doctor who'd treated the sick son. The cot of the cripple, the basket of the boy. Peter had brought a broken oar to show the strength of the storm. And the blind man had left his cup and cane. He didn't need to beg anymore.

"And now," John says, turning to the judge, "we have one final witness to call and one more piece of evidence to submit."

He goes to his table and returns with a white linen sheet. You lean forward, unsure of what he is holding. "This is a burial shroud," he explains. Placing the clothing on the table he requests, "Your honor permitting, I call our final witness to the chair, Lazarus of Bethany."

The Master walked on the water. And the moment he stepped into the boat, we were safe.

Heavy courtroom doors open, and a tall man enters. He strides down the aisle and pauses before Jesus long enough to place a hand on his shoulder and say, "Thank you." You can hear the tenderness in his voice. Lazarus then turns and takes his seat in the witness chair.

"State your name for the court."

"Lazarus."

"Have you heard of a man called Jesus of Nazareth?"

"Who hasn't?"

"How do you know him?"

"He is my friend. We, my sisters and I, have a house in Bethany. When he comes to Jerusalem, he often stays with us. My sisters, Mary and Martha, have become believers in him as well."

"Believers?"

"Believers that he is the Messiah. The Son of God."

"Why do you believe that?"

Lazarus smiles. "How could I not believe? I was dead. I had been dead for four days. I was in the tomb. I was prayed for and buried. I was dead. But Jesus called me out of the grave."

"Tell us what happened."

"Well, I've always been sickly. That's why I've stayed with my sisters, you know. They care for me. My heart never has been the strongest, so I have to be careful. Martha, the oldest sister, she's, well, she's like a mother to me. It was Martha who called Jesus when my heart failed."

*L*azarus smiles. "How could I not believe? I was dead. . . . But Jesus called me out of the grave."

"Is that when you died?"

"No, but almost. I lingered for a few days. But I knew I was near the edge. The doctors would just come in and shake their heads and walk out. I had one sandal in the grave."

"Is that when Jesus came?"

"No, we kept hoping he would. Martha would sit by the bed at night, and she would whisper over and over and over, 'Be strong, Lazarus. Jesus will be here any minute.' We just knew he would come. I mean, he had healed all those strangers; surely he would heal me. I was his friend."

"What delayed him?"

"For the longest time we didn't know. I thought he might be in prison or something. I kept waiting and waiting. Every day I got weaker. My vision faded, and I couldn't see. I drifted in and out. Every time someone entered my room, I thought it might be him. But it never was. He never came."

"Were you angry?"

"More confused than angry. I just didn't understand."

"Then what happened?"

"Well, I woke up one night. My chest was so tight I could hardly breathe. I must have sat up because Martha and Mary came to my bed. They took my hand. I heard them calling my name, but then I began to fall. It was like a dream, I was falling, spinning wildly in midair. Their voices grew fainter and fainter and then nothing. The spinning stopped, the falling stopped. And the hurting stopped. I was at peace."

"At peace?"

"Like I was asleep. Resting. Tranquil. I was dead."

"Then what happened?"

"Well, Martha can tell the details. The funeral was planned. The family came. Friends traveled from Jerusalem. They buried me."

"Did Jesus come to the funeral?"

"No."

"He still wasn't there?"

"No, when he heard I was buried, he waited an extra four days."

"Why?"

Lazarus stopped and looked at Jesus. "To make his point."

John smiled knowingly.

"What happened next?"

"I heard his voice."

"Whose voice?"

"The voice of Jesus."

"But I thought you were dead."

"I was."

"I, uh, thought you were in a grave."

"I was."

"How does a dead man in a grave hear the voice of a man?"

"The spinning stopped, the falling stopped. And the hurting stopped. I was at peace."

"He doesn't. The dead hear only the voice of God. I heard the voice of God."

"What did he say?"

"He didn't say it; he shouted it."

"What did he shout?"

"'Lazarus, come out!'"

"And you heard him?"

"As if he were in the tomb with me. My eyes opened; my fingers moved. I lifted my head. I was alive again. I heard the stone being rolled away. The light poured in. It took a minute for my eyes to adjust."

"What did you see?"

"A circle of faces looking in at me."

"Then what did you do?"

"I stood up. Jesus gave me his hand and pulled me out. He told the people to get me some real clothes, and they did."

"So you died, were in the tomb four days, then Jesus called you back to life? Were there any witnesses to this?"

Lazarus chuckles. "Only a hundred or so."

"That's all, Lazarus, thank you. You may step down."

John returns to the judge. "You have heard the testimonies. I now leave the decision in your hands." With that he returns to the table and takes his seat. The guardian stands. He doesn't identify himself. He doesn't need to. All recognize him. He is Jesus Christ.

He will bring wine to your table, sight to your eyes, strength for your step, and, most of all, power over your grave.

Jesus' voice fills the courtroom. "I represent an orphan who is the sum of all you have seen. Like the party that had no wine, this one has no cause for celebration. Like the dignitary's son, this child is spiritually ill. Like the cripple and the beggar, he can't walk and is blind. He is starving, but earth has no food to fill him. He faces storms as severe as the one on Galilee, but earth has no compass to guide him. And most of all, he is dead. Just like Lazarus. Dead. Spiritually dead.

"I will do for him what I did for them. I'll give him joy, strength, healing, sight, safety, nourishment, new life. All are his. If you will permit."

The judge speaks his answer. "You are my Son, whom I love, and I am very pleased with you" (Luke 3:22 NCV). God looks at you. "I will permit it," he says, "on one condition. That the orphan request it."

John has presented the witnesses.

The witnesses have told their stories.

The Master has offered to do for you what he did for them. He will bring wine to your table, sight to your eyes, strength for your step, and, most of all, power over your grave. He will do for you what he did for them.

The Judge has given his blessing. The rest is up to you.

Now the choice is yours.

—*A GENTLE THUNDER*

Peace

A Tender Tranquility

$\mathcal{I}$ wonder, how many burdens is Jesus carrying for us that we know nothing about? We're aware of some. He carries our sin. He carries our shame. He carries our eternal debt. But are there others? Has he lifted fears before we felt them? Has he carried our confusion so we wouldn't have to? Those times when we have been surprised by our own sense of peace? Could it be that Jesus has lifted our anxiety onto his shoulders and placed a yoke of kindness on ours?

—*A Love Worth Giving*

"$\mathcal{S}$ince we have been made right with God by our faith, we have peace with God" (Rom. 5:1 NCV).

Peace with God. What a happy consequence of faith! Not

just peace between countries, peace between neighbors, or peace at home; salvation brings peace with God.

Once a monk and his apprentice traveled from the abbey to a nearby village. The two parted at the city gates, agreeing to meet the next morning after completing their tasks. According to plan, they met and began the long walk back to the abbey. The monk noticed that the younger man was unusually quiet. He asked him if anything was wrong. "What business is it of yours?" came the terse response.

Now the monk was sure his brother was troubled, but he said nothing. The distance between the two began to increase. The apprentice walked slowly, as if to separate himself from his teacher. When the abbey came in sight, the monk stopped at the gate and waited on the student. "Tell me, my son. What troubles your soul?"

The boy started to react again, but when he saw the warmth in his master's eyes, his heart began to melt. "I have sinned greatly," he sobbed. "Last night I slept with a woman and abandoned my vows. I am not worthy to enter the abbey at your side."

The teacher put his arm around the student and said, "We will enter the abbey together. And we will enter the cathedral together. And together we will confess your sin. No one but God will know which of the two of us fell." (I heard this story at a ministers' retreat featuring Gordon MacDonald in February 1990.)

Doesn't that describe what God has done for us? When we kept our sin silent, we withdrew from him. We saw him as an enemy. We took steps to avoid his presence. But our confession of faults alters our perception. God is no longer a foe but a friend. We are at peace with him. He did more than the monk did, much more. More than share in our sin, Jesus was "crushed for the evil we did. The punishment, which made us well, was given to him" (Isa. 53:5 NCV). "He accepted the shame" (Heb. 12:2 NCV). He leads us into the presence of God.

—*IN THE GRIP OF GRACE*

*S*acred delight is good news coming through the back door of your heart. It's what you'd always dreamed but never expected. It's the too-good-to-be-true coming true. It's having God as your pinch hitter, your lawyer, your dad, your biggest fan, and your best friend. God on your side, in your heart, out in front, and protecting your back. It's hope where you least expected it: a flower in life's sidewalk.

It is *sacred* because only God can grant it. It is a *delight* because it thrills. Since it is sacred, it can't be stolen. And since it is delightful, it can't be predicted.

It was this gladness that danced through the Red Sea. It was this joy that blew the trumpet at Jericho. It was this secret that made Mary sing. It was this surprise that put the springtime into Easter morning.

It is God's gladness. It's sacred delight.

And it is this sacred delight that Jesus promises in the Sermon on the Mount.

Nine times he promises it. And he promises it to an unlikely crowd:

- *The poor in spirit.* Beggars in God's soup kitchen.
- *Those who mourn.* Sinners Anonymous bound together by the truth of their introduction: "Hi, I am me. I'm a sinner."
- *The meek.* Pawnshop pianos played by Van Cliburn. (He's so good no one notices the missing *keys*.)
- *Those who hunger and thirst.* Famished orphans who know the difference between a TV dinner and a Thanksgiving feast.
- *The merciful.* Winners of the million-dollar lottery who share the prize with their enemies.
- *The pure in heart.* Physicians who love lepers and escape infection.
- *The peacemakers.* Architects who build bridges with wood from a Roman cross.
- *The persecuted.* Those who manage to keep an eye on heaven while walking through hell on earth.

It is to this band of pilgrims that God promises a special blessing. A heavenly joy. A sacred delight.

But this joy is not cheap. What Jesus promises is not a gimmick to give you goose bumps nor a mental attitude that has to be pumped up at pep rallies. No, Matthew 5 describes God's radical reconstruction of the heart.

*H*is is a joy that consequences cannot quench. His is a peace that circumstances cannot steal.

Observe the sequence. First, we recognize we are in need (we're poor in spirit). Next, we repent of our self-sufficiency (we mourn). We quit calling the shots and surrender control to God (we're meek). So grateful are we for his presence that we yearn for more of him (we hunger and thirst). As we grow closer to him, we become more like him. We forgive others (we're merciful). We change our outlook (we're pure in heart). We love others (we're peacemakers). We endure injustice (we're persecuted).

It's no casual shift of attitude. It is a demolition of the old structure and a creation of the new. The more radical the change, the greater the joy. And it's worth every effort, for this is the joy of God.

It's no accident that the same word used by Jesus to promise sacred delight is the word used by Paul to describe God:

The blessed God . . . (1 Tim. 1:11 NIV)

God, the blessed and only Ruler . . . (1 Tim. 6:15 NIV)

Think about God's joy. What can cloud it? What can quench it? What can kill it? Is God ever in a bad mood because of bad weather? Does God get ruffled over long lines or traffic jams? Does God ever refuse to rotate the earth because his feelings are hurt?

No. His is a joy that consequences cannot quench. His is a peace that circumstances cannot steal.

—*THE APPLAUSE OF HEAVEN*

*A*ah . . . an hour of contentment. A precious moment of peace. A few minutes of relaxation. Each of us has a setting in which contentment pays a visit.

Early in the morning while the coffee is hot and everyone else is asleep.

Late at night as you kiss your six-year-old's sleepy eyes.

In a boat on a lake when memories of a life well lived are vivid.

In the companionship of a well-worn, dog-eared, even tear-stained Bible.

In the arms of a spouse.

At Thanksgiving dinner or sitting near the Christmas tree.

An hour of contentment. An hour when deadlines are forgotten and strivings have ceased. An hour when what we have overshadows what we want. An hour when we realize that a lifetime of blood-sweating and headhunting can't give us what the cross gave us in one day—a clean conscience and a new start.

But unfortunately, in our squirrel cages of schedules, contests, and side-glancing, hours like these are about as common as one-legged monkeys. In our world, contentment is a strange street vendor, roaming, looking for a home, but seldom finding an open door. This old salesman moves slowly from house to house, tapping on windows, knocking on doors, offering his wares: an hour of peace, a smile of acceptance, a sigh of relief. But his goods are seldom taken. We are too busy to be content (which is crazy since the reason we kill ourselves today is because we think it will make us content tomorrow).

"Not now, thank you. I've too much to do," we say. "Too many marks to be made, too many achievements to be achieved, too many dollars to be saved, too many promotions to be earned. And besides, if I'm content, someone might think I've lost my ambition."

So the street vendor named Contentment moves on. When I asked him why so few welcomed him into their homes, his answer left me convicted. "I charge a high price, you know. My fee is steep. I ask people to trade in their schedules, frustrations, and anxieties. I demand that they put a torch to their fourteen-hour days and sleepless nights. You'd think I'd have more buyers." He scratched his beard, then added pensively, "But people seem strangely proud of their ulcers and headaches."

Can I say something a bit personal? I'd like to give a testimony. A live one. I'm here to tell you that I welcomed this bearded friend into my living room this morning.

It wasn't easy.

My list of things was, for the most part, undone. My responsibilities were just as burdensome as ever. Calls to be made. Letters to be written. Checkbooks to be balanced.

Good-bye, schedule. See you later, routine.
Come back tomorrow, deadlines . . .
hello Contentment, come on in.

But a funny thing happened on the way to the rat race that made me slip into neutral. Just as I got my sleeves rolled up, just as the old engine was starting to purr, just as I was getting up a good head of steam, my infant daughter, Jenna, needed to be held. She had a stomachache. Mom was in the bath so it fell to Daddy to pick her up.

She's three weeks old today. At first I started trying to do things with one hand and hold her with the other. You're smiling. You've tried that too? Just when I realized that it was impossible, I also realized that it was not at all what I was wanting to do.

I sat down and held her tight little tummy against my chest. She began to relax. A big sigh escaped her lungs. Her whimpers became gurgles. She slid down my chest until her little ear was right on top of my heart. That's when her arms went limp and she fell asleep.

And that's when the street vendor knocked at my door.

Good-bye, schedule. See you later, routine. Come back tomorrow, deadlines . . . hello Contentment, come on in.

So here we sit, Contentment, my daughter, and I. Pen in hand, notepad on Jenna's back. She'll never remember this moment and I'll never forget it. The sweet fragrance of a moment captured fills the room. The taste of an opportunity seized sweetens my mouth. The sunlight of a lesson learned illuminates my understanding. This is one moment that didn't get away.

The tasks? They'll get done. The calls? They'll get made. The letters? They'll be written. And you know what? They'll get done with a smile.

I don't do this enough, but I'm going to do it more. In fact, I'm thinking of giving that street vendor a key to my door. "By the way, Contentment, what are you doing this afternoon?"

—*No Wonder They Call Him the Savior*

*M*ark well this promise: "{God} will keep in perfect peace all who trust in {God}, whose thoughts are fixed on {God}" (Isa. 26:3 NLT). God promises not just peace but perfect peace. Undiluted, unspotted, unhindered peace. To whom? To those whose minds are "fixed" on God. Forget occasional glances. Dismiss random ponderings. Peace is promised to the one who fixes thoughts and desires on the king.

—*Facing Your Giants*

Perseverance

Whatever You Do, Don't Quit

The Christian's race is not a jog but rather a demanding and grueling, sometimes agonizing race. It takes a massive effort to finish strong.

Likely you've noticed that many don't? Surely you've observed there are many on the side of the trail? They used to be running. There was a time when they kept the pace. But then weariness set in. They didn't think the run would be this tough. Or they were discouraged by a bump and daunted by a fellow runner. Whatever the reason, they don't run anymore. They may be Christians. They may come to church. They may put a buck in the plate and warm a pew, but their hearts aren't in the race. They retired before their time. Unless something changes, their best work will have been their first work, and they will finish with a whimper.

By contrast, Jesus' best work was his final work, and his strongest step was his last step. Our Master is the classic example of one who endured. The writer of Hebrews goes on to say that Jesus "held on while wicked people were doing evil things to him" (Heb. 12:3 NCV). The Bible says Jesus "held on," implying that Jesus could have "let go." The runner could have given up, sat down, gone home. He could have quit the race. But he didn't. "He held on while wicked people were doing evil things to him."

—*JUST LIKE JESUS*

*G*od never promises to remove us from our struggles. He does promise, however, to change the way we look at them. The apostle Paul dedicates a paragraph to listing trash bags: troubles, problems, sufferings, hunger, nakedness, danger, and violent death. These are the very Dumpsters of difficulty we hope to escape. Paul, however, states their value. "In all these things we have full victory through God" (Rom. 8:37 NCV). We'd prefer another preposition. We'd opt for "*apart* from all these things," or "*away* from all these things," or even "*without* all these things." But Paul says, "*in* all these things." The solution is not to avoid trouble but to change the way we see our troubles.

God can correct your vision.

—*HE STILL MOVES STONES*

*Y*ou and I are on a great climb. The wall is high, and the stakes are higher. You took your first step the day you confessed Christ as the Son of God. He gave you his harness–the Holy Spirit. In your hands he placed a rope–his Word.

Your first steps were confident and strong, but with the journey came weariness, and with the height came fear. You lost your footing. You lost your focus. You lost your grip, and you fell. For a moment, which seemed like forever, you tumbled wildly. Out of control. Out of self-control. Disoriented. Dislodged. Falling.

But then the rope tightened, and the tumble ceased. You hung in the harness and found it to be strong. You grasped the rope and found it to be true. You looked at your guide and found Jesus securing your soul. With a sheepish confession, you smiled at him and he smiled at you, and the journey resumed.

Now you are wiser. You have learned to go slowly. You are careful. You are cautious, but you are also confident. You trust the rope. You rely on the harness. And though you can't see your guide, you know him. You know he is strong. You know he is able to keep you from falling.

And you know you are only a few more steps from the top. So whatever you do, don't quit. Though your falls are great, his strength is greater. You will make it. You will see the summit. You will stand at the top. And when you get there, the first thing you'll do is join with all the others who have made the climb and sing this verse:

To him who is able to keep you from falling and to present you before his glorious presence without fault and with great joy–to the only God our Savior be glory, majesty, power and authority, through Jesus Christ our Lord, before all ages, now and forevermore! Amen. (Jude vv. 24-25 NIV)

—A Gentle Thunder

*G*od gets into things! Red Seas. Big fish. Lions' dens and furnaces. Bankrupt businesses and jail cells. Judean wildernesses, weddings, funerals, and Galilean tempests. Look and you'll find what everyone from Moses to Martha discovered. God in the middle of our storms.

That includes yours.

—Next Door Savior

*D*id God hear the prayer of his Son? Enough to send an angel. Did God spare his Son from death? No. The glory of God outranked the comfort of Christ. So Christ suffered, and God's grace was displayed and deployed.

Are you called to endure a Gethsemane season? Have you

"been granted for Christ's sake, not only to believe in Him, but also to suffer for His sake" (Phil. 1:29 NASB)?

If so, then come thirsty and drink deeply from his lordship. He authors all itineraries. He knows what is best. No struggle will come your way apart from his purpose, presence, and permission. What encouragement this brings! You are never the victim of nature or the prey of fate. Chance is eliminated. You are more than a weather vane whipped about by the winds of fortune. Would God truly abandon you to the whims of drug-crazed thieves, greedy corporate raiders, or evil leaders? Perish the thought!

> *When you pass through the waters, I will be with you;*
> *And through the rivers, they will not overflow you.*
> *When you walk through the fire, you will not be scorched,*
> *Nor will the flame burn you.*
> *For I am the LORD your God. (Isa. 43:2–3 NASB)*

We live beneath the protective palm of a sovereign King who superintends every circumstance of our lives and delights in doing us good.

Nothing comes your way that has not first passed through the filter of his love.

—*COME THIRSTY*

*M*eet today's problems with today's strength. Don't start tackling tomorrow's problems until tomorrow. You do not have tomorrow's strength yet. You simply have enough for today.

—*TRAVELING LIGHT*

*S*ome of you have never won a prize in your life. Oh, maybe you were quartermaster in your Boy Scout troop or in charge of sodas at the homeroom Christmas party, but that's about it. You've never won much. You've watched the Mark McGwires of this world carry home the trophies and walk away with the ribbons. All you have are "almosts" and "what ifs."

If that hits home, then you'll cherish this promise: "And when the Chief Shepherd appears, you will receive the crown of glory that will never fade away" (1 Pet. 5:4 NIV).

Your day is coming. What the world has overlooked, your Father has remembered, and sooner than you can imagine, you will be blessed by him. Look at this promise from the pen of Paul: "God will praise each one of them" (1 Cor. 4:5 NCV).

What an incredible sentence. *God will praise each one of them.* Not "the best of them" nor "a few of them" nor "the achievers among them," but "God will praise each one of them."

God himself will look you in the eye and bless you with the words, "Well done, good and faithful servant!"

You won't be left out. God will see to that. In fact, God himself will give the praise. When it comes to giving recognition, God does not delegate the job. Michael doesn't hand out the crowns. Gabriel doesn't speak on behalf of the throne. God himself does the honors. God himself will praise his children.

And what's more, the praise is personal! Paul says, "God will praise each one of them" (1 Cor. 4:5 NCV). Awards aren't given a nation at a time, a church at a time, or a generation at a time. The crowns are given one at a time. God himself will look you in the eye and bless you with the words, "Well done, good and faithful servant! You have been faithful with a few things; I will put you in charge of many things. Come and share your master's happiness!" (Matt. 25:23 NIV).

With that in mind, let me urge you to stay strong. Don't give up. Don't look back. Let Jesus speak to your heart as he says, "Hold on to what you have, so that no one will take your crown" (Rev. 3:11 NIV).

—*When Christ Comes*

*R*eal courage embraces the twin realities of current difficulty and ultimate triumph. Yes, life stinks. But it won't forever. As one of my friends likes to say, "Everything will work out in the end. If it's not working out, it's not the end."

—*Fearless*

*A*re you hoping that a change in circumstances will bring a change in your attitude? If so, you are in prison, and you need to learn a secret of traveling light. *What you have in your Shepherd is greater than what you don't have in life.*

May I meddle for a moment? What is the one thing separating you from joy? How do you fill in this blank: "I will be happy when _____"? When I am healed. When I am promoted. When I am married. When I am single. When I am rich. How would you finish that statement?

Now, with your answer firmly in mind, answer this. If your ship never comes in, if your dream never comes true, if the situation never changes, could you be happy? If not, then you are sleeping in the cold cell of discontent. You are in prison. And you need to know what you have in your Shepherd.

You have a God who hears you, the power of love behind you, the Holy Spirit within you, and all of heaven ahead of you. If you have the Shepherd, you have grace for every sin, direction for every turn, a candle for every corner, and an anchor for every storm. You have everything you need.

—*TRAVELING LIGHT*

A season of suffering is a small assignment when compared to the reward.

Rather than begrudge your problem, explore it. Ponder it. And most of all, use it. Use it to the glory of God.

—*IT'S NOT ABOUT ME*

*B*e quick to pray, seek healthy counsel, and don't give up.

Don't make the mistake of Florence Chadwick. In 1952, she attempted to swim the chilly ocean waters between Catalina Island and the California shore. She swam through foggy weather and choppy seas for fifteen hours. Her muscles began to cramp, and her resolve weakened. She begged to be taken out of the water, but her mother, riding in a boat alongside, urged her not to give up. She kept trying but grew exhausted and stopped swimming. Aides lifted her out of the water and into the boat. They paddled a few more minutes, the mist broke, and she discovered that the shore was less than a half mile away. "All I could see was the fog," she explained at a news conference. "I think if I could have seen the shore, I would have made it."[3] Take a long look at the shore that awaits you. Don't be fooled by the fog of the slump. The finish may be only strokes away. God may be, at this moment, lifting his hand to signal Gabriel to grab the trumpet. Angels may be assembling, saints gathering, demons trembling. Stay at it! Stay in the water. Stay in the race. Stay in the fight. Give grace, one more time. Be generous, one more time. Teach one more class, encourage one more soul, swim one more stroke.

—*FACING YOUR GIANTS*

God has hung his diplomas in the universe. Rainbows, sunsets, horizons, and star-sequined skies. He has recorded his accomplishments in Scripture. We're not talking six thousand hours of flight time. His résumé includes Red Sea openings. Lions' mouths closings. Goliath topplings. Lazarus raisings. Storm stillings and strollings.

His lesson is clear. He's the commander of every storm.

—*FEARLESS*

Jesus didn't quit. But don't think for one minute that he wasn't tempted to. Watch him wince as he hears his apostles backbite and quarrel. Look at him weep as he sits at Lazarus's tomb or hear him wail as he claws the ground of Gethsemane.

Did he ever want to quit? You bet.

That's why his words are so splendid.

"It is finished."

Stop and listen. Can you imagine the cry from the cross? The sky is dark. The other two victims are moaning. The jeering mouths are silent. Perhaps there is thunder. Perhaps there is weeping. Perhaps there is silence. Then Jesus draws in a deep breath, pushes his feet down on that Roman nail, and cries, "It is finished!"

What was finished?

The history-long plan of redeeming man was finished. The message of God to man was finished. The works done by Jesus as a man on earth were finished. The task of selecting and training ambassadors was finished. The job was finished. The song had been sung. The blood had been poured. The sacrifice had been made. The sting of death had been removed. It was over.

A cry of defeat? Hardly. Had his hands not been fastened down I dare say that a triumphant fist would have punched the dark sky. No, this is no cry of despair. It is a cry of completion. A cry of victory. A cry of fulfillment. Yes, even a cry of relief.

The fighter remained. And thank God that he did. Thank God that he endured.

Are you close to quitting? Please don't do it. Are you discouraged as a parent? Hang in there. Are you weary with doing good? Do just a little more. Are you pessimistic about your job? Roll up your sleeves and go at it again. No communication in your marriage? Give it one more shot. Can't resist temptation? Accept God's forgiveness, and go one more round. Is your day framed with sorrow and disappointment? Are your tomorrows turning into nevers? Is *hope* a forgotten word?

*I*t is not just for those who make the victory laps or drink champagne. No sir. The Land of Promise is for those who simply remain to the end.

Remember, a finisher is not one with no wounds or weariness. Quite to the contrary, he, like the boxer, is scarred and bloody. Mother Teresa is credited with saying, "God didn't call us to be successful, just faithful." The fighter, like our Master, is pierced and full of pain. He, like Paul, may even be bound and beaten. But he remains.

The Land of Promise, says Jesus, awaits those who endure (Matt. 10:22).

It is not just for those who make the victory laps or drink champagne. No sir. The Land of Promise is for those who simply remain to the end.

Let's endure.

—NO WONDER THEY CALL HIM THE SAVIOR

Focus on giants
you stumble.
Focus on God
your giants tumble.

Lift your eyes, giant-slayer. The God who made a miracle out of David stands ready to make one out of you.

—FACING YOUR GIANTS

I understand where Jesus found his strength. He lifted his eyes beyond the horizon and saw the table. He focused on the feast. And what he saw gave him strength to finish–and finish strong.

Such a moment awaits us. In a world oblivious to power abs and speed reading, we'll take our place at the table. In an hour that has no end, we will rest. Surrounded by saints and engulfed by Jesus himself, the work will, indeed, be finished. The final harvest will have been gathered, we will be seated, and Christ will christen the meal with these words: "Well done, good and faithful servant" (Matt. 25:23 KJV).

And in that moment, the race will have been worth it.

—*JUST LIKE JESUS*

*T*he God of surprises strikes again. It's as if he said, "I can't wait any longer. They came this far to see me; I'm going to drop in on them."

God does that for the faithful. Just when the womb gets too old for babies, Sarai gets pregnant. Just when the failure is too great for grace, David is pardoned. And just when the road is too dark for Mary and Mary, the angel glows and the Savior shows and the two women will never be the same.

The lesson? Three words. Don't give up.

Is the trail dark? Don't sit.

Is the road long? Don't stop.

Is the night black? Don't quit.

God is watching. For all you know right at this moment he may be telling the angel to move the stone.

The check may be in the mail.

The apology may be in the making.

The job contract may be on the desk.

Don't quit. For if you do, you may miss the answer to your prayers.

God still sends angels. And God still moves stones.

—*He Still Moves Stones*

At the right time, God comes. In the right way, he appears. So don't bail out. Don't give up! Don't lay down the oars! He is too wise to forget you, too loving to hurt you. When you can't see him, trust him. He is praying a prayer that he himself will answer.

—*A Gentle Thunder*

*C*harles Hall blows up bombs for a living. He is a part of the EOD—the Explosive Ordinance Demolition. He is paid $4,500

a week to walk the sands of post-war Kuwait searching for live mines or discarded grenades. . . .

You and I and these EODs have a lot in common: treacherous trails through explosive territories. Problems that lay partly obscured by the sand. A constant threat of losing life or limb.

And most significant, we, like the demolition team, are called to walk through a minefield that we didn't create. Such is the case with many of life's struggles. We didn't create them, but we have to live with them.

We didn't make alcohol, but our highways have drunk drivers. We don't sell drugs, but our neighborhoods have those who do. We didn't create international tension, but we have to fear the terrorists. We didn't train the thieves, but each of us is a potential victim of their greed.

We, like the EODs, are tiptoeing through a minefield that we didn't create. . . .

If you live on a shooting range chances are you are going to catch a bullet. If you live on a battlefield a cannon ball will likely land in your yard. If you walk through a dark room, you may stub your toe. If you walk through a minefield you may lose your life.

And if you live in a world darkened by sin, you may be its victim.

Jesus is honest about the life we are called to lead. There is no guarantee that just because we belong to him we will go unscathed. No promise is found in Scripture that says when you follow the king you are exempt from battle. No, often just the opposite is the case.

Jesus is honest about the life we are called to lead. There is no guarantee that just because we belong to him we will go unscathed.

How do we survive the battle? How do we endure the fray?

Jesus gives three certainties. Three assurances. Three absolutes. Imagine him leaning closer and looking deeply into the wide eyes of the disciples. Knowing the jungle they are about to enter he gives them three compasses that, if used, will keep them on the right trail.

First, assurance of victory: "Those people who keep their faith until the end will be saved" (Matt. 24:13 NCV).

He doesn't say if you succeed you will be saved. Or if you come out on top you will be saved. He says if you endure. An accurate rendering would be, "If you hang in there until the end . . . if you go the distance."

The Brazilians have a great phrase for this. In Portuguese, a person who has the ability to hang in and not give up has *garra*. *Garra* means "claws." What imagery! A person with *garra* has claws that burrow into the side of the cliff and keep him from falling.

So do the saved. They may get close to the edge; they may even stumble and slide. But they will dig their nails into the rock of God and hang on.

Jesus gives you this assurance. If you hang on, he'll make sure you get home.

Secondly, Jesus gives the assurance of accomplishment: "The Good News about God's kingdom will be preached in all the world, to every nation" (Matt. 24:14 NCV).

In 1066, one of the most decisive battles in the history of the world was fought. William, Duke of Normandy, dared to invade England. The English were a formidable opponent anywhere, but next to invincible in their own land.

But William had something the English did not. He had invented a device that gave his army a heavy advantage in battle. He had an edge: the stirrup.

Conventional wisdom of the day was that a horse was too unstable a platform from which to fight. As a result soldiers would ride their horses to the battlefield and then dismount before engaging in combat. But the Norman army, standing secure in their stirrups, were able to ride down the English. They were faster and they were stronger.

The stirrup led to the conquest of England. Without it, William might never have challenged such an enemy. And this book might have been written in Old English.

Because they had a way to stand in the battle, they were victorious after the battle. Jesus' assurance of victory was daring. Look at his listeners: upcountry fishermen and laborers whose eyes bug at the sight of a big city. You'd have been hard-pressed to find anyone who would wage that the prophecy would come to pass.

But it did, just fifty-three days later. Fifty-three days later Jews were in Jerusalem from "every country in the world" (Acts 2:5 NCV).

Peter stood before them and told them about Jesus.

The disciples were emboldened with the assurance that the

task would be completed. Because they had a way to stand in the battle, they were victorious after the battle. They had an edge . . . and so do we.

Lastly, Jesus gives us assurance of completion: "Then the end will come" (Matt. 24:14 NCV).

An intriguing verse is found in 1 Thessalonians 4:16: "The Lord himself will come down from heaven with a loud command" (NCV).

Have you ever wondered what that command will be? It will be the inaugural word of heaven. It will be the first audible message most have heard from God. It will be the word that closes one age and opens a new one.

I think I know what the command will be. I could very well be wrong, but I think the command that puts an end to the pains of the earth and initiates the joys of heaven will be two words:

"No more."

The King of kings will raise his pierced hand and proclaim, "No more."

The angels will stand and the Father will speak, "No more."

Every person who lives and who ever lived will turn toward the sky and hear God announce, "No more."

No more loneliness.

No more tears.

No more death. No more sadness. No more crying. No more pain.

*J*esus gives you this assurance. If you hang on, he'll make sure you get home.

As John sat on the Island of Patmos surrounded by sea and separated from friends he dreamed of the day when God would say, "No more."

This same disciple who, over half a century before, had heard Jesus speak these words of assurance now knew what they meant. I wonder if he could hear the voice of Jesus in his memory.

"The end will come."

For those who live for this world, that's bad news. But for those who live for the world to come, it's an encouraging promise.

You're in a minefield, my friend, and it's only a matter of time: "In this world you will have trouble . . ." (John 16:33 NCV). Next time you are tossed into a river as you ride the rapids of life, remember his words of assurance.

Those who endure will be saved.

The gospel will be preached.

The end will come.

You can count on it.

—*AND THE ANGELS WERE SILENT*

Prayer

Your Voice Matters in Heaven

$\mathcal{D}$erek Redmond, a twenty-six-year-old Briton, was favored to win the four-hundred-meter race in the 1992 Barcelona Olympics. Halfway into his semifinal heat, a fiery pain seared through his right leg. He crumpled to the track with a torn hamstring.

As the medical attendants were approaching, Redmond fought to his feet. "It was animal instinct," he would later say. He set out hopping, pushing away the coaches in a crazed attempt to finish the race.

When he reached the stretch, a big man pushed through the crowd. He was wearing a T-shirt that read "Have you hugged your child today?" and a hat that challenged, "Just Do It." The man was Jim Redmond, Derek's father.

"You don't have to do this," he told his weeping son.

"Yes, I do," Derek declared.

"Well, then," said Jim, "we're going to finish this together."

And they did. Jim wrapped Derek's arm around his shoulder and helped him hobble to the finish line. Fighting off security men, the son's head sometimes buried in the father's shoulder, they stayed in Derek's lane to the end.

The crowd clapped, then stood, then cheered, and then wept as the father and son finished the race.

What made the father do it? What made the father leave the stands to meet his son on the track? Was it the strength of his child? No, it was the pain of his child. His son was hurt and fighting to complete the race. So the father came to help him finish.

God does the same. Our prayers may be awkward. Our attempts may be feeble. But since the power of prayer is in the one who hears it and not the one who says it, our prayers do make a difference.

—*He Still Moves Stones*

*L*et me ask the obvious. If Jesus, the Son of God, the sinless Savior of humankind, thought it worthwhile to clear his calendar to pray, wouldn't we be wise to do the same?

—*Just Like Jesus*

*I*magine considering every moment as a potential time of communion with God. By the time your life is over, you will have spent six months at stoplights, eight months opening junk mail, a year and a half looking for lost stuff (double that number in my case), and a whopping five years standing in various lines.[4]

Why don't you give these moments to God? By giving God your whispering thoughts, the common becomes uncommon. Simple phrases such as "Thank you, Father," "Be sovereign in this hour, O Lord," "You are my resting place, Jesus" can turn a commute into a pilgrimage. You needn't leave your office or kneel in your kitchen. Just pray where you are. Let the kitchen become a cathedral or the classroom a chapel.

—*JUST LIKE JESUS*

*K*now answered prayer when you see it, and don't give up when you don't.

—*WHEN GOD WHISPERS YOUR NAME*

*F*or ten days the disciples prayed. Ten days of prayer plus a few minutes of preaching led to three thousand saved souls. Perhaps we invert the numbers. We're prone to pray for a few minutes and preach for ten days. Not the apostles. Like the boat waiting for Christ, they lingered in his presence. They never left the place of prayer.

Biblical writers spoke often of this place. Early Christians were urged to

- "pray without ceasing" (1 Thess. 5:17 NASB);
- "always be prayerful" (Rom. 12:12 NLT); and
- "pray at all times and on every occasion" (Eph. 6:18 NLT).

Remember the adverb *continually* that described the Upper Room prayer of the apostles? It's used to describe our prayers as well: "Continue earnestly in prayer, being vigilant in it with thanksgiving" (Col. 4:2 NKJV).

Sound burdensome? Are you wondering, *My business needs attention, my children need dinner, my bills need paying. How can I stay in a place of prayer?* Unceasing prayer may sound complicated, but it needn't be that way.

Do this. Change your definition of prayer. Think of prayers less as an activity for God and more as an awareness of God. Seek to live in uninterrupted awareness. Acknowledge his presence everywhere you go. As you stand in line to register your car, think, *Thank you, Lord, for being here.* In the grocery as you shop, *Your presence, my King, I welcome.* As you wash the dishes, worship your Maker.

—*COME THIRSTY*

*H*ow vital that we pray, armed with the knowledge that God is in heaven. Pray with any lesser conviction and your prayers are timid, shallow, and hollow. But spend some time walking in the workshop of the heavens, seeing what God has done, and watch how your prayers are energized.

—*THE GREAT HOUSE OF GOD*

*W*ant to worry less? Then pray more. Rather than look forward in fear, look upward in faith. This command surprises no one. Regarding prayer, the Bible never blushes. Jesus taught people that "it was necessary for them to pray consistently and never quit" (Luke 18:1 MSG). Paul told believers, "Devote yourselves to prayer with an alert mind and a thankful heart" (Col. 4:2 NLT). James declared, "Are any among you suffering? They should keep on praying about it" (James 5:13 NLT).

Rather than worry about anything, "pray about everything" (Phil. 4:6 NLT). Everything? Diaper changes and dates? Business meetings and broken bathtubs? Procrastinations and prognostications? Pray about everything. "In everything . . . let your requests be made known to God" (Phil. 4:6 NKJV).

When we lived in Rio de Janeiro, Brazil, I used to take my daughters on bus rides. For a few pennies, we could board a bus and ride all over the city. May sound dull to us, but if you are two years old, such a day generates World Cup excitement. The girls did nothing on the trip. I bought the token, carried the backpack, and selected the route. My only request of them was this: "Stay close to me." Why? I knew the kind of characters who might board a bus. And God forbid that my daughters and I got separated.

Our Father makes the same request. "Stay close to me. Talk to me. Pray to me. Breathe me in and exhale your worry." Worry diminishes as we look upward. God knows what can happen on this journey, and he wants to bring us home.

Pray about everything.

—*COME THIRSTY*

*I*t's no accident that New Mexico is called the "Land of Enchantment." Sprawling deserts spotted with sage. Purple mountains wreathed with clouds. Adobe homes hidden on hillsides. Majestic pines. Endless artifacts. A cloverleaf of cultures from the conquistador to the Comanche to the cowboy. New Mexico enchants.

And in this land of enchantment, there is a chapel of wonder.

A block south of the La Fonda Hotel in Santa Fe, on the corner of Water Street and Old Santa Fe Trail, you will find Loretto Chapel. As you step through its iron gate, you enter more than a chapel courtyard. You enter another era. Pause for a moment under the sprawling branches of the ancient trees. Imagine what it was like when the Mexican carpenters completed the chapel in 1878.

Can you see the settlers stomping through the muddy streets? Can you hear the donkeys braying? The wagon wheels groaning? And can you see the early morning sun spotlighting this gothic chapel–so simple, so splendid–as it sits against the backdrop of the desert hills?

Loretto Chapel took five years to complete. Modeled after the Sainte-Chapelle in Paris, its delicate sanctuary contains an altar, a rose window, and a choir loft.

The choir loft is the reason for wonder.

Were you to stand in the newly built chapel in 1878, you might see the Sisters of Loretto looking forlornly at the balcony. Everything else was complete: the doors had been hung, the pews had been placed, the floor had been laid. Everything was finished. Even the choir loft. Except for one thing. No stairs.

The chapel was too small to accommodate a conventional stairway. The best builders and designers in the region shook their heads when consulted. "Impossible," they murmured. There simply wasn't enough room. A ladder would serve the purpose, but mar the ambiance.

The Sisters of Loretto, whose determination had led them from Kentucky to Santa Fe, now faced a challenge greater than their journey: a stairway that couldn't be built.

What they had dreamed of and what they could do were separated by fifteen impossible feet. So what did they do? The only thing they could do. . . . They climbed the mountain of prayer.

What they had dreamed of and what they could do were separated by fifteen impossible feet.

So what did they do? The only thing they could do. They ascended the mountain. Not the high mountains near Santa Fe. No, they climbed even higher. They climbed the same mountain that Jesus climbed 1,800 years earlier in Bethsaida. They climbed the mountain of prayer. . . . As the story goes, the nuns prayed for nine days. On the last day of the novena, a Mexican carpenter with a beard and a wind-burned face appeared at the convent. He explained that he had heard they needed a stairway to a chapel loft. He thought he could help.

The mother superior had nothing to lose, so she gave him permission.

He went to work with crude tools, painstaking patience, and uncanny skill. For eight months he worked.

One morning the Sisters of Loretto entered the chapel to find their prayers had been answered. A masterpiece of carpentry spiraled from the floor to the loft. Two complete three-hundred-sixty-degree turns. Thirty-three steps held together with wooden pegs and no central support. The wood is said to be a variety of hard fir, one nonexistent in New Mexico!

When the sisters turned to thank the craftsman, he was gone. He was never seen again. He never asked for money. He never asked for praise. He was a simple carpenter who did what no one else could do so singers could enter a choir loft and sing.

See the stairway for yourself, if you like. Journey into the Land of Enchantment. Step into this chapel of amazement and witness the fruit of prayer.

Or if you prefer, talk to the Master Carpenter yourself. He has already performed one impossible feat in your world. He, like the Santa Fe carpenter, built a stairway no one else could build. He, like the nameless craftsman, used material from another place. He, like the visitor to Loretto, came to span the gap between where you are and where you long to be.

Each year of his life is a step. Thirty-three paces. Each step of the stair is an answered prayer. He built it so you can climb it.

And sing.

—In the Eye of the Storm

*H*ave you taken your disappointments to God? You've shared them with your neighbor, your relatives, your friends. But have you taken them to God? James says, "Anyone who is having troubles should pray" (James 5:13 NCV).

Before you go anywhere else with your disappointments, go to God.

—Traveling Light

ou can talk to God because God listens. Your voice matters in heaven. He takes you very seriously. When you enter his presence, the attendants turn to you to hear your voice. No need to fear that you will be ignored. Even if you stammer or stumble, even if what you have to say impresses no one, it impresses God—and he listens. He listens to the painful plea of the elderly in the rest home. He listens to the gruff confession of the death-row inmate. When the alcoholic begs for mercy, when the spouse seeks guidance, when the businessman steps off the street into the chapel, God listens.

Intently. Carefully. The prayers are honored as precious jewels. Purified and empowered, the words rise in a delightful fragrance to our Lord. "The smoke from the incense went up from the angel's hand to God" (Rev. 8:4 NCV). Incredible. Your words do not stop until they reach the very throne of God.

Then, the angel "filled the incense pan with fire from the altar and threw it on the earth" (Rev. 8:5 NCV). One call and Heaven's fleet appears. Your prayer on earth activates God's power in heaven, and God's will is "done here on earth as it is in heaven" (Matt 6:10 NCV).

You are the someone of God's kingdom. You have access to God's furnace. Your prayers move God to change the world. You may not understand the mystery of prayer. You don't need to. But this much is clear: Actions in heaven begin when someone prays on earth. What an amazing thought!

When you speak, Jesus hears.

And when Jesus hears, thunder falls.

And when thunder falls, the world is changed.
All because someone prayed.

—*THE GREAT HOUSE OF GOD*

*O*ur passionate prayers move the heart of God. "The effective, fervent prayer of a righteous man avails much" (James 5:16 NKJV). Prayer does not change God's nature; who he is will never be altered. Prayer does, however, impact the flow of history. God has wired his world for power, but he calls on us to flip the switch.

—*OUTLIVE YOUR LIFE*

*S*in-hoarding stiffens us. Confession softens us.

When my daughters were small, they liked to play with Play-Doh. They formed figures out of the soft clay. If they forgot to place the lid on the can, the substance hardened. When it did, they brought it to me. My hands were bigger. My fingers stronger. I could mold the stony stuff into putty.

Is your heart hard? Take it to your Father. You're only a prayer away from tenderness. You live in a hard world, but you don't have to live with a hard heart.

—*3:16: THE NUMBERS OF HOPE*

*I*t's a long way from Boston, Massachusetts, to Edmonton, Canada. No matter how you cut it or route it, it's a long way.

My journey began around 4:30 P.M. I spoke where I was supposed to speak and changed into my Reeboks just in time to fight traffic all the way to Logan Airport.

The plane was overbooked; some folks were mad. The plane was also designed by a five-foot, four-inch engineer who hates tall people. (I ate my knees for lunch.) The plane arrived late into Minneapolis, where I was to change planes.

Now, I know I'm not supposed to complain. I've heard myself preach sermons on gratitude. And I know that a million people in the world would love to have the airline peanuts I threw away today. But still, I got off the plane with a cramp in my leg, an empty stomach, a bad attitude, and three more hours of travel to go.

On the way to my next plane, I saw a McDonald's. Looked good. Did I have time? Then I saw something better: a phone.

I walked over, set down my bags, and called home. Denalyn answered. I love it when she answers. She's always glad when I call. When she gets to heaven, Saint Peter will give her the receptionist job at the gate.

We spent twenty minutes talking about major Pentagon-level topics like the weather in New England and the weather in

San Antonio. We talked about the fact that Jenna had a friend coming over to spend the night and that Sara might have a fever. I told her about the Canadian, French-speaking English teacher I sat next to on the plane, and she told me about the new elementary school.

We made no decisions. We solved no problems. We resolved no major conflicts. We just talked. And I felt better.

Jenna got on the phone and asked me when I was coming home, and it felt good to be wanted.

Andrea got on the phone and told me she loved me, and it felt good to be loved.

Jenna put the phone next to baby Sara's ear, and I talked baby talk in the middle of the airport. (Some people turned to stare.) But I didn't care because Sara cooed, and it felt good to be cooed at.

Denalyn got back on the phone and said, "I'm glad you called." And I hung up happy.

Now I'm back on the plane and my attitude is back on track. The plane is delayed because the runway is backed up, which means I'll get into Edmonton an hour later than I planned. I don't know who is going to pick me up, and I can't remember to whom I'm supposed to speak tomorrow. But that's OK.

I can handle being a pilgrim as long as I know that I can call home whenever I want.

Now it occurs to me that Jesus needed to call home in the middle of the hassles as much as I did.

Jesus could . . . and he did.

Maybe that's the rationale behind verse 19 of Matthew 14: "Taking the five loaves and the two fish and looking up to heaven, he gave thanks and broke the loaves" (NIV). I'd always chalked this prayer up to, at best, a good example–at worst, a good habit.

Until now.

Now it occurs to me that Jesus needed to call home in the middle of the hassles as much as I did. He was surrounded by people who wanted food and disciples who wanted a break. His heart was heavy from the death of John the Baptist.

He needed a minute with someone who would understand.

Maybe he, like me, got a bit weary of the hassles of getting a job done in a distant land and needed to call home.

So he did. He chatted with the One he loved. He heard the sound of the home he missed. And he was reminded that when all hell breaks loose, all heaven draws near.

Maybe you should call home, too. God will be glad when you do–but not half as glad as you will be.

—In the Eye of the Storm

*G*od used (and uses!) people to change the world. *People!* Not saints or superhumans or geniuses but people. Crooks, creeps, lovers, and liars–he uses them all. And what they may lack in perfection, God makes up for in love.

—*No Wonder They Call Him the Savior*

*B*rick by brick, life by life, God is creating a kingdom, a "spiritual house" (1 Pet. 2:5 CEV). He entrusted you with a key task in the project. Examine your tools and discover it. Your ability unveils your destiny. "If anyone ministers, let him do it as *with the ability which God supplies*, that in all things God may be glorified through Jesus Christ" (1 Pet. 4:11 NKJV). When God gives an assignment, he also gives the skill. Study your skills, then, to reveal your assignment.

Look at you. Your uncanny ease with numbers. Your quench-less curiosity about chemistry. Others stare at blueprints and yawn; you read them and drool. "I was made to do this," you say.

Heed that inner music. No one else hears it the way you do.

At this very moment in another section of the church build-ing in which I write, little kids explore their tools. Preschool classrooms may sound like a cacophony to you and me, but God hears a symphony.

A five-year-old sits at a crayon-strewn table. He seldom talks. Classmates have long since set aside their papers, but he ponders his. The colors compel him. He marvels at the gallery of kelly green and navy blue and royal purple. Masterpiece in hand, he'll race to Mom and Dad, eager to show them his kindergarten Picasso.

His sister, however, forgets her drawing. She won't consume the home commute with tales of painted pictures. She'll tell tales of tales. "The teacher told us a new story today!" And the girl will need no prodding to repeat it.

Another boy cares less about the story and the drawings and more about the other kids. He spends the day wearing a "Hey, lis-ten to me!" expression, lingering at the front of the class, testing the patience of the teacher. He relishes attention, evokes reac-tions. His theme seems to be "Do it this way. Come with me. Let's try this."

Our Maker gives assignments to people. . . . As he calls, he equips.

Meaningless activities at an insignificant age? Or subtle hints of hidden strengths? I opt for the latter. The quiet boy with the color fascination may someday brighten city walls with murals. His sister may pen a screenplay or teach literature to curious coeds. And the kid who recruits followers today might eventually do the same on behalf of a product, the poor, or even his church.

What about you? Our Maker gives assignments to people. . . . As he calls, he equips. Look back over your life. What have you consistently done well? What have you loved to do? Stand at the intersection of your affections and successes and find your uniqueness.

You have one. . . . An uncommon call to an uncommon life.

—*CURE FOR THE COMMON LIFE*

*G*od doesn't call the qualified. He qualifies the called.

Don't let Satan convince you otherwise. He will try. He will tell you that God has an IQ requirement or an entry fee. That he employs only specialists and experts, governments and high-powered personalities. When Satan whispers such lies, dismiss him with this truth: God stampeded the first-century society with swaybacks, not thoroughbreds. Before Jesus came along, the disciples were loading trucks, coaching soccer, and selling Slurpee drinks at the convenience store. Their collars were blue, and their hands were calloused, and there is no evidence that Jesus chose them because they were smarter or nicer than the guy next door. The one thing they had going for them was a willingness to take a step when Jesus said, "Follow me."

—*OUTLIVE YOUR LIFE*

*H*ave you been called to go out on a limb for God? You can bet it won't be easy. Limb climbing has never been easy. Ask Joseph. Or, better yet, ask Jesus.

He knows better than anyone the cost of hanging on a tree.

—*GOD CAME NEAR*

*E*xhibit God with your uniqueness. When you magnify your Maker with your strengths, when your contribution enriches God's reputation, your days grow suddenly sweet. And to really dulcify your world, use your uniqueness to make a big deal about God . . . *every day of your life*.

—*CURE FOR THE COMMON LIFE*

*W*ant to know God's will for your life? Then answer this question: What ignites your heart? Forgotten orphans? Untouched nations? The inner city? The outer limits?

Heed the fire within!

Do you have a passion to sing? Then sing!

Are you stirred to manage? Then manage!

Do you ache for the ill? Then treat them!

Do you hurt for the lost? Then teach them!

As a young man I felt the call to preach. Unsure if I was correct in my reading of God's will for me, I sought the counsel of a minister I admired. His counsel still rings true. "Don't preach," he said, "unless you have to."

As I pondered his words I found my answer: "I *have* to. If I don't, the fire will consume me."

What is the fire that consumes you?

Mark it down: Jesus comes to set you on fire! He walks as a torch from heart to heart, warming the cold and thawing the chilled and stirring the ashes. He is at once a Galilean wildfire and a welcome candle. He comes to purge infection and illuminate your direction.

The fire of your heart is the light of your path. Disregard it at your own expense. Fan it at your own delight. Blow it. Stir it. Nourish it. Cynics will doubt it. Those without it will mock it. But those who know it–those who know *him*–will understand it.

To meet the Savior is to be set aflame.

To discover the flame is to discover his will.

And to discover his will is to access a world like none you've ever seen.

—*The Great House of God*

$\mathscr{G}$od made you and broke the mold. "The Lord looks from heaven; He sees all the sons of men. From the place of His dwelling He looks on all the inhabitants of the earth; *He fashions their hearts individually*; He considers all their works" (Ps. 33:13–15 NKJV). Every single baby is a brand-new idea from the mind of God.

Scan history for your replica; you won't find it. God tailor-made you. He "personally formed and made each one" (Isa. 43:7 MSG). No box of "backup yous" sits in God's workshop. You aren't one of many bricks in the mason's pile or one of a dozen bolts in the mechanic's drawer. You are it! And if you aren't you, we don't get you. The world misses out.

You are heaven's Halley's comet; we have one shot at seeing you shine. You offer a gift to society that no one else brings. If you don't bring it, it won't be brought.

—*Cure for the Common Life*

*A*re you more dinghy than cruise ship? More stand-in than movie star? More plumber than executive? More blue jeans than blueblood? Congratulations. God changes the world with folks like you.

—*OUTLIVE YOUR LIFE*

*Y*ou play no small part because there is no small part to be played. "All of you together are Christ's body, and each one of you is a separate and necessary part of it" (1 Cor. 12:27 NLT). "Separate" and "necessary." Unique and essential. No one else has been given your lines. God "shaped each person in turn" (Ps. 33:15 MSG). The Author of the human drama entrusted your part to you alone. Live your life, or it won't be lived. We need you to be you.

You need you to be you.

You can't be your hero, your parent, or your big brother. You might imitate their golf swing or hairstyle, but you can't be them. You can only be you. All you have to give is what you've been given to give. Concentrate on who you are and what you have. "Don't compare yourself with others. Each of you must take responsibility for doing the creative best you can with your own life" (Gal. 6:4–5 MSG).

—*CURE FOR THE COMMON LIFE*

*W*hy are you good at what you do? For your comfort? For your retirement? For your self-esteem? No. Deem these as bonuses, not as the reason.

Why are you good at what you do? For God's sake. Your success is not about what you do. It's all about him–his present and future glory.

—IT'S NOT ABOUT ME

*W*e are created by a great God to do great works. He invites us to outlive our lives, not just in heaven but here on earth.

—OUTLIVE YOUR LIFE

"*G*od made all things, and everything continues through him and *for* him. To him be the glory forever" (Rom. 11:36 NCV). "There is only one God, the Father, who created everything, and *we exist for him*" (1 Cor. 8:6 NLT).

Why does the earth spin? For him.

Why do you have talents and abilities? For him.

Why do you have money or poverty? For him.

Strength or struggles? For him.

Everything and everyone exists to reveal his glory.

Including you.

—IT'S NOT ABOUT ME

$\mathcal{G}$od never called you to be anyone other than you. But he does call on you to be the best *you* you can be.

—*Cure for the Common Life*

$\mathcal{G}$od lets you excel so you can make him known. And you can be sure of one thing: God will make you good at something.

—*It's Not About Me*

Once there was a man who dared God to speak.

Burn the bush like you did for Moses, God.

And I will follow.

Collapse the walls like you did for Joshua, God.

And I will fight.

Still the waves like you did on Galilee, God.

And I will listen.

And so the man sat by a bush, near a wall, close to the sea, and waited for God to speak.

And God heard the man, so God answered.

He sent fire, not for a bush but for a church.

He brought down a wall, not of brick but of sin.

He stilled a storm, not of the sea, but of a soul.

And God waited for the man to respond.

And he waited . . .

And he waited . . .

And waited.

But because the man was looking at bushes, not hearts,

bricks and not lives, seas and not souls,

he decided that God had done nothing.

Finally he looked to God and asked, Have you lost your power?

And God looked at him and said, Have you lost your hearing?

—*A GENTLE THUNDER*

*W*hen you do the most what you do the best, you pop the pride buttons on the vest of God.

—*CURE FOR THE COMMON LIFE*

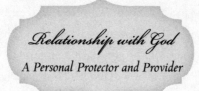

Relationship with God

A Personal Protector and Provider

$\mathcal{L}$istening to God is a firsthand experience. When he asks for your attention, God doesn't want you to send a substitute; he wants you. He invites *you* to vacation in his splendor. He invites *you* to feel the touch of his hand. He invites *you* to feast at his table. He wants to spend time with *you*. And with a little training, your time with God can be the highlight of your day.

—*Just Like Jesus*

$\mathcal{G}$od will always be the same.

No one else will. Lovers call you today and scorn you tomorrow. Companies follow pay raises with pink slips. Friends applaud you when you drive a classic and dismiss you when you drive a dud. Not God. God is "always the same" (Ps. 102:27 NLT).

With him "there is no variation or shadow due to change" (James 4:17 ESV).

Catch God in a bad mood? Won't happen. Fear exhausting his grace? A sardine will swallow the Atlantic first. Think he's given up on you? Wrong. Did he not make a promise to you? "God is not a human being, and he will not lie. He is not a human, and he does not change his mind. What he says he will do, he does. What he promises, he makes come true" (Num. 23:19 NCV). He's never sullen or sour, sulking or stressed. His strength, truth, ways, and love never change. He is "the same yesterday and today and forever" (Heb. 13:8 ESV).

—*IT'S NOT ABOUT ME*

*G*od rewards those who seek *him*. Not those who seek doctrine or religion or systems or creeds. Many settle for these lesser passions, but the reward goes to those who settle for nothing less than Jesus himself. And what is the reward? What awaits those who seek Jesus? Nothing short of the heart of Jesus. "And as the Spirit of the Lord works within us, we become more and more like him" (2 Cor. 3:18 TLB).

Can you think of a greater gift than to be like Jesus? Christ felt no guilt; God wants to banish yours. Jesus had no bad habits; God wants to remove yours. Jesus had no fear of death; God wants you to be fearless. Jesus had kindness for the diseased and mercy for the rebellious and courage for the challenges. God wants you to have the same.

—*JUST LIKE JESUS*

*G*od will whisper. He will shout. He will touch and tug. He will take away our burdens; he'll even take away our blessings. If there are a thousand steps between us and him, he will take all but one. But he will leave the final one for us. The choice is ours.

Please understand. His goal is not to make you happy. His goal is to make you his.

—*A GENTLE THUNDER*

*G*od *in* us! Have we sounded the depth of this promise?

God was *with* Adam and Eve, walking with them in the cool of the evening.

God was *with* Abraham, even calling the patriarch his friend.

God was *with* Moses and the children of Israel. Parents could point their children to the fire by night and cloud by day; *God is with us*, they could assure.

With God *in* you, you have a million resources that you did not have before!

Between the cherubim of the ark, in the glory of the temple, God was *with* his people. He was *with* the apostles. Peter could touch God's beard. John could watch God sleep. Multitudes could hear his voice. God was *with* them!

But he is *in* you. You are a modern-day Mary. Even more so. He was a fetus in her, but he is a force in you. He will do what you cannot. Imagine a million dollars being deposited into your checking account. To any observer you look the same, except for the goofy smile, but are you? Not at all! With God *in* you, you have a million resources that you did not have before!

Can't stop drinking? Christ can. And he lives within you.

Can't stop worrying? Christ can. And he lives within you.

Can't forgive the jerk, forget the past, or forsake your bad habits? Christ can! And he lives within you.

Paul knew this. "For this purpose also I labor, striving according to His power, which mightily works with*in* me" (Col. 1:29, NASB).

Like Mary, you and I are indwelt by Christ.

—NEXT DOOR SAVIOR

*G*od calls us in a real world. He doesn't communicate by performing tricks. He doesn't communicate by stacking stars in the heavens or reincarnating grandparents from the grave. He's not going to speak to you through voices in a cornfield or a little fat man in a land called Oz. There is about as much power in the plastic Jesus that's on your dashboard as there is in the Styrofoam dice on your rearview mirror.

It doesn't make a lick of difference if you are an Aquarius or a Capricorn or if you were born the day Kennedy was shot. God's not a trickster. He's not a genie. He's not a magician or a good luck charm or the man upstairs. He is, instead, the Creator of the universe who is right here in the thick of our day-to-day world, who speaks to you more through cooing babies and hungry bellies than he ever will through horoscopes, zodiac papers, or weeping Madonnas.

If you get some supernatural vision or hear some strange voice in the night, don't get too carried away. It could be God or it could be indigestion, and you don't want to misinterpret one for the other.

Nor do you want to miss the impossible by looking for the incredible. God speaks in our world. We just have to learn to hear him.

Listen for him amidst the ordinary.

—*AND THE ANGELS WERE SILENT*

*C*hrist meets you outside the throne room, takes you by the hand, and walks you into the presence of God. Upon entrance we find grace, not condemnation; mercy, not punishment. Where we would never be granted an audience with the king, we are now welcomed into his presence.

If you are a parent you understand this. If a child you don't know appears on your doorstep and asks to spend the night, what would you do? Likely you would ask him his name, where he lives, find out why he is roaming the streets, and contact his parents. On the other hand, if a youngster enters your house escorted by your child, that child is welcome. The same is true with God. By becoming friends with the Son we gain access to the Father.

Jesus promised, "All those who stand before others and say they believe in me, I will say before my Father in heaven that they belong to me" (Matt. 10:32 NCV). Because we are friends of his Son, we have entrance to the throne room. He ushers us into that "blessing of God's grace that we now enjoy" (Rom. 5:2 NCV).

This gift is not an occasional visit before God but rather a permanent "access by faith into this grace in which we now stand" (v. 2 NIV).

—*IN THE GRIP OF GRACE*

I like John most for the way he loved Jesus. His relationship with Jesus was, again, rather simple. To John, Jesus was a good friend with a good heart and a good idea. A once-upon-a-time story-teller with a somewhere-over-the-rainbow promise.

ohn teaches us . . . that the greatest webs of loyalty are spun, not with airtight theologies or foolproof philosophies, but with friendships.

One gets the impression that to John, Jesus was above all a loyal companion. Messiah? Yes. Son of God? Indeed. Miracle worker? That, too. But more than anything Jesus was a pal. Someone you could go camping with or bowling with or count the stars with.

Simple. To John, Jesus wasn't a treatise on social activism, nor was he a license for blowing up abortion clinics or living in a desert. Jesus was a friend.

Now what do you do with a friend? (Well, that's rather simple too.) You stick by him.

Maybe that is why John is the only one of the twelve who was at the cross. He came to say good-bye. By his own admission he hadn't quite put the pieces together yet. But that didn't really matter. As far as he was concerned, his closest friend was in trouble and he came to help.

"Can you take care of my mother?"

Of course. That's what friends are for.

John teaches us that the strongest relationship with Christ may not necessarily be a complicated one. He teaches us that the greatest webs of loyalty are spun, not with airtight theologies or foolproof philosophies, but with friendships; stubborn, selfless, joyful friendships.

After witnessing this stubborn love, we are left with a burning desire to have one like it. We are left feeling that if we could have been in anyone's sandals that day, we would have been in young

John's and would have been the one to offer a smile of loyalty to this dear Lord.

—*NO WONDER THEY CALL HIM THE SAVIOR*

*W*ould you be bold tomorrow? Then be with Jesus today. Be in his Word. Be with his people. Be in his presence. And when persecution comes (and it will), be strong. Who knows, people may realize that you, like the disciples, have been with Christ.

—*OUTLIVE YOUR LIFE*

"*If* God is for us, who can be against us?" (ROM 8:31 NIV).

The question is not simply, "Who can be against us?" You could answer that one. Who is against you? Disease, inflation, corruption, exhaustion. Calamities confront, and fears imprison. Were Paul's question, "Who can be against us?" we could list our foes much easier than we could fight them. But that is not the question. The question is, if *God is for us*, who can be against us?

Indulge me for a moment. Four words in this verse deserve your attention. Read slowly the phrase, "God is for us." Please pause for a minute before you continue. Read it again, aloud. (My apologies to the person next to you.) *God is for us*. Repeat the phrase four times, this time emphasizing each word. (Come on, you're not in that big of a hurry.)

God is for us.

God *is* for us.

God is *for* us.

God is for *us*.

God is for you. Your parents may have forgotten you, your teachers may have neglected you, your siblings may be ashamed of you; but within reach of your prayers is the maker of the oceans. God!

God *is* for you. Not "may be," not "has been," not "was," not "would be," but "God is!" He *is* for you. Today. At this hour. At this minute. As you read this sentence. No need to wait in line or come back tomorrow. He is with you. He could not be closer than he is at this second. His loyalty won't increase if you are better nor lessen if you are worse. He *is* for you.

God is *for* you. Turn to the sidelines; that's God cheering your run. Look past the finish line; that's God applauding your steps. Listen for him in the bleachers, shouting your name. Too tired to continue? He'll carry you. Too discouraged to fight? He's picking you up. God is *for* you.

God is for *you*. Had he a calendar, your birthday would be circled. If he drove a car, your name would be on his bumper. If there's a tree in heaven, he's carved your name in the bark. We know he has a tattoo, and we know what it says. "I have written your name on my hand," he declares (Isa. 49:16 NCV).

Though hell itself may set itself against you, no one can defeat you. You are protected. God is with you.

"Can a mother forget the baby at her breast and have no compassion on the child she has borne?" God asks in Isaiah 49:15 (NIV). What a bizarre question. Can you mothers imagine feeding your infant and then later asking, "What was that baby's name?" No. I've seen you care for your young. You stroke the hair, you touch the face, you sing the name over and over. Can a mother forget? No way. But "even if she could forget, . . . I will not forget you," God pledges (Isa. 49:15 NCV).

God is with you. Knowing that, who is against you? Can death harm you now? Can disease rob your life? Can your purpose be taken or your value diminished? No. Though hell itself may set itself against you, no one can defeat you. You are protected. God is with you.

—*IN THE GRIP OF GRACE*

Salvation

A Heart Cleansed by Christ

To see sin without grace is despair. To see grace without sin is arrogance. To see them in tandem is conversion.

—*When God Whispers Your Name*

My family did something thoughtful for me last night. They had a party in my honor—a surprise birthday party. Early last week I told Denalyn not to plan anything except a nice, family evening at a restaurant. She listened only to the restaurant part. I was unaware that half a dozen families were going to join us.

In fact, I tried to talk her into staying at home. "Let's have the dinner on another night," I volunteered. Andrea had been sick. Jenna had homework, and I'd spent the afternoon watching football games and felt lazy. Not really in a mood to get up and clean up and go out. I thought I'd have no problem convincing the girls to postpone the dinner. Boy, was I surprised! They wouldn't think of it. Each of my objections was met with a united front and a unanimous defense. My family made it clear–we were going out to eat.

Not only that, we were leaving on time. I consented and set about getting ready. But to their dismay, I moved too slowly. We were a study in contrasts. My attitude was *why hurry?* My daughters' attitude was *hurry up!* I was ho-hum. They were gung-ho. I was content to stay. They were anxious to leave. To be honest, I was bewildered by their actions. They were being uncharacteristically prompt. Curiously enthused. Why the big deal? I mean, I enjoy a night out as much as the next guy, but Sara giggled all the way to the restaurant.

Only when we arrived did their actions make sense. One step inside the door and I understood their enthusiasm. *Surprise!* No wonder they were acting differently. They knew what I didn't. They had seen what I hadn't. They'd already seen the table and stacked the gifts and smelled the cake. Since they knew about the party, they did everything necessary to see that I didn't miss it.

Jesus does the same for us. He knows about *the party.* In one of the greatest chapters in the Bible, Luke 15, he tells three stories. Each story speaks of something lost and of something found. A lost sheep. A lost coin. And a lost son. And at the end of each one, Jesus describes a party, a celebration. The shepherd throws the party for the lost-now-found sheep. The housewife throws a party because of the lost-now-found coin. And the father throws a party in honor of his lost-now-found son.

Three parables, each with a party. Three stories, each with the appearance of the same word: *happy*. Regarding the shepherd who found the lost sheep, Jesus says: "And when he finds it, he *happily* puts it on his shoulders and goes home" (vv. 5-6 NCV). When the housewife finds her lost coin, she announces, "Be *happy* with me because I have found the coin that I lost" (v. 9 NCV). And the father of the prodigal son explains to the reluctant older brother, "We had to celebrate and be *happy* because your brother was dead, but now he is alive. He was lost, but now he is found" (v. 32 NCV).

The point is clear. Jesus is happiest when the lost are found. For him, no moment compares to the moment of salvation. For my daughter the rejoicing began when I got dressed and in the car and on the road to the party. The same occurs in heaven. Let one child consent to be dressed in righteousness and begin the journey home and heaven pours the punch, strings the streamers, and throws the confetti. "There is joy in the presence of the angels of God when one sinner changes his heart and life" (v. 10 NCV).

—*JUST LIKE JESUS*

*J*esus is happiest when the lost are found. For him, no moment compares to the moment of salvation.

At our new birth God remakes our souls and gives us what we need, again. New eyes so we can see by faith. A new mind so we can have the mind of Christ. New strength so we won't grow tired. A new vision so we won't lose heart. A new voice for praise and new hands for service. And most of all, a new heart. A heart that has been cleansed by Christ.

—A Gentle Thunder

God's plan for you is nothing short of a new heart. If you were a car, God would want control of your engine. If you were a computer, God would claim the software and the hard drive. If you were an airplane, he'd take his seat in the cockpit. But you are a person, so God wants to change your heart.

—Just Like Jesus

The walk to freedom is never forgotten. The path taken from slavery to liberation is always vivid. It's more than a road; it's a release. The shackles are opened and, for perhaps the first time, freedom dawns. "I reckons I will always remember that walk . . ."

Do you remember yours? Where were you the night the door was opened? Do you remember the touch of the Father? Who walked with you the day you were set free? Can you still see the scene? Can you feel the road beneath your feet?

I hope so. I hope that permanently planted in your soul is the moment the Father stirred you in the darkness and led you down the path. It's a memory like no other. For when he sets you free, you are free indeed.

Ex-slaves describe well the hour of deliverance.

Can I tell you mine?

A Bible class in a small West Texas town. I don't know what was more remarkable, that a teacher was trying to teach the book of Romans to a group of ten-year-olds or that I remember what he said.

The classroom was mid-sized, one of a dozen or so in a small church. My desk had carving on it and gum under it. Twenty or so others were in the room, though only four or five were taken.

We all sat at the back, too sophisticated to appear interested. Starched jeans. High-topped tennis shoes. It was summer and the slow-setting sun cast the window in gold.

The teacher was an earnest man. I can still see his flattop, his belly bulging from beneath his coat that he doesn't even try to button. His tie stops midway down his chest. He has a black mole on his forehead, a soft voice, and a kind smile. Though he is hopelessly out of touch with the kids of 1965, he doesn't know it.

His notes are stacked on a podium underneath a heavy black Bible. His back is turned to us and his jacket goes up and down his beltline as he writes on the board. He speaks with genuine passion. He is not a dramatic man, but tonight he is fervent.

God only knows why I heard him that night. His text was Romans chapter six. The blackboard was littered with long words and diagrams. Somewhere in the process of describing how Jesus went into the tomb and came back out, it happened. The jewel of grace was lifted and turned so I could see it from a new angle . . . and it stole my breath.

I didn't see a moral code. I didn't see a church. I didn't see ten commandments or hellish demons. I saw what another ten-year-old—Mary Barbour—saw. I saw my Father enter my dark night, awaken me from my slumber, and gently guide me—no, carry me—to freedom.

"I reckons I will always remember that walk."

—*AND THE ANGELS WERE SILENT*

According to Jesus our decisions have a thermostatic impact on the unseen world. Our actions on the keyboard of earth trigger hammers on the piano strings of heaven. Our obedience pulls the ropes that ring the bells in heaven's belfries. Let a child call and the ear of the Father inclines. Let a sister weep and tears begin to flow from above. Let a saint die and the gate is opened. And, most important, let a sinner repent, and every other activity ceases, and every heavenly being celebrates. . . . When a soul is saved, the heart of Jesus becomes the night sky on the Fourth of July, radiant with explosions of cheer.

—*JUST LIKE JESUS*

*H*ow does one receive Christ? By coming thirsty and drinking deeply. How, then, does one live in Christ? By coming thirsty and drinking deeply.

When you do, saving power becomes staying power. "God, who began the good work within you, will continue his work until it is finally finished on that day when Christ Jesus comes back again" (Phil. 4:6 NLT).

Christ did not give you a car and tell you to push it. He didn't even give you a car and tell you to drive it. You know what he did? He threw open the passenger door, invited you to take a seat, and told you to buckle up for the adventure of your life.

—*COME THIRSTY*

Ponder the achievement of God.

He doesn't condone our sin, nor does he compromise his standard.

He doesn't ignore our rebellion, nor does he relax his demands.

Rather than dismiss our sin, he assumes our sin and, incredibly, sentences himself.

God's holiness is honored. Our sin is punished . . . and we are redeemed.

God does what we cannot do so we can be what we dare not dream: perfect before God.

—In the Grip of Grace

*I*t would be enough if God just cleansed your name, but he does more. He gives you *his* name. It would be enough if God just set you free, but he does more. He takes you home. He takes you home to the Great House of God.

Adoptive parents understand this more than anyone. I certainly don't mean to offend any biological parents—I'm one myself. We biological parents know well the earnest longing to have a child. But in many cases our cribs were filled easily. We decided to have a child and a child came. In fact, sometimes the child came with no decision. I've heard of unplanned pregnancies, but I've never heard of an unplanned adoption.

That's why adoptive parents understand God's passion to adopt us. They know what it means to feel an empty space inside. They know what it means to hunt, to set out on a mission, and to take responsibility for a child with a spotted past and a dubious future. If anybody understands God's ardor for his children, it's someone who has rescued an orphan from despair, for that is what God has done for us.

God has adopted you. God sought you, found you, signed the papers, and took you home.

—*THE GREAT HOUSE OF GOD*

*W*hy do Jesus and his angels rejoice over one repenting sinner? Can they see something we can't? Do they know something we don't? Absolutely. They know what heaven holds. They've seen the table, and they've heard the music, and they can't wait to see your face when you arrive. Better still, they can't wait to see you.

—*JUST LIKE JESUS*

*T*here is never a point at which you are any less saved than you were the first moment he saved you. Just because you were grumpy at breakfast doesn't mean you were condemned at breakfast. When you lost your temper yesterday, you didn't lose your salvation. Your name doesn't disappear and reappear in the book of life according to your moods and actions. Such is the message of grace. "There is now no condemnation for those who are in Christ Jesus" (Rom. 8:1 NIV).

You are saved, not because of what you do, but because of what Christ did. And you are special, not because of what you do, but because of whose you are. And you are his.

And because we are his, let's forget the shortcuts and stay on the main road. He knows the way. He drew the map. He knows the way home.

—IN THE GRIP OF GRACE

*B*ack in our elementary school days, my brother received a BB gun for Christmas. We immediately set up a firing range in the back-yard and spent the afternoon shooting at an archery target. Growing bored with the ease of hitting the circle, my brother sent me to fetch a hand mirror. He placed the gun backward on his shoulder, spotted the archery bull's-eye in the mirror, and did his best Buffalo Bill imitation. But he missed the target. He also missed the storehouse behind the target and the fence behind the storehouse. We had no idea where the BB pellet flew. Our neighbor across the alley knew, however. He soon appeared at the back fence, asking who had shot the BB gun and who was going to pay for his sliding glass door.

At this point I disowned my brother. I changed my last name and claimed to be a holiday visitor from Canada. My father was more noble than I. Hearing the noise, he appeared in the backyard, freshly rousted from his Christmas Day nap, and talked with the neighbor.

Among his words were these:

"Yes, they are my children."

"Yes, I'll pay for their mistakes."

Christ says the same about you. He knows you miss the target. He knows you can't pay for your mistakes. But he can. "God sent Jesus to take the punishment for our sins" (Rom. 3:25 NLT).

Since he was sinless, he could.

Since he loves you, he did. "This is real love. It is not that we loved God, but that he loved us and sent his Son as a sacrifice to take away our sins" (1 John 4:10 NLT).

He became one of us to redeem all of us. "Jesus, who makes people holy, and those who are made holy are from the same family. So he is not ashamed to call them his brothers and sisters" (Heb. 2:11 NCV).

He wasn't ashamed of David. He isn't ashamed of you. He calls you brother; he calls you sister. The question is, do you call him Savior?

Take a moment to answer this question. Perhaps you never have. Perhaps you never knew how much Christ loves you. Now you do. Jesus didn't disown David. He won't disown you. He simply awaits your invitation. One word from you and God will do again what he did with David and millions like him: he'll claim you, save you, and use you. Any words will do, but these seem appropriate:

*C*hrist . . . knows you can't pay for your mistakes. But he can.

Jesus, my Savior and Giant-killer, I ask for mercy, strength, and eternal life. I trust you with my heart and give you my life. Amen.

Pray such words with an honest heart, and be assured of this: your greatest Goliath has fallen. Your failures are flushed and death defanged. The power that made pygmies out of David's giants has done the same with yours.

You can face your giants. Why? Because you faced God first.

—*Facing Your Giants*

*I*n many ways your new birth is like your first: In your new birth God provides what you need; someone else feels the pain, and someone else does the work. And just as parents are patient with their newborn, so God is patient with you. But there is one difference. The first time you had no choice about being born; this time you do. The power is God's. The effort is God's. The pain is God's. But the choice is yours.

—*A Gentle Thunder*

*S*alvation is God-given, God-driven, God-empowered, and God-originated. The gift is not from man to God. It is from God to man. "It is not our love for God; it is God's love for us. He sent his Son to die in our place to take away our sins" (1 John 4:10 NCV).

Grace is created by God and given to man. "Sky above, make victory fall like rain; clouds, pour down victory. Let the earth receive it, and let salvation grow, and let victory grow with it. I, the Lord, have created it" (Isa. 45:8 NCV).

On the basis of this point alone, Christianity is set apart from any other religion in the world.

—IN THE GRIP OF GRACE

*H*e has spotted you. He has heard you, and he has invited you. What once separated you has been removed: "Now in Christ Jesus, you who were far away from God are brought near" (Eph. 2:13 NCV). Nothing remains between you and God but an open door.

—HE CHOSE THE NAILS

Second Chances

Count on God's Kindness

God's faithfulness has never depended on the faithfulness of his children. He is faithful even when we aren't. When we lack courage, he doesn't. He has made a history out of using people in spite of people. . . . God is faithful even when his children are not. That's what makes God, God.

—*A Gentle Thunder*

Whoever—God's wonderful word of welcome.

I love to hear my wife say "whoever." Sometimes I detect my favorite fragrance wafting from the kitchen: strawberry cake. I follow the smell just like a bird dog follows a trail until I'm standing over the just-baked, just-iced pan of pure pleasure. Yet I've learned to still my fork until Denalyn gives clearance.

"Who is it for?" I ask.

She might break my heart. "It's for a birthday party, Max. Don't touch it!"

Or "For a friend. Stay away!"

Or she might throw open the door of delight. "Whoever." And since I qualify as a "whoever," I say, "yes."

I so hope you will too. Not to the cake, but to God.

No status too low.

No hour too late.

No place too far.

However. Whenever. Wherever.

Whoever includes you . . . forever.

—*3:16: THE NUMBERS OF HOPE*

*D*on't give up on your Saul. When others write him off, give him another chance. Stay strong. Call her sister. Call him brother. Tell your Saul about Jesus, and pray. And remember this: God never sends you where he hasn't already been. By the time you reach your Saul, who knows what you'll find.

My favorite Ananias-type story involves a couple of college roommates. The Ananias of the pair was a tolerant soul. He tolerated his friend's late night drunkenness, midnight throw-ups, and all day sleep-ins. He didn't complain when his friend disappeared for the weekend or smoked cigarettes in the car. He could have requested a roommate who went to church more or cursed less or cared about something other than impressing girls.

But he hung with his personal Saul, seeming to think that something good could happen if the guy could pull his life together. So he kept cleaning up the mess, inviting his roommate to church, and covering his back.

I don't remember a bright light or a loud voice. I've never traveled a desert road to Damascus. But I distinctly remember Jesus knocking me off my perch and flipping on the light. It took four semesters, but Steve's example and Jesus' message finally got through.

So if this book lifts your spirit, you might thank God for my Ananias, Steve Green. Even more, you might listen to that voice in your heart and look on your map for a street called Straight.

—*Outlive Your Life*

*C*ontrary to what you may have been told, Jesus doesn't limit his recruiting to the stouthearted. The beat up and worn out are prime prospects in his book, and he's been known to climb into boats, bars, and brothels to tell them, "It's not too late to start over."

—*Next Door Savior*

*N*othing drags more stubbornly than a sack of failures.

Could you do it all over again, you'd do it differently. You'd be a different person. You'd be more patient. You'd control your tongue. You'd finish what you started. You'd turn the other cheek instead of slapping his. You'd get married first. You wouldn't marry at all. You'd be honest. You'd resist the temptation. You'd run with a different crowd.

But you can't. And as many times as you tell yourself, "What's done is done," what you did can't be undone.

That's part of what Paul meant when he said, "The wages of sin is death" (Rom. 6:23 NIV). He didn't say, "The wages of sin is a bad mood." Or, "The wages of sin is a hard day." Nor, "The wages of sin is depression." Read it again. "The wages of sin is death." Sin is fatal.

Can anything be done with it?

Your therapist tells you to talk about it. So you do. You pull the bag into his office and pour the rocks out on his floor and analyze each one. And it's helpful. It feels good to talk and he's nice. But when the hour is up, you still have to carry the bag out with you.

Your friends tell you not to feel bad. "Everyone slumps a bit in this world," they say. "Not very comforting," you say.

Feel-great-about-life rallies tell you to ignore the thing and be happy! Which works–until you wipe the fog off your mirror and take an honest look. Then you see, it's still there.

*D*on't we all long for a father who, even though our mistakes are written all over the wall, will love us anyway?

Legalists tell you to work the weight off. A candle for every rock. A prayer for every pebble. Sounds logical, but what if I run out of time? Or what if I didn't count correctly? You panic.

What *do* you do with the stones from life's stumbles?

When my oldest daughter, Jenna, was four years old, she came to me with a confession. "Daddy, I took a crayon and drew on the wall." (Kids amaze me with their honesty.)

I sat down and lifted her up into my lap and tried to be wise. "Is that a good thing to do?" I asked her.

"No."

"What does Daddy do when you write on the wall?"

"You spank me."

"What do you think Daddy should do this time?"

"Love."

Don't we all want that? Don't we all long for a father who, even though our mistakes are written all over the wall, will love us anyway? Don't we want a father who cares for us in spite of our failures?

We *do* have that type of a father. A father who is at his best when we are at our worst. A father whose grace is strongest when our devotion is weakest. If your bag is big and bulky, then you're in for some thrilling news: your failures are not fatal.

—*SIX HOURS ONE FRIDAY*

$\mathcal{P}$eter never again fished for fish. He spent the rest of his days telling anyone who would listen, "It's not too late to try again."

Is it too late for you? Before you say yes, before you fold up the nets and head for the house–two questions. Have you given Christ your boat? Your heartache? Your dead-end dilemma? Your struggle? Have you really turned it over to him? And have you gone deep? Have you bypassed the surface-water solutions you can see in search of the deep-channel provisions God can give? Try the other side of the boat. Go deeper than you've gone. You may find what Peter found. The payload of his second effort was not the fish he caught but the God he saw.

The God-man who spots weary fishermen, who cares enough to enter their boats, who will turn his back on the adoration of a crowd to solve the frustration of a friend. The next door Savior who whispers this word to the owners of empty nets, "Let's try again–this time with me on board."

—*NEXT DOOR SAVIOR*

$\mathcal{E}$ver since Eve hemmed the fig leaves to fit Adam, we have been disguising our truths.

And we've gotten better with each generation.

Michelangelo's creativity is nothing compared to a bald man's use of a few strands of hair. Houdini would stand in awe at our capacity to squeeze lumberjack waistlines into ballerina-sized pants.

We are masters of the masquerade. Cars are driven to make a statement. Jeans are purchased to portray an image. Accents are acquired to hide a heritage. Names are dropped. Weights are lifted. Yarns are spun. Toys are purchased. Achievements are professed.

And the pain is ignored. And, with time, the real self is forgotten.

The Indians used to say that within every heart there is a knife. This knife turns like the minute hand on a clock. Every time the heart lies, the knife rotates an increment. As it turns, it cuts into the heart. As it turns, it carves a circle. The more it turns, the wider the circle becomes. After the knife has rotated one full circle, a path has been carved. The result? No more hurt, no more heart.

One option the boy in the pigpen had was to walk back into the masquerade party and pretend everything was fine. He could have carved his integrity until the pain disappeared. He could have done what millions do. He could have spent a lifetime in the pig-pen pretending it was a palace. But he didn't.

Something told him that this was the moment of–and for–truth.

He looked into the water. The face he saw wasn't pretty–muddy and swollen. He looked away. "Don't think about it. You're no worse off than anybody else. Things will get better tomorrow."

The lies anticipated a receptive ear. They'd always found

one before. "Not this time," he muttered. And he stared at his reflection.

"How far I have fallen." His first words of truth.

He looked into his own eyes. He thought of his father. "They always said I had your eyes." He could see the look of hurt on his father's face when he told him he was leaving.

"How I must have hurt you."

A crack zigzagged across the boy's heart.

A tear splashed into the pool. Another soon followed. Then another. Then the dam broke. He buried his face in his dirty hands as the tears did what tears do so well; they flushed out his soul.

His face was still wet as he sat near the pool. For the first time in a long time he thought of home. The memories warmed him. Memories of dinner-table laughter. Memories of a warm bed. Memories of evenings on the porch with his father as they listened to the hypnotic ring of the crickets.

"Father." He said the word aloud as he looked at himself. "They used to say I looked like you. Now you wouldn't even recognize me. Boy, I blew it, didn't I?"

He stood up and began to walk.

The road home was longer than he remembered. When he last traveled it, he turned heads because of his style. If he turned heads this time, it was because of his stink. His clothes were torn, his hair matted, and his feet black. But that didn't bother him because for the first time in a calendar of heartaches, he had a clean conscience.

He had no money. He had no excuses. And he had no idea how much his father had missed him.

He was going home. He was going home a changed man. Not demanding that he get what he deserved, but willing to take whatever he could get. "Give me" had been replaced with "help me," and his defiance had been replaced with repentance.

He came asking for everything with nothing to give in return. He had no money. He had no excuses.

And he had no idea how much his father had missed him.

He had no idea the number of times his father had paused between chores to look out the front gate for his son. The boy had no idea the number of times his father had awakened from restless sleep, gone into the son's room, and sat on the boy's bed. And the son would have never believed the hours the father had sat on the porch next to the empty rocking chair, looking, longing to see that familiar figure, that stride, that face.

As the boy came around the bend that led up to his house, he rehearsed his speech one more time.

"Father, I have sinned against heaven and against you."

He approached the gate and placed his hand on the latch. He began to lift it, then he paused. His plan to go home suddenly seemed silly. "What's the use?" he heard himself asking himself. "What chance do I have?" He ducked, turned around, and began to walk away.

Then he heard the footsteps. He heard the slap, slap, slap of sandals. Someone was running. He didn't turn to look. *It's probably a servant coming to chase me away or my big brother wanting to know what I'm doing back home.* He began to leave.

But the voice he heard was not the voice of a servant or the voice of his brother; it was the voice of his father.

"Son!"

"Father?"

He turned to open the gate, but the father already had. The son looked at his father standing at the entrance. Tears glistened on his cheeks as arms stretched from east to west inviting the son to come home.

"Father, I have sinned." The words were muffled as the boy buried his face in his father's shoulder.

The two wept. For a forever they stood at the gate intertwined as one. Words were unnecessary. Repentance had been made; forgiveness had been given.

The boy was home.

—*Six Hours One Friday*

*D*on't forget the classic case study on the value of a person by Luke. It is called "The Tale of the Crucified Crook."

If anyone was ever worthless, this one was. If any man ever deserved dying, this man probably did. If any fellow was ever a loser, this fellow was at the top of the list.

All of us—even the purest of us—deserve heaven about as much as that crook did.

Perhaps that is why Jesus chose him to show us what he thinks of the human race.

Maybe this criminal had heard the Messiah speak. Maybe he had seen him love the lowly. Maybe he had watched him dine with the punks, pickpockets, and pot-mouths on the streets. Or maybe not. Maybe the only thing he knew about this Messiah was what he now saw: a beaten, slashed, nail-suspended preacher. His face crimson with blood, his bones peeking through torn flesh, his lungs gasping for air.

Something, though, told him he had never been in better company. And somehow he realized that even though all he had was prayer, he had finally met the One to whom he should pray.

"Any chance that you could put in a good word for me?" (Loose translation.)

"Consider it done."

Now why did Jesus do that? What in the world did he have to gain by promising this desperado a place of honor at the banquet table? What in the world could this chiseling quisling ever offer in return? I mean, the Samaritan woman I can understand. She could go back and tell the tale. And Zacchaeus had some money that he could give. But this guy? What is he going to do? Nothing! . . .

I smile because I know I don't deserve love like that. None of us do. When you get right down to it, any contribution that any of us make is pretty puny. All of us—even the purest of us—deserve heaven about as much as that crook did. All of us are signing on Jesus' credit card, not ours.

And it also makes me smile to think that there is a grinning ex-con walking the golden streets who knows more about grace than a thousand theologians. No one else would have given him a prayer. But in the end that is all that he had. And in the end, that is all it took.

No wonder they call him the Savior.

—No Wonder They Call Him the Savior

*S*omewhere, sometime, somehow you got tangled up in garbage, and you've been avoiding God. You've allowed a veil of guilt to come between you and your Father. You wonder if you could ever feel close to God again. The message of the torn flesh is *you can*. God welcomes you. God is not avoiding you. God is not resisting you. The curtain is down, the door is open, and God invites you in.

Don't trust your conscience. Trust the cross. The blood has been spilt and the veil has been split. You are welcome in God's presence.

—He Chose the Nails

*I*t was like discovering the prize in a box of Crackerjacks or spotting a little pearl in a box of buttons or stumbling across a ten dollar bill in a drawer full of envelopes.

It was small enough to overlook. Only two words. I know I'd read that passage a hundred times. But I'd never seen it. Maybe I'd passed over it in the excitement of the resurrection. Or since Mark's account of the resurrection is by far the briefest of the four, maybe I'd just not paid too much attention. Or maybe since it's in the last chapter of the gospel, my weary eyes had always read too quickly to note this little phrase.

But I won't miss it again. It's highlighted in yellow and underlined in red. You might want to do the same. Look in Mark, chapter 16. Read the first five verses about the women's surprise when they find the stone moved to the side. Then feast on that beautiful phrase spoken by the angel, "He has risen, he is not here" (v. 6 RSV), but don't pause for too long. Go a bit further. Get your pencil ready and enjoy this jewel in the seventh verse (here it comes). The verse reads like this: "But go, tell his disciples and Peter that he is going before you to Galilee" (RSV).

Did you see it? Read it again. (This time I've italicized the words.)

"But go, tell his disciples *and Peter* that he is going before you to Galilee."

Now tell me if that's not a hidden treasure.

"He has risen, he is not here. . . . But go, tell his disciples and Peter that he is going before you to Galilee." (Mark 16:6–7)

If I might paraphrase the words, "Don't stay here, go tell the disciples," a pause, then a smile, "and especially tell Peter, that he is going before you to Galilee."

What a line. It's as if all of heaven had watched Peter fall—and it's as if all of heaven wanted to help him back up again. "Be sure and tell Peter that he's not left out. Tell him that one failure doesn't make a flop."

Whew!

No wonder they call it the gospel of the second chance.

Not many second chances exist in the world today. Just ask the kid who didn't make the Little League team or the fellow who got the pink slip or the mother of three who got dumped for a "pretty little thing."

Not many second chances. Nowadays it's more like, "It's now or never." "Around here we don't tolerate incompetence." "Gotta get tough to get along." "Not much room at the top." "Three strikes and you're out." "It's a dog-eat-dog world!"

Jesus has a simple answer to our masochistic mania. "It's a dog-eat-dog world?" he would say. "Then don't live with the dogs." That makes sense, doesn't it? Why let a bunch of other failures tell you how much of a failure you are?

Sure you can have a second chance.

No wonder they call it the gospel of the second chance.

Just ask Peter. One minute he felt lower than a snake's belly, and the next minute he was the high hog at the trough. Even the angels wanted this distraught netcaster to know that it wasn't over. The message came loud and clear from the celestial Throne Room through the divine courier. "Be sure and tell Peter that he gets to bat again."

Those who know these types of things say that the Gospel of Mark is really the transcribed notes and dictated thoughts of Peter. If this is true, then it was Peter himself who included these two words! And if these really are his words, I can't help but imagine that the old fisherman had to brush away a tear and swallow a lump when he got to this point in the story.

It's not every day that you get a second chance. Peter must have known that. The next time he saw Jesus, he got so excited that he barely got his britches on before he jumped into the cold water of the Sea of Galilee. It was also enough, so they say, to cause this backwoods Galilean to carry the gospel of the second chance all the way to Rome where they killed him. If you've ever wondered what would cause a man to be willing to be crucified upside down, maybe now you know.

It's not every day that you find someone who will give you a second chance—much less someone who will give you a second chance every day.

But in Jesus, Peter found both.

—No Wonder They Call Him the Savior

I was thanking the Father today for his mercy. I began listing the sins he'd forgiven. One by one I thanked God for forgiving my stumbles and tumbles. My motives were pure and my heart was thankful, but my understanding of God was wrong. It was when I used the word *remember* that it hit me.

"Remember the time I . . ." I was about to thank God for another act of mercy. But I stopped. Something was wrong. The word *remember* seemed displaced. It was an off-key note in a sonata, a misspelled word in a poem. It was a baseball game in December. It didn't fit. "Does he remember?"

Then *I* remembered. I remembered his words. "And I will remember their sins no more" (Heb. 8:12 RSV).

Wow! Now, *that* is a remarkable promise.

God doesn't just forgive, he forgets. He erases the board. He destroys the evidence. He burns the microfilm. He clears the computer.

He doesn't remember my mistakes. For all the things he does do, this is one thing he refuses to do. He refuses to keep a list of my wrongs. When I ask for forgiveness he doesn't pull out a clipboard and say, "But I've already forgiven him for that five hundred and sixteen times."

He doesn't remember.

"As far as the east is from the west, so far has he removed our transgressions from us" (Ps. 103:12 NIV).

"I will be merciful toward their iniquities" (Heb. 8:12 RSV).

"Even if you are stained as red as crimson, I can make you white as wool!" (Isa. 1:18 TLB).

No, he doesn't remember. But I do, you do. You still remember. You're like me. You still remember what you did before you changed. In the cellar of your heart lurk the ghosts of yesterday's sins. Sins you've confessed; errors of which you've repented; damage you've done your best to repair.

And though you're a different person, the ghosts still linger. Though you've locked the basement door, they still haunt you. They float to meet you, spooking your soul and robbing your joy. With wordless whispers they remind you of moments when you forgot whose child you were.

That horrid lie.

That business trip you took away from home, that took you so far away from home.

The time you exploded in anger.

Those years spent in the hollow of Satan's hand.

That day you were needed, but didn't respond.

That date.

That jealousy.

That habit.

Poltergeists from yesterday's pitfalls. Spiteful specters that slyly suggest, "Are you really forgiven? Sure, God forgets most of our mistakes, but do you think he could actually forget the time you . . ."

*G*od doesn't just forgive, he forgets. He erases the board. He destroys the evidence. He burns the microfilm.

As a result, your spiritual walk has a slight limp. Oh, you're still faithful. You still do all the right things and say all the right words. But just when you begin to make strides, just when your wings begin to spread and you prepare to soar like an eagle, the ghost appears. It emerges from the swamps of your soul and causes you to question yourself.

"You can't teach a Bible class with your background."

"You, a missionary?"

"How dare you ask him to come to church. What if he finds out about the time you fell away?"

"Who are *you* to offer help?"

The ghost spews waspish words of accusation, deafening your ears to the promises of the cross. And it flaunts your failures in your face, blocking your vision of the Son and leaving you the shadow of a doubt.

Now, honestly. Do you think God sent that ghost? Do you think God is the voice that reminds you of the putridness of your past? Do you think God was teasing when he said, "I will remember your sins no more"? Was he exaggerating when he said he would cast our sins as far as the east is from the west? Do you actually believe he would make a statement like "I will not hold their iniquities against them" and then rub our noses in them whenever we ask for help?

Of course you don't. You and I just need an occasional reminder of God's nature, his forgetful nature.

God is either the God of perfect grace . . . or he is not God.

To love conditionally is against God's nature. Just as it's against your nature to eat trees and against mine to grow wings, it's against God's nature to remember forgiven sins.

You see, God is either the God of perfect grace . . . or he is not God. Grace forgets. Period. He who is perfect love cannot hold grudges. If he does, then he isn't perfect love. And if he isn't perfect love, you might as well put this book down and go fishing because both of us are chasing fairy tales.

But I believe in his loving forgetfulness. And I believe he has a graciously terrible memory.

Think about this. If he didn't forget, how could we pray? How could we sing to him? How could we dare enter into his presence if the moment he saw us he remembered all our pitiful past? How could we enter his throne room wearing the rags of our selfishness and gluttony? We couldn't.

And we don't. Read this powerful passage from Paul's letter to the Galatians and watch your pulse rate. You're in for a thrill. "For as many of you as were baptized into Christ have *put on* Christ" (Gal. 3:27 RSV).

You read it right. We have "put on" Christ. When God looks at us he doesn't see us; he sees Christ. We "wear" him. We are hidden in him; we are covered by him. As the song says, "Dressed in his righteousness alone, faultless to stand before the throne."

Presumptuous, you say? Sacrilegious? It would be if it were my idea. But it isn't; it's his. We are presumptuous not when we marvel at his grace, but when we reject it. And we're sacrilegious not when we claim his forgiveness, but when we allow the haunting sins of yesterday to convince us that God forgives but he doesn't forget.

Do yourself a favor. Purge your cellar. Exorcise your basement. Take the Roman nails of Calvary and board up the door.

And remember . . . he forgot.

—*GOD CAME NEAR*

Spiritual Refreshment

Rivers of Living Water

*I*t's quiet. It's early. My coffee is hot. The sky is still black. The world is still asleep. The day is coming.

In a few moments the day will arrive. It will roar down the track with the rising of the sun. The stillness of the dawn will be exchanged for the noise of the day. The calm of solitude will be replaced by the pounding pace of the human race. The refuge of the early morning will be invaded by decisions to be made and deadlines to be met.

For the next twelve hours I will be exposed to the day's demands. It is now that I must make a choice. Because of Calvary, I'm free to choose. And so I choose.

I choose love . . .

No occasion justifies hatred; no injustice warrants bitterness. I choose love. Today I will love God and what God loves.

I choose joy . . .

I choose love. Today I will love God and what God loves.

I will invite my God to be the God of circumstance. I will refuse the temptation to be cynical . . . the tool of the lazy thinker. I will refuse to see people as anything less than human beings, created by God. I will refuse to see any problem as anything less than an opportunity to see God.

I choose peace . . .

I will live forgiven. I will forgive so that I may live.

I choose patience . . .

I will overlook the inconveniences of the world. Instead of cursing the one who takes my place, I'll invite him to do so. Rather than complain that the wait is too long, I will thank God for a moment to pray. Instead of clinching my fist at new assignments, I will face them with joy and courage.

I choose kindness . . .

I will be kind to the poor, for they are alone. Kind to the rich, for they are afraid. And kind to the unkind, for such is how God has treated me.

I choose goodness . . .

I will go without a dollar before I take a dishonest one. I will be overlooked before I will boast. I will confess before I will accuse. I choose goodness.

I choose faithfulness . . .

Today I will keep my promises. My debtors will not regret their trust. My associates will not question my word. My wife will not question my love. And my children will never fear that their father will not come home.

I choose gentleness . . .

Nothing is won by force. I choose to be gentle. If I raise my voice may it be only in praise. If I clench my fist, may it be only in prayer. If I make a demand, may it be only of myself.

I choose self-control . . .

I am a spiritual being. After this body is dead, my spirit will soar. I refuse to let what will rot, rule the eternal. I choose self-control. I will be drunk only by joy. I will be impassioned only by my faith. I will be influenced only by God. I will be taught only by Christ. I choose self-control.

Love, joy, peace, patience, kindness, goodness, faithfulness, gentleness, and self-control. To these I commit my day. If I succeed, I will give thanks. If I fail, I will seek his grace. And then, when this day is done, I will place my head on my pillow and rest.

—*When God Whispers Your Name*

*E*ternal instants. You've had them. We all have.

Sharing a porch swing on a summer evening with your grandchild.

Seeing her face in the glow of a candle.

Putting your arm into your husband's as you stroll through the golden leaves and breathe the brisk autumn air.

Listening to your six-year-old thank God for everything from goldfish to Grandma.

Such moments are necessary because they remind us that everything is okay. The King is still on the throne and life is still worth living. Eternal instants remind us that love is still the greatest possession and the future is nothing to fear.

The next time an instant in your life begins to be eternal, let it. Put your head back on the pillow and soak it in. Resist the urge to cut it short. Don't interrupt the silence or shatter the solemnity. You are, in a very special way, on holy ground.

—*GOD CAME NEAR*

*C*an you still remember? Are you still in love with him? Remember, Paul begged, remember Jesus. Before you remember anything, remember him. If you forget anything, don't forget him.

Oh, but how quickly we forget. So much happens through the years. So many changes within. So many alterations without. And, somewhere, back there, we leave him. We don't turn away from him . . . we just don't take him with us. Assignments come. Promotions come. Budgets are made. Kids are born, and the Christ . . . the Christ is forgotten.

A man is never the same after
he simultaneously sees his utter
despair and Christ's unbending grace.

Has it been a while since you stared at the heavens in speechless amazement? Has it been a while since you realized God's divinity and your carnality?

If it has, then you need to know something. He is still there. He hasn't left. Under all those papers and books and reports and years. In the midst of all those voices and faces and memories and pictures, he is still there.

Do yourself a favor. Stand before him again. Or, better, allow him to stand before you. Go into your upper room and wait. Wait until he comes. And when he appears, don't leave. Run your fingers over his feet. Place your hand in the pierced side. And look into those eyes. Those same eyes that melted the gates of hell and sent the demons scurrying and Satan running. Look at them as they look at you. You'll never be the same.

A man is never the same after he simultaneously sees his utter despair and Christ's unbending grace. To see the despair without the grace is suicidal. To see the grace without the despair is upper-room futility. But to see them both is conversion.

—*Six Hours One Friday*

*S*omething happened a few weeks ago that could be filed in the folder labeled "Remarkable."

I was playing basketball at the church one Saturday morning.

(A good number of guys show up each week to play.) Some are flat-bellies–guys in their twenties who can touch their toes when they stretch and touch the rim when they jump. The rest of us are fat-bellies–guys who are within eyesight of, if not over the top of, the hill. Touching our toes is no longer an option. Looking down and *seeing* our toes is the current challenge. We never touch the rim when we jump and seldom touch it when we shoot.

But the flat-bellies don't mind if the fat-bellies play. (They don't have a choice. We have the keys to the building.)

Anyway, a few Saturdays back we were in the middle of a game when I went up for a rebound. I must have been pretty slow because, just as I was going up for the ball, someone else was already coming down with it. And the only thing I got from the jump was a finger in the eye.

When I opened my eye, everything was blurry. I knew my contact lens was not where it used to be. I thought I felt it in the corner of my eye, so I waved out of the game and ran to the rest room. But after I looked in the mirror, I realized that it must have fallen out on the floor somewhere.

I ran back onto the court. The guys were at the opposite end, leaving the goal under which I had lost my contact lens vacant.

I hurried out, got down on my knees, and began to search. No luck. When the fellows started bringing the ball downcourt, they saw what I was doing and came to help. All ten of us were down on our knees, panting like puppies and sweating like Pony Express horses.

But no one could find the silly lens.

We were just about to give up when one fellow exclaimed, "There it is." I looked up. He was pointing at a player's shoulder. The same guy whose finger had explored my cornea.

There, on his shoulder, was my lens. It had fallen on him . . . stuck to his skin . . . stayed on his back all the way down the court while he jumped and bounced . . . and then ridden all the way back.

Remarkable.

Even more remarkable when you consider that the contact lens made this round trip on the back of a flat-belly. One of the guys who can touch the rim and his toes. Had it landed on the shoulder of one of the top-of-the-hill guys, no one would have been impressed. Some of us have the mobility of grazing buffalo. But when you think of the ride the tiny piece of plastic took, when you think of the odds of it being found, you have only one place to put this event: in the folder labeled "Remarkable."

The more I thought about this event, the more remarkable it became.

The more remarkable it became, the more I learned about remarkable things.

I learned that remarkable things usually occur in unremarkable situations, i.e., Saturday morning basketball games.

Every day I have the honor of sitting down with a book that contains the words of the One who created me. . . . Remarkable.

I also noticed that there are more remarkable things going on than those I usually see. In fact, as I began to look around, I found more and more things that I'd labeled "To be expected" that deserve to be labeled "Well, what do you know."

Examples?

My money is in a bank with at least several thousand other folks' money. Who knows how many transactions are made every day? Who knows how much money goes into that place and is taken out? But somehow, if I want some money or just want to know how much money I have, the bank teller can give me what I want.

Remarkable.

Each morning I climb into a truck that weighs half a ton and take it out on an interstate where I–and a thousand other drivers–turn our vehicles into sixty-mile-per-hour missiles. Although I've had a few scares and mishaps, I still whistle while I drive at a speed that would have caused my great-grandfather to pass out.

Remarkable.

Every day I have the honor of sitting down with a book that contains the words of the One who created me. Every day I have the opportunity to let him give me a thought or two on how to live.

If I don't do what he says, he doesn't burn the book or cancel my subscription. If I disagree with what he says, lightning doesn't split my swivel chair or an angel doesn't mark my name off the holy list. If I don't understand what he says, he doesn't call me a dummy.

In fact, he calls me "Son" and on a different page explains what I don't understand.

Remarkable.

At the end of the day when I walk through the house, I step into the bedrooms of three little girls. Their covers are usually kicked off, so I cover them up. Their hair usually hides their faces, so I brush it back. And one by one, I bend over and kiss the foreheads of the angels God has loaned me. Then I stand in the doorway and wonder why in the world he would entrust a stumbling, fumbling fellow like me with the task of loving and leading such treasures.

Remarkable.

Then I go and crawl into bed with a woman far wiser than I . . . a woman who deserves a man much better-looking than I . . . but a woman who would argue that fact and tell me from the bottom of her heart that I'm the best thing to come down her pike.

After I think about the wife I have, and when I think that I get to be with her for a lifetime, I shake my head and thank the God of grace for grace and think, *Remarkable.*

In the morning, I'll do it all again. I'll drive down the same road. Go to the same office. Call on the same bank. Kiss the same girls. And crawl into bed with the same woman. But I'm learning not to take these everyday miracles for granted.

Just think; it all came out of a basketball game. Ever since I found that contact, I've seen things a lot clearer.

I shake my head and thank the God of grace for grace and think, *Remarkable*.

I'm discovering many things: traffic jams eventually clear up, sunsets are for free, Little League is a work of art, and most planes take off and arrive on time. I'm learning that most folks are good folks who are just as timid as I am about starting a conversation.

I'm meeting people who love their country and their God and their church and would die for any of the three.

I'm learning that if I look . . . if I open my eyes and observe . . . there are many reasons to take off my hat, look at the Source of it all, and just say thanks.

—IN THE EYE OF THE STORM

*T*he Christ of the galaxies is the Christ of your Mondays. The Starmaker manages your travel schedule. Relax. You have a friend in high places. Does the child of an Olympic weightlifter worry about tight pickle-jar lids? Does the son of Nike founder Phil Knight sweat a broken shoestring? If the daughter of Bill Gates can't turn on her computer, does she panic?

No. Nor should you. The universe's Commander in Chief knows your name. He has walked your streets.

—NEXT DOOR SAVIOR

*T*he wise captain shifts the direction of his craft according to the signal of the lighthouse. A wise person does the same.

Herewith, then, are the lights I look for and the signals I heed:

- Love God more than you fear hell.
- Once a week let a child take you on a walk.
- Make major decisions in a cemetery.
- When no one is watching, live as if someone is.
- Succeed at home first.
- Don't spend tomorrow's money today.
- Pray twice as much as you fret.
- Listen twice as much as you speak.
- Only harbor a grudge when God does.
- Never outgrow your love of sunsets.
- Treat people like angels; you will meet some and help make some.
- 'Tis wiser to err on the side of generosity than on the side of scrutiny.
- God has forgiven you; you'd be wise to do the same.
- When you can't trace God's hand, trust his heart.
- Toot your own horn, and the notes will be flat.
- Don't feel guilty for God's goodness.
- The book of life is lived in chapters, so know your page number.
- Never let the important be the victim of the trivial.
- Live your liturgy.

To sum it all up:

Approach life like a voyage on a schooner. Enjoy the view.
Explore the vessel. Make friends with the captain. Fish a little.
And then get off when you get home.

—*IN THE EYE OF THE STORM*

*I*sn't it incredible to think that God has saved a name just for
you? One you don't even know? We've always assumed that the
name we got is the name we will keep. Not so. Imagine what that
implies. Apparently your future is so promising it warrants a new
title. The road ahead is so bright a fresh name is needed. Your
eternity is so special no common name will do.

So God has one reserved just for you. There is more to your
life than you ever thought. There is more to your story than what
you have read. There is more to your song than what you have
sung. A good author saves the best for last. A great composer keeps
his finest for the finish. And God, the author of life and composer
of hope, has done the same for you.

The best is yet to be.

And so I urge you, don't give up.

And so I plead, finish the journey.

And so I exhort, be there.

Be there when God whispers your name.

—*When God Whispers Your Name*

*R*eligion pacifies, but never satisfies. Church activities might hide a thirst, but only Christ quenches it. Drink *him*.

And drink often. Jesus employs a verb that suggests repeated swallows. Literally, "Let him come to me and drink and keep drinking." One bottle won't satisfy your thirst. Regular sips satisfy thirsty throats. Ceaseless communion satisfies thirsty souls.

Toward this end, I give you this tool: a prayer for the thirsty heart. Carry it just as a cyclist carries a water bottle. The prayer outlines four essential fluids for soul hydration: God's work, God's energy, his lordship, and his love. You'll find the prayer easy to remember. Just think of the word *W-E-L-L*.

Lord, I come thirsty. I come to drink, to receive. I receive your *work* on the cross and in your resurrection. My sins are pardoned, and my death is defeated. I receive your *energy*. Empowered by your Holy Spirit, I can do all things through Christ, who gives me strength. I receive your *lordship*. I belong to you. Nothing comes to me that hasn't passed through you. And I receive your *love*. Nothing can separate me from your love.

Don't you need regular sips from God's reservoir? I do. I've offered this prayer in countless situations: stressful meetings, dull days, long drives, demanding trips, character-testing decisions. Many times a day I step to the underground spring of God and receive anew his work for my sin and death, the energy of his Spirit, his lordship, and his love.

Drink with me from his bottomless well. You don't have to live with a dehydrated heart.

Receive Christ's *work* on the cross,

the *energy* of his Spirit,

his *lordship* over your life,

his unending, unfailing *love*.

Drink deeply and often. And out of you will flow rivers of living water.

—*Come Thirsty*

In a world rocky with human failure, there is a land lush with divine mercy. Your Shepherd invites you there. He wants you to lie down. Nestle deeply until you are hidden, buried, in the tall shoots of his love, and there you will find rest.

—*Traveling Light*

Value to God

He's Crazy About You

"*B*ecause he delights in me, he saved me" (Ps. 18:19 NCV).

And you thought he saved you because of your decency. You thought he saved you because of your good works or good attitude or good looks. Sorry. If that were the case, your salvation would be lost when your voice went south or your works got weak. There are many reasons God saves you: to bring glory to himself, to appease his justice, to demonstrate his sovereignty. But one of the sweetest reasons God saved you is because he is fond of you. He likes having you around. He thinks you are the best thing to come down the pike in quite awhile. "As a man rejoices over his new wife, so your God will rejoice over you" (Isa. 62:5 NCV).

If God had a refrigerator, your picture would be on it. If he had a wallet, your photo would be in it. He sends you flowers every spring and a sunrise every morning. Whenever you want to talk, he'll listen. He can live anywhere in the universe, and he chose your heart. And the Christmas gift he sent you in Bethlehem? Face it, friend. He's crazy about you.

—*A Gentle Thunder*

In my closet hangs a sweater that I seldom wear. It is too small. The sleeves are too short, the shoulders too tight. Some of the buttons are missing, and the thread is frazzled. I should throw that sweater away. I have no use for it. I'll never wear it again. Logic says I should clear out the space and get rid of the sweater.

That's what *logic* says.

But *love* won't let me.

Something unique about that sweater makes me keep it. What is unusual about it? For one thing, it has no label. Nowhere on the garment will you find a tag that reads, "Made in Taiwan," or "Wash in Cold Water." It has no tag because it wasn't made in a factory. It has no label because it wasn't produced on an assembly line. It isn't the product of a nameless employee earning a living. It's the creation of a devoted mother expressing her love.

That sweater is unique. One of a kind. It can't be replaced. Each strand was chosen with care. Each thread was selected with affection.

And though the sweater has lost all of its use, it has lost none of its value. It is valuable not because of its function, but because of its maker.

You were deliberately planned, specifically gifted, and lovingly positioned on this earth by the Master Craftsman.

That must have been what the psalmist had in mind when he wrote, "you knit me together in my mother's womb" (Ps. 139:13 NIV).

Think on those words. You were knitted together. You aren't an accident. You weren't mass-produced. You aren't an assembly-line product. You were deliberately planned, specifically gifted, and lovingly positioned on this earth by the Master Craftsman.

"For we are God's workmanship, created in Christ Jesus to do good works, which God prepared in advance for us to do" (Eph. 2:10 NIV).

In a society that has little room for second fiddles, that's good news. In a culture where the door of opportunity opens only once and then slams shut, that is a revelation. In a system that ranks the value of a human by the figures of his salary or the shape of her legs . . . let me tell you something: Jesus' plan is a reason for joy!

Jesus told John that a new kingdom was coming–a kingdom where people have value not because of what they do, but because of *whose* they are.

—The Applause of Heaven

We are his idea. We are his. His face. His eyes. His hands. His touch. We are him. Look deeply into the face of every human being on earth, and you will see his likeness. Though some appear to be distant relatives, they are not. God has no cousins, only children.

—*A Gentle Thunder*

*W*ith God in your world, you aren't an accident or an incident; you are a gift to the world, a divine work of art, signed by God.

One of the finest gifts I ever received is a football signed by thirty former professional quarterbacks. There is nothing unique about this ball. For all I know it was bought at a discount sports store. What makes it unique are the signatures.

The same is true with us. In the scheme of nature *Homo sapiens* are not unique. We aren't the only creatures with flesh and hair and blood and hearts. What makes us special is not our body but the signature of God on our lives. We are his works of art. We are created in his image to do good deeds. We are significant, not because of what we do, but because of whose we are.

—*In the Grip of Grace*

*I*magine, for a moment, yourself in this situation. Your final hour with a son about to be sent overseas. Your last moments with your dying spouse. One last visit with your parent. What do you say? What do you do? What words do you choose?

It's worth noting that Jesus chose prayer. He chose to pray for us. "I pray for these men. But I am also praying for all people who will believe in me because of the teaching of these men. Father, I pray that all people who believe in me can be one. . . . I pray that these people can also be one in us, so that the world will believe that you sent me" (John 17:20–21, author's paraphrase).

You need to note that in this final prayer, Jesus prayed for you. You need to underline in red and highlight in yellow his love: "I am also praying for all people who will believe in me because of the teaching." That is you. As Jesus stepped into the garden, you were in his prayers. As Jesus looked into heaven, you were in his vision. As Jesus dreamed of the day when we will be where he is, he saw you there.

His final prayer was about you. His final pain was for you. His final passion was you.

He then turns, steps into the garden, and invites Peter, James, and John to come. He tells them his soul is "overwhelmed with sorrow to the point of death," and begins to pray.

Never has he felt so alone. What must be done, only he can do. An angel can't do it. No angel has the power to break open hell's gates. A man can't do it. No man has the purity to destroy sin's claim. No force on earth can face the force of evil and win—except God.

As Jesus stepped into the garden, you were in his prayers. As Jesus looked into heaven, you were in his vision.

"The spirit is willing, but the flesh is weak," Jesus confesses (Matt. 26:41 NASB).

His humanity begged to be delivered from what his divinity could see. Jesus, the carpenter, implores. Jesus, the man, peers into the dark pit and begs, "Can't there be another way?"

Did he know the answer before he asked the question? Did his human heart hope his heavenly Father had found another way? We don't know. But we do know he asked to get out. We do know he begged for an exit. We do know there was a time when if he could have, he would have turned his back on the whole mess and gone away.

But he couldn't.

He couldn't because he saw you. Right there in the middle of a world that isn't fair. He saw you cast into a river of life you didn't request. He saw you betrayed by those you love. He saw you with a body that gets sick and a heart that grows weak.

He saw you in your own garden of gnarled trees and sleeping friends. He saw you staring into the pit of your own failures and the mouth of your own grave.

He saw you in your Garden of Gethsemane–and he didn't want you to be alone.

He wanted you to know that he has been there too. He knows what it's like to be plotted against. He knows what it's like to be confused. He knows what it's like to be torn between two desires. He knows what it's like to smell the stench of Satan. And, perhaps most of all, he knows what it's like to beg God to change his mind and to hear God say so gently but firmly, "No."

For that is what God says to Jesus. And Jesus accepts the answer. At some moment during that midnight hour an angel of mercy comes over the weary body of the man in the garden. As he stands, the anguish is gone from his eyes. His fist will clench no more. His heart will fight no more.

The battle is won. You may have thought it was won on Golgotha. It wasn't. You may have thought the sign of victory is the empty tomb. It isn't. The final battle was won in Gethsemane. And the sign of conquest is Jesus at peace in the olive trees.

For it was in the garden that he made his decision. He would rather go to hell for you than go to heaven without you.

—*AND THE ANGELS WERE SILENT*

*W*hen everyone else rejects you, Christ accepts you. When everyone else leaves you, Christ finds you. When no one else wants you, Christ claims you. When no one else will give you the time of day, Jesus will give you the words of eternity.

—*A GENTLE THUNDER*

"*For* God caused Christ, who himself knew nothing of sin, actually to *be* sin for our sakes, so that in Christ we might be made good with the goodness of God" (2 Cor. 5:21 PHILLIPS).

Note the last four words: "the goodness of God." God's goodness is your goodness. You are absolute perfection. Flawless. Without defects or mistakes. Unsullied. Unrivaled. Unmarred. Peerless. Virgin pure. Undeserved yet unreserved perfection.

No wonder heaven applauds when you wake up. A masterpiece has stirred.

"*Shhh*," whisper the stars, "look at the wonder of that child."

"My!" gasp the angels. "What a prodigy God has created."

So while you groan, eternity gasps with wonder. As you stumble, angels are star struck. What you see in the mirror as morning disaster is, in reality, a morning miracle. Holiness in a bathrobe.

Go ahead and get dressed. Go ahead and put on the rings, shave the whiskers, comb the hair, and cover the moles. Do it for yourself. Do it for the sake of your image. Do it to keep your job. Do it for the benefit of those who have to sit beside you. But don't do it for God.

He has already seen you as you really are. And in his book, you are perfect.

—*IN THE EYE OF THE STORM*

*W*hat matters to you matters to God.

You probably think that's true when it comes to the big stuff. When it comes to the major-league difficulties like death, disease, sin, and disaster–you know that God cares.

But what about the smaller things? What about grouchy bosses or flat tires or lost dogs? What about broken dishes, late flights, toothaches, or a crashed hard drive? Do these matter to God?

I mean, he's got a universe to run. He's got the planets to keep balanced and presidents and kings to watch over. He's got wars to worry with and famines to fix. Who am I to tell him about my ingrown toenail?

I'm glad you asked. Let me tell you who you are. In fact, let me *proclaim* who you are.

You are an heir of God and a coheir with Christ (Rom. 8:17).

You are eternal, like an angel (Luke 20:36).

You have a crown that will last forever (1 Cor. 9:25).

You are a holy priest (1 Pet. 2:5), a treasured possession (Exod. 19:5).

You were chosen before the creation of the world (Eph. 1:4).

You are destined for "praise, fame, and honor, and you will be a holy people to the LORD your God" (Deut. 26:19 NCV).

But more than any of the above–more significant than any title or position–is the simple fact that you are God's child. "The Father has loved us so much that we are called children of God. And we really are his children" (1 John 3:1 NCV).

I love that last phrase! "We really are his children." It's as if John knew some of us would shake our heads and say, "Naw, not me. Mother Teresa, maybe. Billy Graham, all right. But not me." If those are your feelings, John added that phrase for you.

"We *really* are his children."

As a result, if something is important to you, it's important to God.

—*HE STILL MOVES STONES*

In God's book man is heading somewhere. He has an amazing destiny. We are being prepared to walk down the church aisle and become the bride of Jesus. We are going to live with him. Share the throne with him. Reign with him. We count. We are valuable. And what's more, our worth is built in! Our value is inborn.

You see, if there was anything that Jesus wanted everyone to understand it was this: a person is worth something simply because he is a person. That is why he treated people like he did. Think about it. The girl caught making undercover thunder with someone she shouldn't–he forgave her. The untouchable leper who asked for cleansing–he touched him. And the blind welfare case that cluttered the roadside–he honored him. And the worn-out old windbag addicted to self-pity near the pool of Siloam–he healed him!

. . . Listen closely. Jesus' love does not depend upon what

we do for him. Not at all. In the eyes of the King, you have value simply because you are. You don't have to look nice or perform well. Your value is inborn.

Period.

Think about that for just a minute. You are valuable just because you exist. Not because of what you do or what you have done, but simply because you are. Remember that. Remember that the next time you are left bobbing in the wake of someone's steamboat ambition. Remember that the next time some trickster tries to hang a bargain basement price tag on your self-worth. The next time someone tries to pass you off as a cheap buy, just think about the way Jesus honors you . . . and smile.

—*No Wonder They Call Him the Savior*

Worship

A Big View of God

$\mathcal{T}$he day Jesus went to worship, his very face was changed.

"You're telling me that Jesus went to worship?"

I am. The Bible speaks of a day when Jesus took time to stand with friends in the presence of God. Let's read about the day Jesus went to worship:

> Six days later, Jesus took Peter, James, and John, the brother of James, up on a high mountain by themselves. While they watched, Jesus' appearance was changed; his face became bright like the sun, and his clothes became white as light. Then Moses and Elijah appeared to them, talking with Jesus.
>
> Peter said to Jesus, "Lord, it is good that we are here. If you want, I will put up three tents here—one for you, one for Moses, and one for Elijah."
>
> While Peter was talking, a bright cloud covered them. A

voice came from the cloud and said, "This is my Son, whom I love, and I am very pleased with him. Listen to him!" (Matt. 17:1–5 NCV)

The words of Matthew presuppose a decision on the part of Jesus to stand in the presence of God. The simple fact that he chose his companions and went up on a mountain suggests this was no spur-of-the-moment action. He didn't awaken one morning, look at the calendar and then at his watch, and say, "Oops, today is the day we go to the mountain." No, he had preparations to make. Ministry to people was suspended so ministry to his heart could occur. Since his chosen place of worship was some distance away, he had to select the right path and stay on the right road. By the time he was on the mountain, his heart was ready. Jesus prepared for worship.

Let me ask you, do you do the same? Do you prepare for worship? What paths do you take to lead you up the mountain? The question may seem foreign, but my hunch is, many of us simply wake up and show up. We're sadly casual when it comes to meeting God.

Would we be so lackadaisical with, oh, let's say, the president? Suppose you were granted a Sunday morning breakfast at the White House? How would you spend Saturday night? Would you get ready? Would you collect your thoughts? Would you think about your questions and requests? Of course you would. Should we prepare any less for an encounter with the Holy God?

We're sadly casual when it comes to meeting God. Would we be so lackadaisical with, oh, let's say, the president?

Let me urge you to come to worship prepared to worship. Pray before you come so you will be ready to pray when you arrive. Sleep before you come so you'll stay alert when you arrive. Read the Word before you come so your heart will be soft when you worship. Come hungry. Come willing. Come expecting God to speak.

—*JUST LIKE JESUS*

*W*e worship God because we need to.

But our need runs a turtle-paced distant second to the thoroughbred reason for worship.

The chief reason for applauding God? He deserves it. If singing did nothing but weary your voice, if giving only emptied your wallet–if worship did nothing for you–it would still be right to do. God warrants our worship.

How else do you respond to a Being of blazing, blistering, unadulterated, unending holiness? No mark. Nor freckle. Not a bad thought, bad day, or bad decision. Ever! What do you do with such holiness if not adore it?

And his power. He churns forces that launch meteors, orbit planets, and ignite stars. Commanding whales to spout salty air, petunias to perfume the night, and songbirds to chirp joy into spring. Above the earth, flotillas of clouds endlessly shape and reshape; within the earth, strata of groaning rocks shift and turn.

Who are we to sojourn on a trembling, wonderful orb so shot through with wonder?

And tenderness? God has never taken his eyes off you. Not for a millisecond. He's always near. He lives to hear your heartbeat. He loves to hear your prayers. He'd die for your sin before he'd let you die in your sin, so he did.

What do you do with such a Savior? Don't you sing to him? Don't you celebrate him in baptism, elevate him in Communion? Don't you bow a knee, lower a head, hammer a nail, feed the poor, and lift up your gift in worship? Of course you do.

Worship God. Applaud him loud and often. For your sake, you need it.

And for heaven's sake, he deserves it.

—*CURE FOR THE COMMON LIFE*

The purpose of worship {is} to change the face of the worshiper. This is exactly what happened to Christ on the mountain. Jesus' appearance was changed: "His face became bright like the sun" (Matt. 17:2 NCV).

The connection between the face and worship is more than coincidental. Our face is the most public part of our bodies, covered less than any other area. It is also the most recognizable part of our bodies. We don't fill a school annual with photos of people's feet but rather with photos of faces. God desires to take our faces, this exposed and memorable part of our bodies, and use them to reflect his goodness. Paul writes: "Our faces, then, are not covered. We all show the Lord's glory, and we are being changed to be like him. This change in us brings ever greater glory, which comes from the Lord, who is the Spirit" (2 Cor. 3:18 NCV).

God invites us to see his face so he can change ours. He uses our uncovered faces to display his glory. The transformation isn't easy. The sculptor of Mount Rushmore faced a lesser challenge than does God. But our Lord is up to the task. He loves to change the faces of his children. By his fingers, wrinkles of worry are rubbed away. Shadows of shame and doubt become portraits of grace and trust. He relaxes clenched jaws and smooths furrowed brows. His touch can remove the bags of exhaustion from beneath the eyes and turn tears of despair into tears of peace.

How? Through worship.

We'd expect something more complicated, more demanding. A forty-day fast or the memorization of Leviticus perhaps. No. God's plan is simpler. He changes our faces through worship.

Exactly what is worship? I like King David's definition. "O magnify the LORD with me, and let us exalt His name together" (Ps. 34:3 NASB). Worship is the act of magnifying God. Enlarging our vision of him. Stepping into the cockpit to see where he sits and observe how he works. Of course, his size doesn't change, but our perception of him does. As we draw nearer, he seems larger. Isn't that what we need? A *big* view of God? Don't we have *big* problems, *big* worries, *big* questions? Of course we do. Hence we need a big view of God.

Worship offers that. How can we sing, "Holy, Holy, Holy" and not have our vision expanded? Or what about the lines from "It Is Well with My Soul"?

> *My sin—O the bliss of this glorious thought,*
> *My sin—not in part but the whole,*
> *Is nailed to the cross and I bear it no more,*
> *Praise the Lord, praise the Lord, O my soul!*[5]

Can we sing those words and not have our countenance illuminated?

A vibrant, shining face is the mark of one who has stood in God's presence. After speaking to God, Moses had to cover his face with a veil (Exod. 34:33–35). After seeing heaven, Stephen's face glowed like that of an angel (Acts 6:15; 7:55–56).

God is in the business of changing the face of the world.

Let me be very clear. This change is his job, not ours. Our goal is not to make our faces radiant. Not even Jesus did that. Matthew says, "Jesus' appearance was changed" not "Jesus changed his appearance." Moses didn't even know his face was shining (Exod. 34:29). Our goal is not to conjure up some fake, frozen expression. Our goal is simply to stand before God with a prepared and willing heart and then let God do his work.

God is in the business of changing the
face of the world.

And he does. He wipes away the tears. He mops away the perspiration. He softens our furrowed brows. He touches our cheeks. He changes our faces as we worship.

—*JUST LIKE JESUS*

*G*od does not exist to make a big deal out of us. We exist to make a big deal out of him. It's not about you. It's not about me. It's all about him.

—*IT'S NOT ABOUT ME*

*P*arents, what are your children learning from your worship? Do they see the same excitement as when you go to a basketball game? Do they see you prepare for worship as you do for a vacation? Do they see you hungry to arrive, seeking the face of the Father? Or do they see you content to leave the way you came?

They are watching. Believe me. They are watching.

Do you come to church with a worship-hungry heart? Our Savior did.

May I urge you to be just like Jesus? Prepare your heart for worship. Let God change your face through worship. Demonstrate the power of worship.

—*JUST LIKE JESUS*

*G*od has one goal: God. "I have my reputation to keep up" (Isa. 48:11 MSG).

Surprised? Isn't such an attitude, dare we ask, self-centered? Don't we deem this behavior self-promotion? Why does God broadcast himself?

For the same reason the pilot of the lifeboat does. Think of it this way. You're floundering neck-deep in a dark, cold sea. Ship sinking. Life jacket deflating. Strength waning. Through the inky night comes the voice of a lifeboat pilot. But you cannot see him. What do you want the driver of the lifeboat to do?

Be quiet? Say nothing? Stealth his way through the drowning passengers? By no means! You need volume! Amp it up, buddy! In biblical jargon, you want him to show his glory. You need to hear him say, "I am here. I am strong. I have room for you. I can save you!" Drowning passengers want the pilot to reveal his preeminence.

Don't we want God to do the same? Look around. People thrash about in seas of guilt, anger, despair. Life isn't working. We are going down fast. But God can rescue us. And only one message matters. His! We need to see God's glory.

Make no mistake. God has no ego problem. *He does not reveal his glory for his good. We need to witness it for ours.* We need a strong hand to pull us into a safe boat. And, once aboard, what becomes our priority?

Simple. Promote God. We declare his preeminence. "Hey! Strong boat over here! Able pilot! He can pull you out!"

Passengers promote the pilot. "Not to us, O LORD, not to us, but to Your name give glory because of Your lovingkindness, because of Your truth" (Ps. 115:1 NASB). If we boast at all, we "boast in the Lord" (2 Cor. 10:17 NASB).

The breath you took as you read that last sentence was given to you for one reason, that you might for another moment "reflect the Lord's glory" (2 Cor. 3:18 NIV). God awoke you and me this morning for one purpose: "Declare his glory among the nations, his marvelous deeds among all peoples" (1 Chron. 16:24 NIV).

—*IT'S NOT ABOUT ME*

Notes

1. Frederick Dale Bruner, *The Churchbook: Matthew 13–28*, vol. 2 of *Matthew: A Commentary by Frederick Dale Bruner* (Dallas: Word Publishing, 1990), 534.

2. Jack Canfield and Mark Hansen, *Chicken Soup for the Soul* (Deerfield Beach, Fla.: Health Communications, 1993), 273–74.

3. C. J. Mahaney, "Loving the Church," audiotape of message at Covenant Life Church, Gaithersburg, MD, n.d., quoted in Randy Alcorn, *Heaven* (Wheaton, IL: Tyndale House, 2004), xxii.

4. Charles R. Swindoll, *The Finishing Touch* (Dallas: Word Publishing, 1994), 292.

5. Horatio G. Spafford, "It Is Well with My Soul."

Sources Index

All of the material in *The Lucado Inspirational Reader* was originally published in books authored by Max Lucado. All copyrights to the original works are held by Max Lucado.

And the Angels Were Silent (Nashville: W Publishing Group, 2003), 144-47, 172-74, 245, 314-24, 353-54, 366-68, 426-30

Applause of Heaven, The (Nashville: Word, 1990), 207-8, 273-74, 290-93, 423-25

Come Thirsty (Nashville: W Publishing Group, 2004), 54-54, 108, 180-81, 190-91, 244, 302-3, 324-25, 326-27, 369, 420-21

Cure for the Common Life (Nashville: W Publishing Group, 2005), 15-16, 21-22, 26-28, 54-55, 107, 149-50, 338-41, 342, 344, 345, 347, 348, 438-39

Every Day Deserves a Chance (Nashville: Thomas Nelson, Inc., 2007), 226

Facing Your Giants (Nashville: Thomas Nelson, Inc., 2006), 8-10, 44-45, 46-48, 153-57, 169, 298, 308-9, 312, 372-75

Fearless (Nashville: Thomas Nelson, Inc., 2009), 101, 103, 135, 149, 152-53, 236-37, 258-59, 262, 267, 306, 309

Gentle Thunder, A (Nashville: Word, 1995), 15, 23-24, 55, 119-23, 178-79, 191, 201-3, 212-13, 263-67, 275-87, 301-2, 314, 347-48, 354, 366, 375, 377, 422-23, 425-26, 430

God Came Near (Nashville: W Publishing Group, 2003), 37-41, 93-94, 227-31, 239-45, 246-47, 250-53, 268-73, 342, 397-403, 407-8

Topical Index